FIERCE LOVE
A Life of MARY O'MALLEY

To my daughter Polly, her husband Don and their children Patrick, Hannah and Daniel; and to my daughter Amy, her husband Stuart and their children Zachary and Poppy. To my siblings: Michael, Mark and Ruth.

To two proud Belfast women: my mother Marie Rainsford and my mother-in-law Mona McElroy.

To my lovely wife, Mona (1940–2019), my companion on visits to the little theatre in Derryvolgie Avenue, who departed this life far too soon.

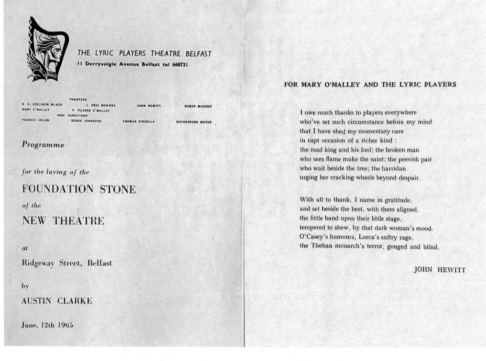

THE LYRIC PLAYERS THEATRE BELFAST
11 Derryvolgie Avenue Belfast tel 668721

TRUSTEES
W. D. COLLISON BLACK   J. NEIL BOWNES   JOHN HEWITT   ROGER McHUGH
MARY O'MALLEY   P. PEARSE O'MALLEY
HON. DIRECTORS
PADRAIC COLUM   DENIS JOHNSTON   THOMAS KINSELLA   RUTHERFORD MAYNE

Programme

for the laying of the

FOUNDATION STONE

of the

NEW THEATRE

at

Ridgeway Street, Belfast

by

AUSTIN CLARKE

June, 12th 1965

FOR MARY O'MALLEY AND THE LYRIC PLAYERS

I owe much thanks to players everywhere
who've set such circumstance before my mind
that I have shed my momentary care
in rapt occasion of a richer kind :
the mad king and his fool; the broken man
who sees flame make the saint; the peevish pair
who wait beside the tree; the harridan
urging her cracking wheels beyond despair.

With all to thank, I name in gratitude,
and set beside the best, with them aligned,
the little band upon their little stage,
tempered to shew, by that dark woman's mood,
O'Casey's humours, Lorca's sultry rage,
the Theban monarch's terror, gouged and blind.

JOHN HEWITT

John Hewitt's poem for the Lyric, celebrating the laying of the foundation stone, 1965. The Lyric motif – Cuchulain with a raven on his shoulder, was designed by Edna and Marie Boyd. (Hewitt's revised version of the poem can be found in Appendix C.)

'The future history of the Ulster Theatre will no doubt find Mary O'Malley at the centre of some controversies but also, and far more significantly, will find her at the source of many achievements … For her the world of theatre has also been the theatre of the world.'
– J.C. Beckett

Citation by the Dean of the Arts Faculty, for an honorary degree at Queen's University, Belfast, July 1969

FIERCE LOVE

A Life of

MARY O'MALLEY

Founder of the Lyric Players Theatre, Belfast

Bernard Adams

THE LILLIPUT PRESS, DUBLIN

First published 2022 by

THE LILLIPUT PRESS
62–63 Sitric Road, Arbour Hill
Dublin 7, Ireland
www.lilliputpress.ie

A CIP record for this publication is available from The British Library.

10 9 8 7 6 5 4 3 2 1

ISBN 978 1 84351 854 9

The Lilliput Press gratefully acknowledges the financial support
of the Arts Council / An Chomhairle Ealaíon.

Set in 11pt on 16pt Adobe Garamond Pro by Niall McCormack.
Printed in Ireland by Walsh Colour Print.

Contents

Illustrations fall between pages 84 and 85 and 244 and 245 respectively.

Preface

MARY O'MALLEY wanted to change the world. In 1947 she came up from the South of Ireland to live in a place which badly needed changing – the Unionist-dominated statelet of Northern Ireland. She wanted to transform her Belfast world, politically and culturally.

She served for three years in the early 1950s as an Irish Labour council-lor on the Belfast Corporation. She had encountered desperate deprivation in the ramshackle homes of her constituents in Smithfield and, as a socialist, laboured hard to alleviate it. But she found the Unionist monolith too hard to crack at that moment. So Mary tried another tack: she directed her considerable energy to asserting her own culture, in her own theatre – trying to add a wider, Irish dimension to theatre-going in Belfast.

In 1951 she had begun to put on verse dramas in the bay window of the front room of her Belfast home; in 1953 she moved to a bigger suburban house with a stable block at the back. There, in Derryvolgie Avenue, she made a fifty-seater theatre out of a room above the stable where she created a fine company of actors, turned distinguished Ulster artists into set designers, found a choreographer and a composer and put on 140 plays in seventeen years on a stage that was only ten feet wide. Until 1960 it was a wholly amateur operation, subsidized by the earnings of Mary's husband, the psychiatrist Patrick Pearse O'Malley, who provided active, lifelong support for her projects.

In her choice of plays, she asserted a broad Irish culture; Belfast kitchen comedies were not part of her repertoire. W.B. Yeats became her standard-bearer. She did all twenty-six of his plays, some of them several times over, evolving a style of acting and movement which elicited surprise, praise, recognition and, it has to be admitted, some persistent local scepticism.

Mary was feisty, awkward, relentless and as her tiny theatre started to burst at the seams, she began to dream of creating a playhouse where thousands rather than hundreds could see the work of her company. That dream took a while to fulfil. Frustrated, she expanded, setting up a whole fleet of cultural enterprises: *Threshold*, a literary magazine with a thirty-year lifespan; a modest drama school; a music academy; a shop selling Irish handcrafts; and an art gallery. It was not surprising that a woman who was a known nationalist and would scuttle out, or remain sitting, for 'God Save the Queen', took a while to get support for building a new theatre in Unionist Belfast, but in the end she did. In October 1968 the 300-seater Lyric Players Theatre opened with Yeats's *Cuchulain* cycle.

What happened after that autumn night of dinner jackets and speeches is the core of this book. Suffice it to say it was probably the worst moment in the twentieth century to open a theatre in Belfast: the Troubles were about to explode, Ulster was politically polarized as never before and going out to the theatre became a potentially dangerous activity as bombings, rioting and assassinations took over from normal life in the city.

Neither Mary nor Pearse had any experience of managing a fully professional theatre. The task was made even harder by the fact that Mary was a nationalist in a Unionist city. She was a socialist, but potential audiences were much more likely to be conservative. She liked poetic dramas, but local taste was for realism and comedy. Compromise was needed. That was always difficult for Mary. But she had courage and tenacity, which she needed as managing her theatre became ever more perilous in the early 1970s. Bombers tried to blow up her brand-new Lyric; audience numbers collapsed because of murder in the streets; the state subsidy was insufficient, so she found herself in relentless financial difficulty. And there were endless problems with the actors' union Equity. But she and her players adapted and coped. As Linda Wray, one of Mary's trusty actresses from the 1970s, told me:

Belfast in the '70s: six o'clock at night, everything stopped. People just barricaded themselves, there was nothing happening. Bars didn't open. But the Lyric was the one constant thing … and it was like a sort of beacon of hope, this little, unassuming building at the bottom of Ridgeway Street, it just stayed open.

It was Mary's achievement to create, from the late 1960s, in the somewhat theatre-averse city of Belfast, a theatre – the Lyric, which now stands out proudly above the River Lagan, in its new, £11 million re-incarnation. Mary was hyperactive, a workaholic. For three decades her work *was* her life. That 'work' was so multifarious, her initiatives so numerous, that too full a description of them might blur the personal portrait. A good example is *Threshold*, the literary magazine she and Pearse founded in 1957. Its thirty-nine issues reveal the full richness of the flowering of prose and poetry from the mid-1960s in Northern Ireland. A full account of the magazine's creation, growth and development could fill a separate volume so brutal selection has been necessary (most of the account is in a separate appendix); nevertheless attention will be paid to significant editions of the magazine, like John Montague's 'Northern Crisis' number. My aim in the book has been to prevent 'public' Mary from overwhelming 'private' Mary – the wife, mother and friend.

In Belfast in the mid-1960s I went to Mary O'Malley's tiny Studio theatre. I met Mary there and wrote benign notices on the plays for the *Belfast Telegraph*. I was impressed by her and her project. I used to see her after the show dispensing coffee to a mingle of actors and audience. I remember little of what she said to me, but I have a strong visual image of her. She was then in her mid-forties, pale-faced, with black hair, elegantly dressed and wearing simple but striking Celtic jewellery. I must have made very little impression on her because in the O'Malley archive I located one of her carefully kept card indexes. Under 'A' for Adams, I'm merely listed as 'declining an invitation to the Lyric's Summer Fiesta'. Looking back, I can see that what I wrote about her productions was unsurprisingly favourable, partly because I loved her tiny theatre and was biased towards her whole cultural project and partly because I, like her, had come up from Dublin.

I remember that when going to a performance in the suburban house in Derryvolgie Avenue I had the feeling that my presence was useful, that I was more than a box-office receipt. Going to the little stable playhouse was somehow culturally a good deed, and certainly an enjoyable one. From such memories biographies grow.

I had only two years in Belfast. When I left for London, I followed Mary's successes and vicissitudes from afar. When she died, I thought I should try to tell her story. Setting the literary satnav to 'objective' has been difficult, but I have tried to navigate the bumpy terrain that lies between hagiography and exposé, navigating towards a truthful biography of a complex woman who was remarkable but not always lovable.

FIERCE LOVE

A Life of

MARY O'MALLEY

1

Youghal

MARY HICKEY was born in Mallow, Co. Cork, on 28 July 1918. Her father, Daniel, had died of tuberculosis just a few months before her birth. Mary says in her autobiography *Never Shake Hands with the Devil* (1990) that never seeing her father made her childhood 'lopsided' – so much so that she came to feel that perhaps her mother, Anne, could have done something about finding a 'replacement'. But the widow concentrated on motherhood rather than searching for a new partner. Mary describes her as 'a splendid home-maker, inventive, artistic and a marvellous story-teller'. Nature passed on most of these gifts to Mary; and her mother's nurture fostered them further. Losing a father shaped Mary, but so did having an exceptional mother.

Her maiden name was Anne Lysaght. She was born in 1875 to a Protestant father, William, and a Catholic mother, Margaret. The couple lived in Mallow, Co. Cork, and Anne was one of their five children. She also lost her father early on: he died of 'spotted typhus fever', which he caught while working to replace drains on a large local estate. He seems to have been a successful building contractor and a generous man. Mary relates a family legend that before his last Christmas William brought home two beautiful and expensive dolls – gifts for Anne and her sister. He was upbraided by his wife, but replied with strange foresight: 'Why not? I may not be here next Christmas.' By New Year's Day he was dead.

Anne's mother, Margaret (Mary's grandmother), then decided – unwisely as it turned out – to remarry. She had her husband's thriving business to run as well as five children to look after, so she sought someone to share the burden. She chose a well-off American called John Fitzgibbon and they were married ten months after William Lysaght's death. Fitzgibbon gave her four more children but turned out to be a spendthrift eccentric who went on long trips to the USA. He didn't allow his children to wear bright clothes and 'they would be constantly castigated for their frivolity'. He later developed a type of religious mania, which entailed creating a chapel in the family home in which he delivered interminable sermons to which the children were forced to listen. Eventually he was committed to a mental institution in Cork.

Family life for the nine children in Mallow was not completely blighted by Fitzgibbon's strange behaviour. Anne had good memories of Canon Sheehan, who lived across the road from the Fitzgibbon household. A poet and writer of popular novels (*My New Curate*, *The Graves of Kilmorna*), Canon Sheehan liked Anne and gave her sweets. On one occasion, probably in the 1890s, she took a towel and a bar of soap to have a bath in the stream at the back of the house. The canon happened to be looking out of his window when he observed the ablutions. He went across the road and told Anne's mother: 'Now don't say anything to her, but Anne is having a bath in the stream; she is naked, go and get her in.'

Mallow was a lively place in the early years of the last century. The presence of a British regiment, the North Cork Militia, in the town added to the gaiety of the social scene, which also benefited from the presence of several Anglo-Irish Big Houses in the area. Anne was vivacious and wilful, despite her stepfather's attempts to restrain her. She had many admirers: photographs from the early 1900s show a handsome woman with formidable coils of auburn hair and fine dark eyes. But in the end, she had, according to Mary, only one love. He was a teacher, Joe Fitzgerald, who was also studying law and involved in politics. He became a Cork county councillor and followed the star of the local politician, agrarian campaigner and journalist William O'Brien. The courtship with Anne was stormy and prolonged by Joe's commitment to looking after his mother. He gave his beloved a gold ring with both their names engraved on it and, finally, it seemed as if they would be able to marry. But Joe died, quite suddenly, on Anne's birthday in April 1906. He was only thirty-three.

Anne was shocked, dismayed and disoriented. But she was by now in her thirties and when Daniel Hickey, who worked for the local authority as an asylum attendant in Youghal and had an East Cork farming background, proposed to her, she accepted. Being a substitute for the adored Joe must have been difficult for Daniel, but the marriage seems to have been a happy one. He and Anne lived in Youghal and produced three children: Gerard, Joe and Mary. Anne rarely spoke of her husband, so Mary's account of her father is scant, reporting only that one of her Mallow step-aunts 'admired him greatly and once told me he had lovely almond eyes'. But he also was to die prematurely, contracting the much-feared disease of tuberculosis. He died in March 1918, only four months before Mary was born. Anne was left bereft once again.

She had, however, good family support from her mother and numerous sisters and half-sisters who lived fifty miles away from Youghal, in Mallow. Mary and her brothers went there frequently to see their grandmother and the aunts. Soon there was another, important, reason for keeping in close contact with these relatives: Mary's middle brother Joe was delicate and when he fell ill, he was swept away to Mallow by one of Anne's sisters and lived there with his grandmother and his aunts for his whole childhood. Anne went to see Joe in Mallow as often as she could, but her means were limited and she accepted the separation as a cruel but inevitable necessity.

Anne's first-born, Gerard, was nine years older than Mary and to some extent came to fill the role of substitute father. And he was kind to Mary as well, eventually providing a huge amount of practical and financial help as she grew up. A pencilled note from eight-year-old Mary to Gerard has been preserved in the O'Malley archive. There is little punctuation, but the hand is clear: 'I hope you are getting on well I was in bed six days. Mammy got your letter and was pleased with it …' She ends: '… your fond sister Mary Hickey.' The three of them lived in a pleasant enough house but it did not have a bathroom. They made light of this with a hip bath in front of the kitchen range – a Saturday night ritual. The house had no electricity; oil lamps and candles provided the light. Eventually gas lighting was installed but not before Mary had acquired a lifelong fear of the dark.

Ireland changed radically in the early years of Mary's life. At the time of her birth, the reverberations of the failed 1916 Easter Rising in Dublin were still being felt. Its brutal suppression by the British simply made the hunger for independence stronger. Agitation and lawlessness spread. Eventually a guerrilla war broke out between hastily assembled British forces, the Black and Tans, and Irish freedom fighters. The British bowed to the inevitable: the Anglo-Irish Treaty of 1922 granted independence and six of the nine counties of Ulster remained British.

Mary could never accept the partition of Ireland and she was to fight with passion against this arrangement and its effect on the people of Northern Ireland. The violent unrest in Co. Cork came close to home when parts of Youghal were burned down by the Black and Tans. And then there was the Holy Well incident in May 1921, when the IRA detonated a roadside bomb as a British army band and a detachment of soldiers from the Hampshire regiment were passing on their way to a rifle range just outside of Youghal. The bomb killed at least seven soldiers and a civilian. One of the bandsmen was only fifteen. Mary was too young to register much of the savage struggle, but she remembers seeing men in civilian clothes and cloth caps with guns at the ready crouching behind a wall in front of the house.

Youghal in the early 1920s was not prosperous. It relied on the erratic returns from tourism: it has the second longest city walls in Ireland, attractive beaches and fishing. In the summer months the Hickey family would move into the back of their home and rent out the front part to holidaymakers. Anne and her children were often short of money. But she was a good enough manager to be able to pay for domestic help (which cost a pittance) and to make improvements to the house.

Mary and Gerard did not have many friends in Youghal. Gerard was a little shy and Mary recalls spending a lot of time together with him in the house. Anne encouraged them to draw and paint. Gerard had considerable artistic talent: he was skilful enough as a boy to do a full-length oil painting of Michael Collins, which his mother loyally insisted on hanging prominently, long after Gerard had outgrown this piece of juvenilia. He benefited from having a good art teacher at school, the local sculptor Joe Higgins, who gave him great encouragement. Mary was to benefit later from Gerard's artistic skills, which came to include stage design.

Stories were the other currency of Mary's childhood. Anne had a fine repertoire: tales of weddings and wakes and strange events in Mallow and its environs. Mary describes the magic of listening to her mother: 'We would sit at the fire in the twilight; she could read the coals and describe so vividly what she saw there. I loved these moments, the sense of closeness and warmth.' Mary constantly asked for repeat performances of her mother's tales and was annoyed if there were any variations in the retelling. This ability to tell a good story Anne passed on to her daughter. It was to come in useful.

Mary's entertainments in her childhood were not confined to the fireside. She remembers a breathtaking ride in a motor car – still a new-fangled wonder in Co. Cork. They drove to the monastery at Mount Melleray, home of the contemplative Cistercians, at a stately speed and the party was so late coming home that they had to light the candles in the sidelamps. Then there was her first experience of the theatre in Youghal Town Hall – the play was Boucicault's *The Colleen Bawn*. In her autobiography Mary says she was 'wildly excited' by it, although she was unable to suspend her disbelief when the unfortunate Colleen was pushed over the side of the boat: 'I thought, cynically, how silly, she is only on the floor of the stage.'

Youghal had a picture house and one day, when her mother was away, Mary went with Nora, the maid, to see *The Gold Rush*. Later she saw Cecil B. DeMille's *The King of Kings* and, on a special outing to Cork that included tea at the Tivoli restaurant, enjoyed *Song o' My Heart* with John McCormack. The maid Nora (annual salary £18, pocketed by her mother) became Mary's confidante. Nora would disappear occasionally from the Hickey household, probably to support her brothers who could not accept the Treaty and were hiding in the hills and fighting for de Valera's Irreconcilables. But, paradoxically, Nora would also spend some of her spare time writing love letters by candlelight to now-departed British soldiers. When Nora eventually returned home to West Cork, Mary missed the tales of her escapades and her love affairs.

During the summer months when the house was part-rented, Gerard spent time with his grandmother and aunts in Mallow. Mary and her mother would visit, and Mary remembers being there for the grand funeral of the local hero William O'Brien in 1928 when she was ten. Her grandmother had been a friend of O'Brien and his Russian wife who lived nearby. When he died suddenly in London, elaborate preparations were made in Mallow for the return of the remains. Candles burned in every window along the route of the procession. Mary watched from an upstairs window and then went to the Requiem Mass and the burial.

During Mary's childhood the Irish Free State began to emphasize its Roman-Catholic identity. There is a vivid account in Mary's autobiography of the remarkable Corpus Christi celebrations in Youghal. Preparations were intense in the weeks beforehand: bunting and flags decked the streets and altars were erected along the route of the procession. Veils and white dresses were laid out for the girls, Sunday outfits refreshed for the boys. On the big day various organizations processed to the Green Park, a pleasant space close to the sea. There they received a benediction and thousands of voices sang 'Oh! Sacrament Divine' before the procession moved off to the quays, where the boats were blessed, and then on to St Mary's Parish Church for the final blessing.

When it was time for school, Anne was able to send Mary, aged four, to the Loreto Convent, a gentle private school for thirty or so children. She was there for two years before her mother moved her to the national school which, like many others throughout the country, was run by the Presentation Order. There she had a good grounding in the three Rs and a startling introduction to life in the raw. Her first day was a shock: 'I can always remember … going into the playground at lunch break, putting my back against the wall and looking in horror at the hundred screaming children around me.'

She survived, but school opened her eyes to a world beyond her relatively comfortable existence. Many of her classmates did not have boots or shoes. One girl would walk, barefoot, the six miles to and from school, carrying her boots on her shoulder so as not to wear them out. Mary became aware of the poverty that marked many lives in the town and the countryside around Youghal – and indeed all over the twenty-six counties as the recently born Irish Free State struggled economically. She knew one family, the McCarthys, who lived on the outskirts of the town in a tiny cottage with a kitchen, a living room and a loft. In this space lived the parents, their six children and an uncle who had been in the Boer War and suffered from recurrent malaria. Their life was hard: the uncle did milk deliveries; the father had a seasonal job on the golf links and the mother took in washing. One of the McCarthy girls died in her teens, another daughter eventually came as a domestic help for Anne and a son emigrated to America: 'I was very fond of this family and was present at the party (or live-wake) the night before their eldest child left for the States. He was about the same age as my brother and I was old enough to have some appreciation of their anguish – despite the singing and dancing on the stone-flagged kitchen floor.' Social concern was to become one of the keynotes of Mary's life.

2

St Michael's

MARY WAS ABOUT eleven when a big change took place in her circumstances. After leaving school Gerard had taken part in the first Open Competitive Examination for the Irish civil service. He passed and was duly called to a post in Dublin. Mary found life without him lonely but there were compensations, like the presents he brought when he returned at Christmas, including, one year, a doll which spoke when it was turned over; and the next, a fancy pair of fur-backed gloves which she took care to see were highly visible at Mass on Christmas Day. Anne missed Gerard too but was delighted that he was becoming independent and that at last there was money coming in which, it turned out, he generously shared with his mother and sister.

When Mary reached the top class of her school, the Presentation nuns told Anne that Mary showed promise and might benefit from a boarding school. They suggested St Michael's Convent in Navan, Co. Meath. Gerard was consulted and agreed to pay the fees, if Anne could find the considerable outlay for what Mary calls her 'trousseau'. The requirements were stern: two veils, one black and one white; all vests had to have a high neck; and a 'school-girl's black cloth coat for best wear in winter, which must be at least 4" below the knee'. Modesty was clearly going to be a watchword at St Michael's.

Mary did not want to leave her mother but was beguiled by the pleasant picture the local nuns painted of boarding-school life. A trunk was packed and arrangements made for the long journey via Dublin. Mary was to be accompanied by another local girl, Nellie, who had already been at the school for some time. Both were reporting late for the autumn term, in Mary's case because the decision to go had taken a while to make. Goodbyes were waved at the station and as she looked out of the window of her carriage, 'realization set in'. She had restrained her tears until that moment, not wishing to distress her mother, but when the train went into a tunnel and the lights went out, she started to cry. She dried her eyes as they came out and the inspector came to check the tickets: 'He clipped mine and as he handed it back said quizzically, "Ah, never shake hands with the devil," and turning as he went out the door, with a smile he added, "until you meet him." No doubt my tear-stained face had told its own story and the ticket-inspector's homespun philosophy was not to be forgotten.'

Before she arrived at the school there was a treat in store. Gerard, who had arranged accommodation, was waiting for them at Kingsbridge Station in Dublin. Nellie went elsewhere while Gerard put into effect his plan to introduce his little sister to the theatre, which had become his passion since moving to the city. He took Mary to the Abbey where they sat in the one-and-sixpenny seats in the gallery. That night the stalls were graced by the appearance of W.B. Yeats and Lady Gregory. Gerard pointed them out but their significance was quite lost on Mary, aged twelve. What she saw was probably Shaw's *Fanny's First Play* and the premiere of Yeats's *The Cat and the Moon*. Mary found the ambience intriguing and was pleased that 'my handsome brother had brought me along'.

The school prospectus for St Michael's bore an impressive picture of a rather severe-looking, many-windowed mansion – standing 'just outside the town of Navan on a gentle eminence overlooking the historic Boyne'. Behind this exterior was a Catholic institution with a harsh daily routine, severe rules and a staff of nuns who varied from the kindly to the strict. Mary cried herself to sleep on her first night but slowly became used to getting up at 6.30 am, to the emphasis on achieving piety (she always felt she had a 'deficit' in this department) and to the intense celebration of the major religious festivals. The austere annual Easter retreat, for example, was a trial:

Such intensity of religious fervour was too much for me. A sceptic at thirteen, I longed for reclamation. I tried to get into the proper mood, maintained silence, said the prayers, listened to the sermons given by the priest and made my Easter Duty, promising to amend my life and deal honestly with the faults in my character.

Mary's schooldays were in no way exceptional. Her school reports show that she did well in English and history and was good at art. Languages were not her forte, but she had one special talent: 'I could tell a story well. Having read more than my companions, I could relate in detail a good love story for their edification. From my mother's vast repertoire, I could select at random.' In her autobiography Mary tends to downplay her academic record at St Michael's, but her performance in English was consistently good. At one point she was top of her class overall, but a weakness in Irish was to limit her later progress.

Making friends was what made the rigours of St Michael's tolerable: the lumpy porridge, the revolting tapioca, the unappetizing potatoes, the intense cold of the early months of the year, the chilblains, the purgatory of long walks with infected heels – all could be forgotten when there were sympathetic friends around. Mary grew close to two girls from Youghal whom she had known earlier at the national school, Peggy and Eileen Flavin. Peggy was a little older than Mary and it was her younger sister Eileen who became a special friend. She was an all-rounder: top of the class, a good tennis player and a musician who also managed to be, in Mary's view, 'generous and thoughtful'.

St Michael's was more interested in music than in drama, but Mary did get a few thespian opportunities. She wrote a script based on a short story called 'The Lost Princess', which she describes as 'dramatic and sad'. The play was short, so Mary arranged an extra programme of songs and poems. She repeated it the next year with a costumed literary quiz. Pupils selected a book title and made a costume to illustrate it and the audience had to guess the book title from the outfit. As usual with Mary this was not all: 'We had some singing and dancing with coloured, pleated crêpe paper providing wings for the butterflies. These primitive efforts on my part absorbed all my energies and gave great satisfaction.'

The next chance to involve herself in 'theatricals' came with the opening of a new gym and chapel at the school. The occasion was marked with a musical entertainment – with sets and lighting by Mary Hickey. She got one more chance to enjoy making theatre when she was given a part in a carefully chosen religious play. 'Now, I knew I had no acting ability but was very pleased to be part of the production.' But then she broke the rules. Mary's friend Maeve Laffan (who was a half-sister of Brendan Bracken, Churchill's wartime aide) used to have a weekly visit from her father. After one of them, she handed Mary a cake. Mary enjoyed this bedtime titbit but left some crumbs in her bedclothes, which were noticed the next morning by the sister in charge of the dormitory and the offence was reported to the Mistress of Schools. Mary and Maeve 'were both dismissed from the play a couple of days before it was due to go on'. Indignation still burned sixty years later when Mary described the incident: 'I felt the punishment far outweighed the crime and I never forgave the sister who had reported the matter.'

Mary counted the days till the holidays. She remembers going home at the end of her first term, meeting her mother in Cork and flying into her arms, 'independence suddenly forgotten'. Three weeks of bliss then ensued, enhanced by Gerard's Christmas visit. However, although the scene at home was unchanging, Mary was growing up. When the long summer holidays came, a much more self-reliant Mary set about enjoying Youghal, which for these months of the year was a lively town. She spent as much time as possible on the beach, swimming and making friends. Many families came year after year and that summer she became aware of boys for the first time – 'as a special species of animal … It was about this time … I got my first kiss. I never told my mother about this of course. I think she resented a little my preoccupation with the good life and my new sense of independence.'

Mary and her mother together did, however, have one spectacular outing that summer of 1932. They were present at an event which signalled perhaps the high-water mark of Irish Catholicism: the thirty-first Eucharistic Congress, held that year in Dublin. They made tram excursions to see the sights of a city bedecked in bunting, papal flags and flowers. There was a big altar on O'Connell Bridge, and they went to a service in Phoenix Park where more than a million people – a quarter of the whole population of the Irish Free State – heard the Papal Legate Cardinal Lauri celebrate Mass and John McCormack singing 'Panis Angelicus'. Cardinal Lauri blessed the throng and Mary reaffirmed her belief in Rome. This emphatic public assertion of Irish Catholicism was a great organizational success. But its sheer scale provoked angry contempt from northern Protestants, which resulted in trains carrying Catholics from Belfast to Dublin for the celebrations being stoned as they passed through the Protestant town of Portadown. The young Mary found this disturbing. In time she would come to experience at first hand the powerful hold anti-popery had in Protestant Northern Ireland, and discover that 'old red-socks' still had his place in Ulster demonology.

There was another big national event that year: the general election of 1932. Mary became interested in politics and enjoyed the fact that the pupils at her school were divided in their loyalties. She was a supporter of de Valera and was delighted when he won his handsome victory. The policies he implemented meant even stronger efforts to Gaelicize the country, more economic and cultural isolationism, the ever-closer integration of church and state and a fierce determination to step out of the shadow of the former colonial master. In these sheltered schooldays, Mary inclined to acceptance of de Valera's vision. Once out in the wider world she found aspects of it less to her taste, although all her life she shared de Valera's intense antipathy to the partition of Ireland.

In 1936, aged eighteen, Mary began to consider what she should do as she approached the end of her schooldays. She had done well in the Intermediate examination in English, history and art. She was entered for university matriculation but failed Irish again and so she missed out on higher education. Mary knew she would have to get a job and become financially independent and confesses to being 'confused and worried' as she approached her final term at St Michael's.

Just as she was about to finish school, Mary had a shock. Her mother had decided to leave Youghal and move to Dublin; she and Mary would join Gerard in his flat in Leinster Square in Rathmines. Anne had begun to feel increasingly lonely now that both Mary and Gerard were no longer at home. Also, she had a low opinion of her daughter's prospects of getting a job in Youghal. Mary was to try for entry to the civil service during the summer, but if that failed the big city offered better job prospects. Dublin was the logical place for the family to reassemble. Mary was sad to be uprooted from her childhood home but recognized that finding a job was paramount. She duly took the civil service exam but although she passed, she was not among 'the lucky few' appointed to jobs. Employment opportunities were few in the depressed economy of late 1930s Ireland and for a while Mary drifted about in a state of indecision. Then the idea of doing a secretarial course came up: 'I grasped this straw and tried to apply myself.' She completed the course and found a temporary job, and thus her life as a Dublin wage-earner began.

Once she had discovered the means of earning a living, Mary was free to enjoy late 1930s Dublin – a strange, impecunious amalgam of high culture and unemployment, of deep religiosity and wild irreverence, of wealthy households with maids and desperate poverty in the tenements. The city now became her unofficial university. So far Mary's life had been fairly conventional. Things were about to get much more interesting.

3

Dublin, War, Theatre

LEINSTER SQUARE is a pleasant set of Victorian houses, close to Rathmines and perhaps two miles from the city centre. Gerard's generosity to his mother and sister was greater than Mary acknowledges in her autobiography. The flat was small – too small for the three of them. So before they arrived Gerard built himself an abode that was somewhere between a mobile home and a large garden shed. He lived in this until he got married – not long after Mary came to Dublin. He was fortunate in that, by now, he had a good job in the civil service and, as his talents were recognized, was able to climb the promotion ladder. So, Mary lived with her mother for most of her Dublin decade – rarely an ideal arrangement for a lively young girl exploring the excitements of a large city. But they seem to have got along well enough although Anne disapproved of her daughter's growing interest in socialism and never quite shared in the obsessive enthusiasm both Mary and Gerard had for the theatre.

In Dublin it is probable that the constant presence of Gerard, who acted as Mary's guide, confidant and mentor, would have reassured Anne that her daughter was in no moral danger and that the worst hazard to Mary's well-being was lack of sleep. (Mary was soon in the habit of staying up all night at Saturday post-performance parties at the Peacock Theatre – and then going straight on to Mass on the Sunday morning.) She is unequivocal about the role Gerard played in her life at this stage: 'He was my second father. For many years now he had taken over completely from my mother in influencing my life.'

Mary was an assiduous reader, and now she took pains to acquire some of the knowledge she might have assimilated at Trinity or University College Dublin (UCD). A fat notebook, covering the period 1938–42, contains reading lists and transcribed quotations. In 1938 she was exploring the Anglo-Irish Literary heritage but also reading Shelley, Tennyson and Charlotte Bronte (*Villette*). Her taste took in contemporary authors – Cecil Day-Lewis, Margaret Mitchell (*Gone with the Wind*), James Hilton (*Goodbye Mr. Chips*) and Helen Waddell's *Peter Abelard*. Irish history gets attention: John Mitchel's *Jail Journal*, the writings of Patrick Pearse, a biography of de Valera by Seán O'Faoláin and, the star attraction for Mary, *Portrait of a Rebel Father*, a life of James Connolly by his daughter Nora Connolly O'Brien. Yeats has his place – she quotes from 'Under Ben Bulben' in the *Selected Poems*. In drama her reading is wide: Donagh MacDonagh, a compendium of Abbey plays, Ibsen's *Brand* (which contains her mantra 'Compromise is the prince of lies'), a study of Oscar Wilde and Andrew Malone's *The Irish Drama* are among the titles she lists. The autodidact's reading was eclectic and formative.

With her first wage packet she was 'able to purchase a blouse and gloves, which was encouraging'. Soon she moved on to a more permanent office post. The hours were long, but she still found energy for a lively social and cultural life in the evenings. Eventually she discovered more interesting employment, working as the private secretary to James Bayley Butler, Professor of Zoology at UCD and the creator, over thirty years, of a replica classical villa and a fine garden on the slopes of Howth Head, just to the north of Dublin. Mary enjoyed working with him and admired his energy and inventiveness. During the war he had developed a process 'for waterproofing military maps and the Americans, with great foresight, purchased the formula for £2000. He was of course very pleased and went around flashing the cheque for some time.' Other areas of Bayley Butler expertise were in the treatment of dry rot and the wood-boring beetle. Such was his reputation that he did a great deal of consultancy, even giving advice on the care of the Stormont Parliament buildings. He was also adept at making furniture and gadgets for his house. Not surprisingly Mary says she was 'never bored'; and it seems likely that the professor recognized Mary's qualities and potential. She and only one other person were the guests when Bayley Butler – who had been a widower for many years – was married for the second time in the University Church in September 1944. His bride was Alice Dromgoole, a medical social worker. A letter Bayley Butler wrote to Mary while on his honeymoon gives some idea of his hyperactive personality and his relationship with her. He comments that 'the wedding was OK, but too much confetti'. He then sends three pages of instructions for her to follow while he is absent. These include 'keeping the upper part of the house locked' and 'Phone Mr Robbins, the Clock and Cabinet Manufacturing Coy, Cork St., to send a French polisher to polish the wardrobe'.

Being in steady employment and paying a modest rent to her mother meant Mary could live reasonably comfortably in a city which, a decade and a half after independence, was far from prosperous. Unemployment was high and there was considerable poverty in the working-class slums. Handsome Georgian exteriors often concealed the squalor of the multi-occupied dwellings behind them. Tuberculosis was rife and the infant mortality rate was well above European norms. De Valera had provoked an economic war with Britain which Éire, as the Irish Free State officially became in 1937, was not winning. The farmers were suffering, and the slow haemorrhage of emigration continued. The self-sufficient Gaelic republic, which 'Dev' had convinced the Irish people was a possibility, seemed further away than ever. This depressing cultural and economic picture was darkened further by the censorship of books and films, which had been in place since the 1920s, and the ubiquitous presence of a paternalistic Catholic Church. So it is hardly surprising that the politics of a natural rebel like Mary, who had also seen poverty at first hand, should take a radical, leftward turn: 'My mind was opening up and I wanted to know everything. I decided to join every conceivable society of interest.'

First she joined a 'ginger' group for women's rights. The Women's Social and Progressive League, founded in 1937, met irregularly at the Peacock Theatre. It opposed the narrow-minded and anti-women pronouncements of various Catholic clerics including the Bishop of Galway (well known for his opposition to 'mixed bathing' on local beaches). The membership of the League comprised a 'remarkable group of women' including Hanna Sheehy-Skeffington, who could oppose traditional values with impunity because she had compelling patriotic credentials. (Her pacifist husband had been shot almost on a whim by an unbalanced British army officer in 1916.) 'She was an excellent public speaker. Small and stout, she was the equal of any battalion.' The group included other women of substance, among them two of Hanna's sisters, Mrs Kathleen Cruise O'Brien and Mrs Mary Kettle, whose husband Tom had been killed while serving in the British army in Flanders in 1916. The young Mary was delighted to be involved with 'such august company' and she became quite friendly with Hanna and her son Owen, later a lecturer in French at TCD and a formidable advocate of progressive causes in Ireland's post-war years.

Next she threw herself into the fight against the censorship of books and films. She became a founder member of the progressive Irish Society for Intellectual Freedom (ISFIF), a body dedicated to opposing the censorship. It did this by publishing a monthly anti-censorship journal. Mary was there at the Society's first meeting in a flat in Baggot Street in January 1941. A living historical figure, Maud Gonne MacBride, now well into her seventies, was in the chair. Mary found her 'formidable' and admired her piercing blue eyes. They had an exchange in which Maud Gonne pronounced: 'Young lady, you still have the most precious thing of all, you have youth, do what you can with it.' Mary admired Maud Gonne's courage; she mentions seeing her some years later in Grafton Street, 'protesting about IRA prisoners in Mountjoy. The Saturday morning shoppers nearly brushed her off the pavement, but she carried on resolute and defiant ...'

Mary's name is recorded as an Executive Officer of the Society. Terence Brown, in his valuable book *Ireland: A Social and Cultural History, 1922–1979*, notes that the foundation of the ISFIF marked the beginning of a cultural watershed in Ireland. For the moment, however, church and state retained their suffocating grip.

All this sociopolitical activity was taking place in a country which had chosen to be neutral when Britain and Germany declared war in 1939. In the late 1930s much of Europe had been shadowed by a cloud of political anxiety. A rampant Germany, a hesitant Anglo-French alliance, fear of bombing (exacerbated by news of the raids on Barcelona and the destruction of Guernica in the Spanish Civil War), the pull of pacifism and a woeful lack of clear leadership – all these concerns kept ordinary European citizens awake at night. Irish men and women were no exception. De Valera's reaction to the threat of a war 'not of our own making' was to move, from 1936 onwards, towards neutrality. He was not the only leader of a small European country to make this political choice. Belgium, Finland, Hungary, Yugoslavia, Romania, Bulgaria, Portugal, Switzerland and the Netherlands (and others) also chose to be neutral when war broke out in 1939. Like Ireland, they felt relatively defenceless against the big battalions. Ireland's army and navy were Lilliputian and its air defences almost non-existent. Strategically, the Irish Free State was a sitting duck. As Clair Wills puts it in *That Neutral Island*, 'If neutrality was dangerous, belligerence looked like suicide.'

Ireland's military vulnerability was, however, only one of the considerations that drove de Valera towards neutrality. The struggle for Irish independence had been long and hard, so when it was achieved in 1921 it was important for the leaders of the new Irish Free State to assert a strong, separate national identity. In the late 1930s de Valera was determined to gain greater political and economic independence from Britain. Dev's simplistic vision of a self-sufficient, agricultural, Gaelic-speaking Ireland was probably unrealizable, but his determination to stand up to his powerful next-door neighbour struck a chord with his people. There was a strong sense of grievance in the Free State that, nearly two decades after independence, the six counties in the north of Ireland remained under British rule. And there were clear indications that the Protestant majority in the statelet of Northern Ireland was discriminating against the Catholic minority while Britain looked the other way. Indeed, nationalist, anti-British sentiment was so strong in 1939 that the Irish Republican Army – probably numbering 5000 adherents at this point – instigated a serious bombing campaign in Britain. There were 127 'incidents' in the first half of the year.

Then, on 25 August 1939, as Britons fearfully contemplated the imminent prospect of a Second World War, an IRA bomb killed five people in Coventry. De Valera knew that the feelings which prompted a young man like Brendan Behan to challenge the might of the British Empire (in his case with an almost ludicrous lack of success) were sufficiently intense and widespread to make it almost inconceivable that, in case of war, there would be general support for the former colonial power. If he took Britain's side, it was more than possible the IRA might turn their bombers towards local targets. De Valera and many others came to believe that neutrality was necessary if the Irish Free State was not to be divided politically to the point of becoming ungovernable. So when hostilities began on 3 September 1939 de Valera reaffirmed his country's stance, citing its democratic right to choose its own path. His choice, says Clair Wills, was 'a sign of Ireland's sovereignty, an expression of its hard-won independence'.

One day in early September 1939, just as the war began, Mary Hickey was at a gathering at College Green in Dublin, attended by the leaders of all political parties. A huge crowd was endorsing Ireland's neutral stance. In her autobiography she says little about the moral complexities of neutrality, but like most Irish people, she had little sympathy for fascist Germany and favoured the Allies. She notes that later, while the war was on, both Allied and German airmen, who had landed or crashed in Ireland, were allowed out from their prison camp at the Curragh on parole. Mary would mix with them at parties, but not always easily. 'Mostly they were relaxed and friendly. I remember one German airman who boasted he had been in the air raid over Coventry. This had occurred shortly before and it had accounted for much damage and great loss of life. I felt chilled by the conversation.' She nevertheless believed that de Valera was exercising his country's sovereign right to choose neutrality.

Mary's account of her Dublin years dwells on her intellectual development but also describes how 'The Emergency', as the wartime period of neutrality came to be known, affected her and her fellow citizens. When war broke out, de Valera imposed a fierce censorship on all news. The Irish newspapers were not allowed to publish more than the most cursory accounts of the battle with Germany. The Irish people found themselves in a state of disoriented isolation. Writing in 1942, Frank O'Connor saw his country as 'a nonentity state, entirely divorced from the rest of the world'. He found the intellectual darkness of the country 'almost palpable'. The novelist Kate O'Brien and other commentators saw wartime Ireland as 'a land outside time'. Complaints about censorship increased, but in a vote following a debate in the Dáil the pro-censorship lobby won easily. At this wartime moment, liberal 'European-Ireland', supported by writers like Seán O'Faoláin and O'Connor, was in particularly sharp conflict with repressive 'Irish-Ireland'. For Mary, the choice had to be for European-Ireland. And, paradoxically, the war created new cultural currents in Dublin, from which she benefited.

In 1939, after the conflict started, there was an influx of writers and artists from Britain and Europe. The painter Norah McGuinness and the poet and editor Geoffrey Taylor came from England. Louis le Brocquy, still in his twenties and eventually to become one of Ireland's great twentieth-century painters, arrived from France with his mother, Sybil. Northern Irish writers like Roy McFadden, Benedict Kiely and Robert Greacen came to Dublin. Another immigrant was Yeats's friend, woman of letters Ethel Mannin. A group of immigrant-artists made a big impact on Mary. Two pacifist painters, Basil Rákóczi and Kenneth Hall, and their close friend the psychiatrist Herbrand Ingouville-Williams, came from England where they became known as the White Stag Group. Rákóczi had a Hungarian father and an Irish mother; Hall was English. They wintered in the West of Ireland in 1940 but then came to Dublin. After their avant-garde work had created a stir when they exhibited in a flat in Baggot Street, they set up the tasteful White Stag Gallery in central Dublin, where they used the label 'subjectivist art' to describe their offerings. The trio brought a fresh perspective to a somewhat conservative Irish art world and, long-term, they had a liberating effect on Irish painters. Their lives were unconventional as well: Hall was gay and loved Rákóczi, who was an active bisexual, which caused Hall grief.

They held lectures at the White Stag Gallery. Rákóczi talked about psychoanalysis and was a disciple of Freud. Other subjects included Darwin's theory of evolution and there was even a talk on 'The Disintegration of the Sexual Impulse'. Mary remembers attending with 'a rather sedate elderly lady'. The talk, illustrated on a blackboard with pink and blue chalk, turned out to be somewhat explicit. Mary's elderly friend was horrified: 'You couldn't be a Catholic and sit here listening to that,' she kept murmuring in Mary's ear. Mary socialized with the White Staggers – going to a bottle party at Basil Rákóczi's, armed with a container of milk; or sitting on white cushions in Ingouville-Williams's all-white Fitzwilliam Square flat.

The refugees did a good deal of evangelizing in the cause of various varieties of modernism. They also recognized in the young Irish painter Patrick Scott an artist of enormous talent (he was later to be persuaded by Mary to paint sets for her in Belfast). Terence de Vere White sums up the White Stag Group very neatly, saying that the arrival in 1940 of 'a corduroy panzer division ... did us good ... for, uninhibited by Dublin backgrounds, they butted their way into public consciousness, living witness of something, if it was not always quite clear what.' In mixing with the White Stag artists, Mary had encountered a group which, as Herbert Read put it in an exhibition programme note, was 'in the mainstream of European culture'. She always had a strong visual sense, inherited from her mother and nurtured by Gerard. The 'corduroy panzers' probably fed in much new raw material to her inner eye.

The eclectic mix of visiting artists was clearly stimulating, but in cultural terms what Dublin offered, above all, was home-grown theatre. Mary had the chance to see good plays well done and to serve a kind of theatrical apprenticeship that was to bear remarkable fruit later on. There were the two Victorian theatres in the city: the Gaiety and the Olympia. Neither had a permanent company but both provided a varied diet of plays, some of them done by touring ensembles. However, Mary's main theatrical education took place at the venues with repertory companies, the Abbey and the Gate. Gerard provided an entrée to the Abbey. He had moved on from the Civil Service Dramatic Society and was designing and painting sets for the Abbey's studio theatre, the Peacock, as well as appearing in small parts. The theatre drew heavily on talented amateurs like Gerard. The Saturday all-night parties at the Peacock were just one facet of Mary's involvement with the Abbey. She went regularly to first nights and saw, among other works, the first performance of Paul Vincent Carroll's *Shadow and Substance* in 1937. She remembers this occasion as the debut of 'a fine young actress' Phyllis Ryan and the presence of a rather flamboyant audience member who announced to all and sundry: 'I am Patrick Kavanagh. I won the A.E. Memorial award.'

The Carroll play was one of the Abbey's better offerings during Mary's time in Dublin. The period 1936–46 was not one of the more distinguished decades in the history of what had once been an exciting, innovative theatre. In 1935 the liberal-minded Frank O'Connor had been appointed to the Abbey Board. From 1937 he ran the theatre, contributing plays such as *In the Train*, but he was deeply frustrated by the caution of his fellow directors. O'Connor was eventually ousted (general impiety and marriage to a divorcee were held against him) and was replaced by F.R. Higgins, who died in 1941, and was followed by the Ulsterman Ernest Blythe. Under Blythe the theatre gave long runs to plays with 'peasant quality' and expended much energy on poorly attended productions in Irish. There were fine actors in the company – like F.J. McCormick, Arthur Shields and Eileen Crowe – and a good director in Lennox Robinson, but groundbreaking new writing had little chance and the theatre settled into a comfortable mediocrity.

Mary's theatrical education benefited much more from the Gate, which was more outward-looking than the Abbey and was fortunate in having at the helm two outstanding theatrical personalities. Micheál MacLiammóir was an actor born in the suburbs of London, but with strong Irish connections, who learnt Irish, was fluent in several other languages, designed imaginative sets and had a stage presence, which few who saw his performances found it possible to forget. He had a caressing West-of-Ireland voice and for thirty years from the late 1920s dominated the Irish stage. His partner, both domestically and theatrically, was Hilton Edwards, an Englishman and a director of genius who brought discipline, focus and an imaginative professionalism to the presentation of plays: allied with the dazzling gifts of his lead actor, this led to some astonishing productions, perhaps the most notable being *The Old Lady Says "No!"* by Denis Johnston.

The Gate company was not always in residence in its theatre, which occupied the old Assembly Rooms of the Rotunda Hospital at the top of O'Connell Street. From 1936 the space was shared with a company run by the portly Frank Pakenham, Seventh Earl of Longford. It did good, varied work as well, but it was Edwards and MacLiammóir whose productions provided the high-voltage drama. Mary lists some of the plays they did in 1940 (many actually staged in the larger Gaiety Theatre), which impressed her: *Where Stars Walk*, a piece by MacLiammóir (playwriting was another of his talents); *The Dreaming Dust*, a play about Jonathan Swift by Denis Johnston; *The Masque of Kings* (Maxwell Anderson); *The Insect Play* by the Capek brothers; and *Mourning becomes Electra* by Eugene O'Neill. It was this last production she remembered best, 'not alone for its length but for its virtuosity; we entered the theatre at 6.30 p.m. and left about 11.00'.

Mary expresses warm feelings about the Gate in her memoirs: 'For 6d I saw some of the world's masterpieces.' And she remembers affectionately the delightful eccentricity of MacLiammóir who, after taking his curtain call, would always 'come back on stage and make a speech and assure us we were the best audience ever'. Tears of joy would often flow, especially if he had just returned to his theatrical home from a long tour. These speeches were one of the delights of Dublin theatrical life for more than thirty years.

She does not mention another theatre group operating during her time in Dublin that was to influence her profoundly. The poet Austin Clarke, in despair at the Abbey's abandonment of Yeats's plays and the way poetry had become a 'silent' art, founded the Dublin Verse-Speaking Society in 1940. This group was influential enough to persuade Radio Éireann to broadcast poetry and verse plays. Then in 1944 Clarke founded the Lyric Theatre Company, which managed to hire the Abbey stage and put on a production of *The Countess Cathleen* – a firm hint to the Abbey to mount more Yeats plays. Clarke wanted to revive Yeats and Lady Gregory's original 'imaginative aims of the dramatic movement'. In his Lyric Company there was to be much emphasis on the spoken word and new verse plays were to be tested, and if necessary revised, in rehearsal. In doing this Clarke learnt the need for shorter speeches and for more action. His company delivered twenty-seven productions over its lifetime of eight years. They included Clarke's own plays, several Yeats works and new verse plays by talented poet/dramatists like Donagh MacDonagh. Clarke also secured the involvement, usually unpaid, of a set of fine actors including Eithne Dunne, Cyril Cusack, Jack MacGowran and Eve Watkinson. Mary does not mention attending any of the Lyric's productions, but it seems likely that she went to them. What is clear is that she was inspired by Clarke's ideals and his Lyric Theatre provided a model she was to follow in her early Belfast days. She was later to correspond with Clarke, meet him and to ask him, the leading poet/dramatist in the Ireland of his day, to come up to Belfast to perform ceremonial functions for her.

Going regularly to see plays in Dublin gave Mary a good idea of what was possible in the theatre. But to make theatre herself it would be necessary to step out from the audience and go backstage to learn the practicalities: this she eventually did when her socialist convictions plunged her into the world of little theatre productions.

———————

In the Irish Free State, the years 1939–45 were neither as harsh nor as frightening as in England. While there was food rationing, it was not so severe as across the water. Eggs, butter and cheese were freely available, and many visitors came from England to enjoy eating and drinking in a city that still had neon lights at night. The café and restaurant scenes were lively. Grafton Street had its coffee houses – Roberts's, Mitchell's and Bewley's. Many of the acting fraternity ate at the Ritz in Middle Abbey Street. This was not as grand as it sounds and there were confirmed reports, according to Mary, of cockroaches in the kitchens. At the top of the scale in both cost and quality was Jammet's, which provided exceptional French cuisine just off Grafton Street. Upstairs an open fire burned in a room of great comfort and atmosphere. Mary was occasionally able to eat there, but only if richer folk footed the bill.

Visitors from across the water seeking R & R in Dublin were mostly well fed, but in winter they would also have been cold. Supplies of imported coal ran out early in the war. Plenty of turf was available; piles of it were provided free in Phoenix Park, but it was often hopelessly damp and provided little heat. Anything that would burn was utilized and 'occasionally a little box of coal would make its way down from the North and this was heaven'. Gas supplies were limited, so its use was restricted and 'the glimmer man', a sort of gas inspector, patrolled the streets to check on any unlawful use of the precious commodity.

Transport was also a problem. The trains ran on turf and the journeys often seemed interminable. Sometimes the engines moved so slowly that passengers found they could take the air on a long journey by walking beside their carriage. The electric trams in Dublin were efficient but did not run late at night. In this immobile world, the bicycle was king. In the evening hundreds – perhaps thousands – of bikes were parked in central Dublin while their owners visited the cinemas and theatres. Mary undertook what were, for her, some rash two-wheeled expeditions, like cycling the ten miles from Dublin to the traditional Easter Monday Fairyhouse Races and back. She had a 'High Nell' bicycle at this point, which she found terrifying to ride because the saddle was so far from the ground.

Mary is clear that the Emergency discomforts described above were very minor 'compared to what was endured across the water'. Bombs *were* dropped on Ireland in 1940 and '41, mostly by mistake. On the night of 30 May 1941, the North Strand area of the city was hit by four bombs – killing twenty-eight people, destroying seventeen houses and making hundreds of families homeless. Mary remembered the events of that night vividly:

> My mother and myself wandered around the house, she clutching her rosary beads while we waited for the next bomb. Then the morning finally dawned, and we were grateful to be alive. The coal shortage didn't seem so bad after that. Immediate danger passed, we were up and doing again.

Up and doing meant more cultural activity for Mary. Her eclectic policy of 'join everything' took her to the Irish Film Society (IFS). Dublin was in thrall to Hollywood; the big cinemas in the centre of the city attracted huge audiences, awed by the glamour and affluence of the American way of life. But there were also the *cineastes* of the IFS who loved the cinema as an art form, enjoyed critical analysis and wanted, if possible, to make their own movies. When Mary joined, she was allowed to pay the subscription of a guinea in instalments. The society, founded in 1936, delivered monthly showings of classic films – usually of the left-wing variety – at various Dublin cinemas. The leading light was Liam O'Laoghaire who, attired in a red shirt and with a wild shock of hair, introduced the films. Mary's viewing included *Battleship Potemkin*, *Kammerschaft*, *The Lonely White Sail*, *All Quiet on the Western Front*, *The Blue Angel* and *The 39 Steps*.

At first, she did office chores at the Society's headquarters in Talbot Street, but then something much more exciting turned up. She 'starred' in a short 16mm film made by the Society in 1943. It was called *Tibradden*, after an area in the foothills of the Dublin mountains. It was shot on Sunday mornings over two summers. Mary and the crew would meet at Rathfarnham Castle and cycle up the steep hills to their locations. The crew consisted of Peter Sherry, director; Jack White, cameraman; Norrie Duff, scriptwriter; and an unnamed continuity girl. The film was silent and told the story of a young man and woman (Mary) who cycle some way up the mountain, then pause to relax for a time in the heather. Then they go further up the mountain and the atmosphere changes 'to one of bleakness and foreboding'. Mary's own summing up of *Tibradden* is: 'Atmosphere was the keynote; it was all too subtle, I felt, but I enjoyed the making.' Mary does not mention the name of her co-star, with whom she must have spent several Sundays lolling in the heather in reasonably close physical contact, if surviving stills from the picture are to be believed. He was an actor called Brendan O'Sé and it is odd that she has absolutely nothing to say about him in her autobiography. One can only speculate; perhaps something happened between them which made remembering and recording difficult.

Socialism and theatre were already two defining strands in Mary's life, so it is not surprising that when she encountered a left-wing theatre group, she grabbed a chance to create a theatrical apprenticeship for herself. The New Theatre Group (NTG) had been founded in 1937. It was connected to the Irish Labour Party and its aim was to produce dramas of social and socialist significance, which also had artistic merit. These two aspirations often clashed when plays were being chosen. Mary says there were 'plays that were overtly political or weighed down with the social message', which were often not very good. And there were good plays that were seen as 'far too lightweight for people in a hurry to change the world'. Her summary is that 'the New Theatre Group did manage, over a period of years, to do mainly good plays, not always, unfortunately, very well.' The NTG was always short of money and performed in a series of primitive and dilapidated venues. When Mary joined, the group was putting on plays in Rutland Place near the Gate Theatre. The roof leaked, which on one occasion caused a distinguished audience member, Lord Longford, to put up his umbrella during a performance. The facilities were basic: the dressing rooms consisted of an open area, divided into Ladies and Gents by a piece of hanging canvas. A stage of sorts had been constructed and the audience sat on chairs borrowed from one of the trade unions. In this unpromising environment, Mary worked hard – 'unremitting toil' is how she describes it. She cleaned, rehearsed, read and 'instructed' fellow members. With amateur and some professional actors working side by side, the NTG did a new play every month and ran it for a week. Amateur dramatic societies were by now proliferating all over the country, with the approval of the hierarchy, which saw them as healthier options than imbibing the worldly romances of Hollywood or pursuing the tactile pleasures of the dance hall. But the NTG regarded itself as trying to do something more serious, more politically committed than most of the proliferating amateur groups.

Mary did not direct plays but describes herself as being 'secretary' to the group for several years. It seems likely that under that title her role was somewhere between producer and general dogsbody. The files of the NTG show the way the company worked and Mary's role in it. Her secretary's minute book for 1942–43 has survived. There is a discussion (11 January 1943) about art versus propaganda. The committee seem to prefer propaganda and agree that their purpose is to do 'plays that for various reasons would not be done by the Gate and the Abbey'. And they want to attract a working-class audience rather than an 'artistic' one. On a more practical level there are grumbles about chairs not being put out before performances, about unfinished sets and lack of discipline in the cast. Two actors are castigated for being late for a dress rehearsal. One is H.A.L. 'Harry' Craig. To sharpen up organization it is decided to employ a 'business manager' and so Joe MacColum makes his appearance. He was paid the munificent sum of £1 per week.

By mid-January 1943 MacColum was in post with a long list of tasks (including 'the upkeep of the premises') as well as considerable powers. He could 'depute members to various duties'; he had the right to suspend them; he was in 'complete control of publicity'; and he had 'general control of the stage during productions'.

MacColum was on the NTG scene for most of 1943 and some of his fortnightly reports on productions make fascinating reading. Towards the end of February, the company put on Ernst Toller's *No More Peace*. It had a cast of more than thirty. All the parts had not been filled when they began rehearsals in January and it emerges from Joe's reports that he, as well as performing all his other duties, was to direct the play as well. He says he wants to 'adhere to the Stanislavsky method of production as far as possible'. Rehearsals were held every evening, and in the afternoons for those who were able to attend. First the cast read the whole piece together, then each cast member had to answer a questionnaire about the play. The second week of rehearsals was devoted to movement; the third to characterization. Joe says he wants cast meetings as often as possible to discuss the latter, and he fervently hopes that the Sunday preceding the performance week can be a free day for the cast.

Writing a fortnight later, on 16 February 1943, he records problems with the cast. Actors have dropped out and replacements have been hard to find. Cast meetings are rare 'because the cast is so large and the time so short'. In a happier report, written nearly three weeks later, MacColum proudly states that, as planned, no rehearsals were necessary on the Sunday before the play began. He seems to have weathered a storm over the important role of Jacob. It was still not cast with a week to go and two possibilities had to drop out. Finally, Harry Craig stepped into the breach and went on after 'only two or three short rehearsals'.

MacColum was pleased with the sets, done by Mary's brother Gerard 'in twelve hours' and perfectly expressing 'the spirit of the play'. Despite the casting difficulties, the public performances went well, in the director's view, with 'no hitch of any importance'. That is until the Saturday night, when 'Keith Adams was incapable of coherent and intelligent acting, owing to his having taken too much drink.' Another cast member failed to turn up at all but was later seen, drunk, at a party. MacColum has a kind word for the inebriated Keith Adams who is 'very stiff but is willing to try and is worth attention'. Then Mary steps into the limelight as stage manager: 'The stage management was as nearly perfect as I have yet seen in the Group and Mary Hickey had complete control, delegated the work as necessary, and was completely responsible for the smooth running of this end of the production.'

Later minutes of the NTG report that they are attempting to take plays out into the provinces; that UCD students have hired the theatre for a party and trashed it; and that the Study Circle is going well. But quite early on there are suggestions that members have been questioning Joe's decisions and by the end of the year he was gone. He was not around to enjoy a move to a much better theatre, a change made possible when a benefactor, Frank Hugh O'Donnell, gave them £25. The company moved to Baggot Court in Ballsbridge in the final years of the war and with the help of Andrew Ganly (dentist and playwright), painted and prepared a small theatre.

The list of NTG productions includes plays which Mary was to return to in her later incarnation as a director. She acted in four: *The Great God Brown* by Eugene O'Neill, *Squaring the Circle* by Valentin Kataev, *The Golden Cuckoo* by Denis Johnston and *Waiting for Lefty* by Clifford Odets. She then abandoned acting, preferring to confine herself to less spectacular backstage functions in what she calls 'the movement'. She adds, cryptically, that 'there were many crises to be overcome and I was strong on the battlements'.

New Theatre plays were not exclusively socialist agitprop; *Volpone* was done and the *Ascent of F6* by Auden and Isherwood. Nevertheless, the main thrust was to present committed left-wing plays and Mary hints that as the forties went on and some of the group's energy began to flag, it suffered for its determined stance. The NTG was too far left for some in the Labour Party. 'We were not on our guard,' Mary says, 'and it appears to me the organization was taken over and deliberately put out of action.' Dublin Labour politics in the 1940s were bedevilled and corrupted by a huge fissure between the leftish party members and the more conventional trade unionists. Mary learnt some political lessons at the NTG, but more importantly she found out what was required to make a small, impecunious, amateur theatre work. She absorbed some of the prosaic secrets of creating theatrical magic.

4

Suitors

SO, WHERE HAD the essential Mary gone in all this welter of cultural activity? This lively, dark-eyed girl with fine coils of black hair had many male friends. But the autobiography is parsimonious with details: only two males are recorded as having made a serious impression on her during her Dublin decade.

One is the poet and, later, diplomat Val (Valentin) Iremonger. She liked him: 'I was taken with his ideas, his gentleness ...' Already trained at the Abbey School of Acting, he directed for the NTG and she admired the 'resilience and sense of fun he showed when disruptions occurred – which they frequently did'. He liked 'the dense smokey atmosphere of the rehearsal scene. He was pale-faced and thin and never took any fresh air, alleging it would be the death of him.' Mary used to try to persuade him to go on bike rides into the countryside and occasionally succeeded:

> Once we visited the ruins in Rathfarnham of Sarah Curran's home. It seemed to me a rather special occasion and he promised to write a poem in memory of the visit. I had always been rather affected by the sad story of Sarah Curran's love for the rebel, Robert Emmet; the whole sorrow of their relationship and her great loneliness when her father cast her out.

Val never wrote the poem. He did, however, write a play about Emmet, *Wrap Up My Green Jacket*, which Louis MacNeice directed on radio for the BBC Third Programme and which Mary herself was to stage in her own theatre. There is a hint of sadness in the final line of her short account of Iremonger: 'Our paths would sever.' But their friendship continued for some time after Mary married and Val may have had stronger feelings for her than she realized.

Mary would perhaps have daunted some young men, with her feisty determination to get a job done. This aspect of her nature does not seem to have discouraged a new suitor when he appeared in 1943. She met Dr Pearse O'Malley at a fundraising dance, which had been organized by the Irish Film Society at the Avoca School in Blackrock:

> I was stage-managing a play the same night and we arrived late to find that the evening was already well under way. I immediately joined a Paul Jones and when the music stopped was claimed by a rather attractive, clean-shaven young man. Most of my acquaintances at this stage were rather ragged and down-at-heel. This fellow looked promising.

He asked her for the next dance but very soon the MC announced that specially laid-on transport arrangements had fallen through and that those dependent on public transport should leave because the trams would be stopping early. They sat beside each other on the bus and as they talked she discovered that he came from the North. When they got into the centre of Dublin, Pearse retrieved his bicycle and gave Mary 'a cross-bar' to Rathmines, delivering a wobbly intimacy she may have relished. Pearse must have liked her well enough because he got in touch again. Mary had found out that he came from a large Co. Armagh family, was just a few days younger than her, had graduated at Queen's University and was now studying psychiatry in Dublin. She was interested. She gave him a this-is-my-address note which has, astonishingly, survived. There is a quotation which is not easily legible, but the gist is, 'Let the philosophers explain the world, our policy is to change it!' Changing the world together did indeed become their joint 'policy', but not just yet.

She took Dr O'Malley to see the NTG production of *Six Men of Dorset* at Liberty Hall, the shrine of the Irish labour movement. They sat together at the back, holding hands. Mary's job that evening was to run up some steps to turn the house lights on and off. As the hall had no sound system, the audience simply sang labour songs in the interval and, at the end, 'The Watchword of Labour'. Pearse seems to have withstood this session of total immersion in socialism because he had a half-crown ready to put on the plate. The handholding at the back of the hall, however, had consequences. Mary was, after all, supposed to be on duty and, almost unbelievably, she was censured by the committee for 'frivolity'.

Mary and Pearse had about a year together in Dublin before he decided to move to England to advance his medical career, specialising in neurology and psychiatry. In Dublin he worked at St Patrick's hospital, founded by Dean Swift as a 'home for fools and the mad'. He had time and money for a leisured lifestyle: fishing, riding and giving dinner parties. Even though the relationship with Mary was developing, Pearse was adamant that he needed more experience elsewhere, so he chose to go to the Bristol Mental Hospital and to do research at the Maudsley in London. His departure caused Mary some stress. She had begun to think 'he was worth pursuing'. She missed him and found it hard to understand why he had left her and the safety and comfort of Dublin. In London the V1s and V2s were causing fear and havoc and Pearse was housed in very rudimentary quarters in a Toc H hostel. He came back to Ireland only twice a year and travel from Ireland to England was difficult because of wartime restrictions. 'As a result, our courtship was rather dilatory and unhappy from my point of view.' They wrote frequently but Mary found pursuing a long-distance relationship by correspondence difficult. Pearse, for his part, was being single-minded about getting the necessary experience to enable him to become a consultant.

An interesting note from this period has survived, which may have been torn out of a pocket diary:

Agreement, August 11, 1944
Between PP O'Mallie [*sic*] (medical doctor?) of St Patrick's Hospital, James Street, Dublin, on the one hand, and Mary Hickey (Private

Secretary) of 37 Grosvenor Road, on the other. The latter agrees to abandon all claim to the former for a period of three months, dating from the above date. The freedom given herewith is free and unconditional. Signed M Hickey, August 11th, 1944.

This communication is probably part of a long string of notes charting their slow courtship. Two letters from Mary have survived, almost certainly from a later period in the relationship. The first, written from home in Rathmines, is undated and teasing:

Dear Pearse

I thought you had given me up for a giddy blonde. Your long letter, 11 lines and a bit, was too tremendous!!! No fear of your getting writer's cramp … Having a quiet life and doing my best to behave myself – a bit of a job of course.

Went to a NTG [New Theatre] party with Val – not very exciting. Make your next epistle more detailed.

Yours, Mary

Pearse's response may have drawn the following bantering reply from Mary, although it very possible that, because of the reference to Belfast, it is written much later, perhaps in 1946:

Dear P

Your extremely long, newsy and invigorating letter received … Two or three games of golf – darling, you're being reckless. I am really disappointed that socialist training availed you so little that you fell victim to 'golf'. Stalin be praised! … Life is quite 'flat' without you, although I am not exactly pining away … The fattening process is progressing favourably. I shall be quite beefy-looking when you return! Hope you behave yourself in Belfast. Keep the 'fat one' at distance, knowing your partiality to the flesh! Mary

The end of the war, which came with Victory in Europe Day in May 1945, was greeted with delight in Ireland. The long limbo of neutrality was over. De Valera's stance had been a step in the dark, but it had worked from Ireland's point of view, even if at some moral cost. Mary was angry when, during peace celebrations in Dublin, she saw a tricolour being burned in front of one of the last bastions of the Ascendancy, Trinity College, which was rashly flying a Union Jack. Attempts were made to remove it and then UCD students led, according to legend, by the youthful Charles Haughey, brought a new tricolour to College Green and fisticuffs ensued.

An immediate consequence of the peace was that many of the interesting and creative 'foreigners' who had lodged in Dublin during the war departed – leaving behind a country which was still culturally impoverished and now economically more dependent on Britain than ever. Unemployment and growing disillusion with the limitations of rural life led to tens of thousands departing across the water to rebuild Britain, where they enjoyed plentiful overtime, usually remembered to send their remittances home and thus propped up the Irish economy.

For Mary the end of the war meant more chances to see Pearse. In 1946 he finally came 'home' when he was offered an opportunity he could not refuse. He was asked to open a department of neurology and psychiatry at the Mater Hospital in Belfast – at which he had trained. (This was a considerable achievement; Pearse was still in his twenties.) Because the Mater was a teaching hospital, he received a small emolument for instructing medical students. But it was understood that his main income would come from private practice, which he began to develop straight away. From Dublin Mary watched his progress in Belfast – noting that while living at the Belgravia Hotel in the Lisburn Road, he was doing cautious house-hunting.

Mary's 'intended', Patrick Pearse O'Malley to give him his full and resonant name, was at this time twenty-nine years old. His background was interesting. His father (also Patrick) was born on a farm in the Dorsey area of Co. Armagh. He seems to have spent time in America, then returned with enough money to buy a hardware business in Newtownhamilton, Co. Armagh. Patrick senior had a drink problem, so the business was run from then on, very effectively, by Pearse's mother, Susan (née McKee). Pearse was a thoughtful, rebellious child who read Dickens and sometimes refused to go to school because of the corporal punishment delivered by the head teacher. His youth was otherwise comfortable enough, with long summers spent camping at Newcastle, Co. Down, and interesting relatives, including an uncle, Father Pat McKee, who was a well-off priest who had returned to Ireland from Sacramento, California. Doctors and priests were numerous in Pearse's family. Several relatives were involved with the IRA during the early 1920s. Pearse's uncle James McKee – another doctor – rose to the rank of commandant general of the Northern Division. In 1922 he was arrested and spent three years in gaol in Belfast, Derry and on the prison boat *Argenta*. He later became a respected doctor with a practice in Dublin and served as best man at Pearse and Mary's wedding.

Mary refers ironically to Pearse as 'my Romeo in Belfast'. He came to Dublin frequently, but Mary says that they 'flew in and out of love regularly'. At one point there was a serious rupture and Mary handed back to Pearse the many letters he had written to her from England. He burnt them, but relations were repaired, and Mary began to pay visits to Belfast, meeting Pearse's friends and attending the staff dance at the Mater Hospital, where she had a strong feeling of being closely scrutinized. House-hunting was going on desultorily, so one day Mary, approaching desperation, pointed to a sizeable establishment for sale on the corner of Ulsterville Avenue, near the centre of the city, said it would do and departed for Dublin. To her astonishment – and eventually dismay – she heard shortly afterwards that Pearse had bought the house. The dismay came when she realized how unsuitable it was:

> This large barracks of a place was on the front of the Lisburn Road, and had done service during the war as a headquarters for the Fire Service. The fine mahogany doors bore witness to intensive darts practice. The bathroom boasted three washbasins and the general décor was dark green and cream.

Whatever Mary's feelings about the house, its purchase was now a *fait accompli*. (Pearse's uncle, Father Pat, had enough spare cash to help with the purchase.)

Marriage was looking more and more likely. A date was finally set: Tuesday, 16 September 1947, at the University Church in St Stephen's Green. Both families were well represented at a reception at the Shelbourne Hotel. Mary's maternal uncle, Bill Lysaght, gave her away; Val Iremonger and her brother Gerard were groomsmen. The NTG gave Mary a fine china tea service and the Irish Film Society made a movie of the occasion (now sadly lost). Mary's mother wore a memorable hat for the occasion. Strangely, the autobiography makes no mention of a honeymoon. A love letter Pearse wrote to Mary ten years after the wedding provides a somewhat opaque explanation. First he reviews their happy times together but adds, 'My chief regret is that we didn't get married sooner and that I inadvertently made our honeymoon and post-honeymoon period a nightmare. Indulgence in self-reproach may be another form of hypocrisy – I am only stating what I feel to be a fact.' He says he is not asking for forgiveness, but 'how we both live our lives in the future is the ultimate answer'. Pearse's references to difficult times on the honeymoon and afterwards probably explains why Mary left out any reference to it in her autobiography. Whatever the problem was, it was solved subsequently in what became an enduring, argumentative but loving marriage.

After describing the wedding, Mary moves swiftly on to Belfast: 'We arrived in the Northern Capital in the first week in October.' There, she says, she felt strange, out of place and a little nervous. As they drove down the Lisburn Road on the first 'black October evening, a little shiver went down my spine.' She had left many good friends behind in Dublin, and she remembered the stories of Protestants stoning the Eucharistic Congress train as it steamed through Portadown. What sort of place had this good Catholic girl from Co. Cork come to live in?

5

Belfast

THERE WERE BOTH personal and political elements in Mary's apprehension as she arrived in Belfast. She already knew the city a little from her wartime expeditions to see Pearse. She had dined at the Crawfordsburn Inn (a welcoming hostelry on the southern shores of Belfast Lough); she had done her tourist duty and climbed the Cave Hill, a bare ridge a thousand feet high and only four miles from the city centre; and she remembered standing outside the City Hall (a grand example of Victorian municipal pride) on a fine night during the war – and been frightened when someone looked up into the sky and quipped, 'What a lovely evening for an air raid.'

As she and Pearse drove around on that dank October evening in 1947, she felt a bit like an exile and ruminated on what she had left behind. 'I had grown to love Dublin and I had a large circle of friends and I seemed to "fit in".' She had indeed found her niche in Dublin. Would she be able to create a new one for herself here? A long, intimate and conversational letter from Val Iremonger, now a trainee diplomat, which arrived not long after the wedding, throws a little light on her state of mind. It begins 'Mary darling,' and he apologizes that he and his girlfriend, Sheila, will not be up in Belfast for Halloween. He is quite upfront about his feelings for Mary:

> I'm looking forward very much to seeing you and talking things over with you. There isn't anybody in town here I want to talk to – I miss you

very much. When we all get together, we can send Pearse off with Sheila and we'll have a good pow-wow on the subject.

Iremonger's letters continued – often jokey and usually entertaining. He tells her that her wedding photos are now to be seen in the window of the *Irish Independent* newspaper offices in Abbey Street and then imagines the kind of rude comments that their socialist friends might have made about them. He goes on: 'You look terrific, and Pearse ... Personally I think *I* look wonderful – very diplomaticky – but that's only my opinion.' He goes on to describe how he was 'elephants' (drunk) after the wedding and then managed to drive a friend to Blackrock.

This cameo of Dublin life must have done little to relieve any separation anxiety which Mary may have implied in an earlier letter to Iremonger. He says: 'It is nice to read in your letter that you had no mental stimulation up there at all. Believe me there's nothing worse for the figure. I hope you won't start organising the Group Theatre, or anything like that ...' He then mischievously asks her to tell Pearse that 'he still stands for Partition and the status quo'. Next, he gives an account of the plays he's seen in Dublin and reports that his own piece, *Wrap Up My Green Jacket*, has been playing to poor houses at the Peacock Theatre. Then, making more mischief:

> Well, how are you liking Belfast? Now shut up. Don't be thinking of it as 'this God-forsaken hole'. You're living in a terrific house and Belfast isn't all that bad. When I go up, I'll introduce you to John Hewitt and Sam Hanna Bell. Hewitt is a stuffy cove – don't care for him overmuch myself, but still ... Anyway, with your car – have you got a petrol allowance? – you will find the outskirts of Belfast very nice indeed. All cities are the same. Belfast will be what you make of it yourself.

Belfast was not the same as Dublin – it was different physically, politically and culturally. To Mary it was a city 'in Ireland' rather than 'of Ireland'. It lacked Dublin's spacious and gracious Georgian squares – although those fine facades sometimes hid grim slums. Belfast's Royal Avenue was a relatively prosaic, business-like main thoroughfare, lacking the grand scale of O'Connell Street. Wrapped around the Victorian heart of the city were tens of thousands of tiny red-brick terrace houses, many proudly maintained by carpet-slippered women enthusiastically brushing their front steps for the greater glory of Ulster (or Ireland) and, perhaps, hoping to acquire godliness through cleanliness. From many parts of the city, it was possible to see the towering cranes of the Harland & Wolff shipyard – their presence a reminder of past glories (the construction of the *Titanic* for example) but also indicating that at this post-war moment, Ulster still had a powerful industrial base.

The Irish Free State had been a good place for Mary to leave, but she was coming to live in a deeply undemocratic statelet. Northern Ireland had been run, since its inception in 1921, by the Unionists, who discriminated against Catholics in housing, education and employment. Lord Brookeborough told his Protestant supporters that 'he had not a Roman Catholic about the place ... because [they] were out with all their force and might to destroy the power and constitution of Ulster'. The Protestants felt they worked harder than Catholics, were more entrepreneurial, more honest and not in thrall to the *diktat* of an elderly gentleman in Rome. This sense of superiority was accompanied by a damaging complacency in government. During the war Belfast had been pathetically undefended against the German air raids. Nine hundred people had died in the Easter blitz of 1941 – more deaths in a single raid than any other British city except London.

Economically the picture was brighter; subventions from the Westminster government fattened Ulster's purse and the traditional industries in Belfast still had life left in them. This was a time of political opportunity when, with living standards rising and inter-communal relations relatively quiet, the Brookeborough government had a chance to try to reconcile the non-violent members of the nationalist community with the political status quo. But the Unionists made little attempt to do so, while the nationalists remained firmly abstentionist. The frustration caused by this political stagnation, not surprisingly, led to sporadic outbreaks of IRA violence in the 1950s.

Being from the South was not an asset in Belfast. The Northern Ireland majority remained suspicious and distrustful of its southern neighbour. Irish neutrality during the war had not helped matters, nor did talk of the Free State becoming a republic, which got louder in 1948 and was enacted in 1949. This meant the final severing of the Anglo-Irish umbilical cord. Even worse from a Northern point of view, this move was accompanied by a great deal of anti-partitionist activity in the South – the backwash of which soon began to flow through the O'Malley drawing room in Ulsterville Avenue. Mary and Pearse, hospitable from the start, gave help and accommodation to visiting representatives of anti-partitionist groups. Various political figures, including Conor Cruise O'Brien, were welcomed at Ulsterville House on their way to speaking at large meetings in Belfast. In the late 1940s there was optimism about the possibility of reuniting Ireland.

Culturally, Belfast was not the 'Siberia of the arts' Mary might have feared. There were painters of talent like Basil Blackshaw, John Luke and Colin Middleton; accomplished poets like John Hewitt and Robert Greacen; and novelists of quality, including Forrest Reid and Michael McLaverty. Belfast was also lucky enough to have in the decade after the war two very lively theatres. Frank Matcham's beautiful Royal Opera House took in visiting productions, but the real vibrancy came from the Arts and the Group theatres. The Group was, as its name implies, an amalgam of several amateur companies, formed in 1940. It survived the Blitz and went on to deliver a wide repertoire of plays including productions of Ibsen, Sheridan, Chekhov, Pinero, Odets and Shaw. It did some Irish dramas, but they often had an Ulster slant, like St John Ervine's *Boyd's Shop*. The Group was fortunate in having in the company Joseph Tomelty, playwright, actor and theatrical manager, and Harold Goldblatt, a director and actor of great talent. An astonishing number of fine performers learned their trade at the Group – and then emigrated. The list includes Patrick Magee, Harry Towb, J.G. Devlin, Denys Hawthorne, Stephen Boyd, Colin Blakely and James Ellis. This talented company was in full voice when Mary arrived in Belfast; it was adventurous in its choice of new plays, which included Tomelty's supernatural tragedy, *All Souls' Night*, in which he also excelled as an actor. The Group was to continue as a force in Ulster drama for another ten years.

Its high standards and the quality of its programming meant that when Mary made her own entry into the Belfast theatrical scene, three years after her arrival, she was stepping into a highly competitive environment.

The Arts was another vibrant theatre. Founded in 1945 by Hubert Wilmot, it presented plays by major European and American dramatists: Ionesco, Miller, Anouilh, Bolt, Giraudoux, Cocteau and T.S. Eliot among others. For a time in the early 1950s the Arts was one of the most exciting theatres in Ireland. It was probably near its peak when Mary arrived, but within a few years drama on television began to provide stiff competition, so to survive, Wilmot had to narrow his choice and veer towards entertainment, which meant doing more Ulster plays and musicals. He came to believe that his theatre could not stay in business if it catered exclusively, or even largely, 'for the 10% of the Ulster audience who want "strong" drama'. But this gloomy conclusion came later and, as Mary settled into her new environment, the Arts was still doing interesting plays well.

Mary's early reservations about Ulsterville House had been amply borne out. It was a sizeable four-storey establishment, but it had only a small front garden and no more than a yard at the back. To get to the top of the house involved climbing forty-one stairs, arranged in five separate flights. She and Pearse chose to dedicate the two main rooms on the ground floor to Pearse's private practice; the lounge became a waiting room and the dining area his consulting room. This meant that the family had to move upstairs to eat. As a result, Mary often worried that the food, which came up from the basement, was cold after journeying up two flights of stairs. However, she made light of these difficulties, and with her mother's resourcefulness and taste made the austere interior friendly and habitable.

By Christmas time Mary felt that Ulsterville House was presentable enough for a housewarming party. Pearse's colleagues and their wives were invited as well as sundry Belfast acquaintances. Dublin friends were encouraged to come, among them Val Iremonger. The Dubliners had to bring not only themselves but Dublin delicacies not then available in rationed Belfast, such as meats, various savouries, cakes and biscuits. The party was held upstairs, with a large octagonal mahogany table – recently purchased for £12 – as the centrepiece. There was an enormous Christmas tree and a roaring fire. The guests had been invited for eight and at this point Mary was in the bath – believing that, like Dublin, no one would be there on time. Wrong: everyone had arrived by ten past eight. She had learnt her first lesson in Belfast punctuality.

One of the guests was the playwright Joseph Tomelty, who felt so much at home that he stayed till 6.30 am. Mary says Tomelty gave her an informal seminar on Belfast humour and the way of life in the small kitchen houses in the little streets. He knew a lot about this subject, which he was to put to good use when, a year or two later, he was to author the immensely popular local radio serial, *The McCooeys*. Also invited were John and Elizabeth Boyle who were on their way to becoming lifelong friends. He was a teacher at the Royal Belfast Academical Institution (known as 'Inst'), alma mater of Michael Longley; she lectured at a teacher-training college and wrote radio plays, one of which, *Falcons in the Square*, Mary was to stage later in her theatre. The Boyles were active in Labour politics and fostered Mary's desire to become similarly committed.

As 1948 wore on pregnancy became Mary's first concern. Her mother was imported from Dublin to help with preparations and seems to have given approval to her daughter's slightly sprawling ménage. For a time, Mrs Hickey's 'stunning floral arrangements' in the waiting room probably improved the mood of the patients queuing for their psychiatric interviews with Dr O'Malley.

Mary filled in the impatient hours as she waited for her first child by painting her front gate orange and entertaining Pearse's relatives from Philadelphia. The baby was three weeks late, but finally on 15 November 1948, at home at Ulsterville House, a healthy boy arrived. The birth was not easy. Mary is laconic: 'I was flat out. When I recovered sufficiently, I admired my handiwork.' Kieran Darragh was christened, with Pearse's father and mother as godparents. Mary's mother devoted herself to the care of Kieran who slept at the top of the house in a room heated by an open fire which constantly needed replenishing with coal – heaved up all forty-one steps every time. Mary took a while to recover from the difficult birth.

At this moment Mary and Pearse were observers of the local political scene rather than participators in it. But Pearse's career and earnings were soon to be seriously affected by a major piece of social legislation introduced by the Westminster parliament. In 1948 a National Health Service was introduced in England, Scotland and Wales. An almost identical system was put in place in Northern Ireland and quickly there were huge improvements in the general level of health. But there was a sectarian fly in the ointment. The newly formed Hospitals Authority insisted on complete control of all hospitals and refused to allow the Mater Hospital – where Pearse worked – to preserve its Catholic ethos. The Mater was denied payment for providing outpatient services and it received no public funding whatsoever. There were sharp debates at Stormont, but the government refused to budge. The doctors working at the Mater (one of only two teaching hospitals in Northern Ireland), continued to provide free treatment for patients, but all funds had to come from charitable sources. This meant that, unlike the consultants in other hospitals, who had adequate NHS salaries, Pearse and his colleagues at the Mater had to manage on £500 a year, plus what they could make from private practice. The salaries improved slowly, but it was not until 1972, well into the Troubles, that the Mater became part of the NHS in Belfast and Pearse began to earn a proper consultant's salary. Fortunately, his private psychiatric practice thrived so the family was able to move eventually to a larger suburban house, which made Mary's future theatrical activities possible.

The other event which impinged on Mary's political thinking was the Stormont election of 1949. She was an admirer of the eloquent socialist Jack Beattie who had represented the constituency of Belfast-Pottinger since 1929. He was a staunch friend of the poor and the unemployed, but in this election, he was caught out by a split in Labour politics in Northern Ireland. One section of the party was pro-partition and called itself the Northern Ireland Labour Party; the other was anti-partitionist and called itself the Irish Labour Party. Beattie was an anti-partitionist, but also a Presbyterian. His defection to an 'Irish' party made him a 'lundy', or traitor, to many

Protestants. Beattie was a fine orator, but at the hustings in this election he was pelted with oranges as he spoke. This now seems an expensive and exotic form of protest, but it had a dangerous edge – literally, because the soft oranges often had razorblades embedded in them. He survived this assault but lost the election (and later took to wearing a tin helmet when he addressed meetings). Mary admired Beattie and later shared a platform with him at Belfast Corporation local elections.

Mary produced her second son, Donal Lysaght, on 10 August 1950 – again a difficult birth. His older brother, Kieran, was not entirely pleased with the arrival and the new baby proved difficult to feed. Domestic help evaporated just as it was most needed and the inconveniences of Ulsterville House made life difficult and exhausting for a time. The forty-one steps up to the nursery seemed more wearisome than ever. Eventually the employment of a children's nurse eased the situation. Pearse, according to Mary, 'seemed to sail through it all, calm and relatively unscathed'.

Domestic management and motherhood were clearly not enough for Mary and it is typical of her that she chose this moment to kindle a small, flickering dramatic fire, which would eventually blaze gloriously as the Lyric Players Theatre. Her beginnings as a director came about in a curious way. Pearse, as if he weren't busy enough already, became the president of the Newman Society at Queen's University, a Catholic organization promoting culture and debate. He did not baulk at the task of organizing a programme of lectures and poetry readings. He would invite poets like Val Iremonger to perform (which he had done in January 1948); or ask the wonderfully outspoken Dublin socialist Owen Sheehy-Skeffington to speak to the motion 'Nationalism equals Socialism'. Skeffington's speech led to an acrid discussion in which a Catholic priest, Cathal Daly, then a young lecturer in scholastic philosophy, reproached the speaker and referred to 'the treachery of the intellectuals'.

Pearse could manage such events easily, but as the 1950 annual Christmas party approached, he 'went into a decline'. Parties he felt were beyond his scope. He needed Mary's help and she thought she could provide it. The event was to take place in the large Aquinas Hall in the Catholic residence at the university. Pearse thought that the tea and the traditional 'sticky buns' should be accompanied by some form of entertainment. This Mary was commissioned to provide.

To some extent, she followed the advice which Val Iremonger had given her two years before. He had told her that 'Belfast will be what you make it yourself.' He then said: 'You don't have to tell me – the Hickey irritability and world-building – she wants to change it overnight. Don't, Mary, don't; it's solid. Be your own civilization and let the rest go to hell.' She followed this advice quite closely.

Mary still had few contacts in the city, and certainly not many with theatrical Belfast. So she started with her hairdresser, Lily Reed. Lily had theatrical connections – she was herself a soprano singer, her sister 'Madame' May Reid, played the organ and her niece, Kathleen Feenan, had toured America as an actress. Luckily Kathleen was at home, 'resting'. Lily gave Mary more names: 'Paddy Coyle, who had once acted with the Abbey Theatre; Frances McShane and Maureen Cremin, both teachers; Nan McGuigan, a well-known local actress; Lucy Young from the Group Theatre; and Bob Haldane from the BBC.' Mary contacted everyone on this eclectic list and clearly her powers of persuasion were already well developed because all agreed to help and, as Mary says, 'We were on our way.'

She had the performers, but what were they going to do? It was decided that the main menu was to consist of two one-act plays, both from the Dublin theatrical stable. One was *The Dear Queen*, a nostalgic piece which had already been put on at the Abbey. The second was a nativity, rendered in the Kiltartan dialect by Lady Gregory. Such a play was already a seasonal touch, but Mary added another: Kathleen Feenan, the holidaying actress, played a Christmas fairy/compère who spoke in verse written by the poet John Irvine. And there were to be songs, provided by a variety of singers. Mary knew the challenge she was facing, of developing a relationship with all those people of different persuasions, not all followers of Newman, to get a good show together. 'I worked like a beaver, taking rehearsals in the consulting rooms in Ulsterville House. I felt there was enough diversity in the material to cover all tastes and make a happy, relaxed evening.'

The opening lines, spoken by the compère/fairy, have been preserved. They catch nicely the slightly tentative informality of the whole venture:

Ladies and gentlemen, although a fairy,
I must admit I'm trembling now with fear.
Proud though we are of this our little play
In which to pleasure you we all appear,
Our hearts would sink if you were bored,
For we have worked and tried in every way
To learn our parts, to act and sing
That you and we may have a happy day.
For you, O Newman friends, this is our test –
To give you, one and all, our very best.

Pictures of the Lady Gregory nativity in the Aquinas Hall show good costumes, a believable crib and nice grouping against a background of stars. The play is a charming retelling of the familiar story. The second piece, *The Dear Queen*, is Chekhov crossed with Elizabeth Bowen – a wistful, delightful piece by Andrew Ganly.

Afterwards a senior university official, who attended the show and enjoyed it greatly, wrote to Mary asking if she could repeat it for the whole university and not just members of the Newman Society. The letter-writer, Max Freeland, the assistant secretary to the university, ended with this tribute: 'It was just wonderful to realise in these benighted times that there is someone with the skill and initiative to do such a lovely thing.' Mary had put on a programme with some local references but also a definite nod southward – mostly in the direction of the Abbey Theatre. The evening had been carried off with skill and panache: a huge success for a first venture. In Dublin Mary had not directed at the New Theatre, but she had obviously silently imbibed the skills needed to direct a piece with a largely amateur cast and little time for rehearsal. In the different environment of Belfast and, perhaps, helped by the ballast of marriage and motherhood, she had found the confidence which enabled her to push forward and deliver something eye-catching and special. (Her success was not completely unqualified: the nuns who ran the Aquinas Hall expressed disapproval of a singer striking a match on the tight leather skirt she wore to sing 'Lili Marlene'.)

Early in 1951 Mary sent out to those who had been there, and to other likely thespians, an invitation to coffee at Ulsterville House. An interesting group turned up to discuss the possibilities of doing plays in the large bay window of Pearse's consulting rooms. There were doctors, including Dr Eileen Hickey (no relation), and teachers and writers like their new friends John and Elizabeth Boyle. The meeting agreed that the one-act play, done before small, invited audiences, was the way to forward. Mary's enthusiasm for poetic drama was reflected in the nine productions she was to put on at Ulsterville – six of them were verse plays. It was also agreed that the productions would be enhanced with live music and that there would be separate evenings of musical entertainment.

One of the actresses who appeared in the productions at Ulsterville House was Sheelagh Garvin. She remembers how strongly Mary bought into Yeats's idea of 'drawing room theatre.' This was what she was going to provide on the bay window stage. There was minimal scenery, the actors were on the same level as the audience, which was rarely above twenty people. Sheelagh remembers Mary as being self-possessed and with a clear vision of the kind of theatre she wanted to create. Sheelagh found her 'determined' and even 'demanding': 'If I wasn't ready to play the part [she wanted] she'd put the script through my letter-box. Then she would ring up and say: "Have you read it? You know it's made for you." That was the way she worked; she used flattery and blackmail.'

The list of plays for the two 'seasons' at Ulsterville House began with a long one-act piece, *Lost Light*, by Robert Farren. It dealt in an intriguing way with a conflict of loyalties within a family during Easter week. The main role was played by Frances McShane, an actress who was to become one of the Lyric stalwarts. McShane later said of the tiny venue: 'It was a stage that demanded a strong nerve, iron discipline and very neat footwork if you hoped to avoid being catapulted into the arms of the audience.' After the show coffee was served and opinions exchanged. The reception of the first play was good enough to encourage more productions. For the next evening Mary chose a Yeats, *At the Hawk's Well*, and *The Kiss* by Austin Clarke. Emboldened by success, she and Pearse now decided to name their company the Lyric

Players Theatre, an admiring nod in the direction of Austin Clarke and his Lyric Theatre in Dublin.

In 1952–53, despite Mary's plunge into the world of local politics and eventually a house move, three more separate programmes were put together for Saturday and Sunday nights, the only time Pearse's consulting rooms were free. They did *Wrap Up My Green Jacket*, Val Iremonger's full-length piece. In directing this Mary had to introduce some of the Ulster cast, including the lead actor, to the tragic, romantic figure of Robert Emmet. (Irish history did not figure much on the curriculum in Protestant schools.) More Yeats and Austin Clarke followed, with the productions becoming visually more ambitious – sometimes using masks made by Gerard. Costumes – with which Mary's mother helped, rather reluctantly – became more detailed. The staging became more enterprising. A roll of lino was discovered in the Ulsterville attic, painted white, and transformed into a serviceable cyclorama. A lighting man, Sammy Armstrong, was acquired. He brought his own equipment and was able to double as cast photographer. New actors appeared, including a promising sixth-former from Inst, Norman Stevenson.

The Lyric Players company was developing. It was a well-balanced mix of Protestants and Catholics. Sheelagh Garvin notes that at this stage, and later, the company 'lived in a kind of vacuum; we never discussed religion or politics'. Considering the subject matter of the plays Mary had chosen, this seems a little unlikely, but the point is that probably people kept their allegiances to themselves and got on with the exciting job of putting on plays that were not available elsewhere in Belfast.

Mary was already laying down markers for the direction she wished to go. Her choice of plays would be both international and Irish-oriented and Yeats's drama would be a central feature of her work. With Yeats, Mary tried to remain true to the specific requirements of the poet himself – as transmitted to her by his brother Jack Yeats during a production of *At the Hawk's Well* at the New Theatre in Dublin. Her programme was, in Belfast terms, exotic and very much more Irish than Ulster. Mary had, indeed, followed her friend Val's advice and created what she wanted rather than what was conventional in Belfast or likely to be widely popular. She had begun to create 'a poets' theatre' in which speech, movement, lighting, sets and costumes would combine to create magical productions in a theatre so small that audiences felt as if they were interacting with the players. She had, very quickly, found a suitable template.

6

Politics

'Political Interlude' is the title of the fourth chapter of the O'Malley autobiography. It implies a gentle dabble in Ulster politics and gives little hint of how hectic the years between 1952 and 1955 were, domestically, theatrically and politically. During that period Mary moved to a new home, 'Beechbank' in Derryvolgie Avenue, set up a small but viable theatre at the back of the house and expanded the activities of her Lyric Players, directing most of the eighteen plays she put on in those three years. This was achieved while she was an active, conscientious and often angry Belfast Corporation councillor representing an impoverished ward. And during this period, she also bore a third son, Conor. Within two weeks of his arrival, she was directing her first production of *Hamlet*.

Mary was still living in inconvenient Ulsterville House at the start of her political career. She had already been involved in Labour politics for more than a decade, in both Dublin and Belfast. Now, as a good socialist, she saw a chance to improve the lives of people in the deeply deprived inner-city ward of Smithfield. She hoped that by standing as a candidate for the anti-partitionist Irish Labour Party in the Belfast Corporation local elections, she might be able to 'stir things up', agitate the stagnant pool of Ulster politics. As 'a member of the minority in Northern Ireland' she wrote a letter in May 1951 to the Westminster MP George Thomas, not mincing her words: 'Political and administrative discrimination have become such an established feature of life in the Six Counties that it is difficult to see how we can obtain some measure of justice without active pressure on the Stormont Government by Westminster.' Mr Thomas duly raised questions in the House about discrimination in Northern Ireland. In her letter Mary had been less than hopeful that even a Labour Government would do anything, as it 'appears to have given active support to the Unionist position of privilege through sectarian rule'. She was right to be pessimistic.

This, then, was the stale political pool into which Mary stepped when she began to canvass on the doorsteps in Smithfield ward. To stir up uncommitted voters she would tell them that she was going to oppose 'discrimination and sectarianism in the services of the Belfast Corporation'. She also gave public and unambiguous support for a 32-county republic. Mary and Pearse were aware that making explicit political statements might affect Pearse's prospects of professional advancement or damage the pleasant camaraderie of her religiously and politically mixed band of actors, which depended, to some extent, on restraint in the expression of political and religious views. True to form, she and Pearse decided 'to go ahead and take the chance'. As it turned out, her political plunge was to make little difference to Pearse's prospects or to her company; she went on directing and they went on playing, more or less exactly as before.

May 1952 was warm for Belfast; canvassing was exhausting. There were four Irish Labour candidates in the ward. One of them was extremely interesting: Jack Beattie, the survivor of the 'razor-blade' election. Another candidate was the diffident T. McIlmurray, who canvassed with Mary and left her to do most of the talking when they knocked on front doors. The accommodation behind the knocked doors was usually desperately inadequate, 'two rooms upstairs, one down, no indoor toilets or any modern conveniences'. Rubbish was emptied into the cobblestoned streets. The deprivation she saw affected Mary deeply and spurred her on; to be able to help she had to win. The election day was 21 May 1952 and an official notice stated that voters had to bring either a medical card or a ration book with them – a precaution presumably designed to scupper those who thought it was their duty to 'vote early and vote often'. Mary, despite – or perhaps because – of being the only female name on the ballot paper, won easily, polling more than any of the other candidates. Jack Beattie was also victorious and became an alderman.

After the count there were photos on the steps of the City Hall and a modest party at Ulsterville House (bananas, sandwiches and stout). This was followed some days later by a victory parade, which involved a slow progress in an open car, ahead of which was a lorry blasting out 'The Bold Fenian Men' in a version by Anne Shelton. 'Beattie and I acknowledged the crowd and I thought to myself – now all I have to do is die for Ireland!' Beattie waved his panama hat at his supporters and Mary promised to strive for 'social justice and political freedom for all Ireland'.

When, a few days later, Councillor O'Malley stepped through the doors of City Hall she was one of ten members of an opposition which she described as 'quite formidable'. They needed to be because the difficulties they faced were also quite formidable. Councillor Mrs O'Malley early on had accepted an invitation to a prize-giving at a borstal – awards to be presented by the minister of finance, a dressy occasion. The audience was seated when suddenly a band appeared and began to play 'God Save the Queen'. Unruffled, Mary made a quick decision: '… the faithful stood as I sat, and in the silence [before the anthem started] a little voice behind me piped up, "Oh, Mummy, look at the lady sitting down!" I could feel my neck reddening …' At the junket afterwards Mary was ostracized and got no tea until a kindly, elderly councillor finally offered her a cup. 'I was relieved to be at least treated civilly by *someone*.' She determined never to subject herself to this sort of political embarrassment again. Her anthem-phobia became an incurable condition. It's worth noting that throughout her time in Northern Ireland she would 'scuttle' (a word often used by observers) out of the room as soon as there was any hint of a 'God Save the Queen' moment. This gesture of keeping seated or leaving the room while others stood was redolent of the failure of nationalists to find a more constructive way of making their entirely justified case against the Unionist establishment. Staying seated, or exiting, may have made the protestors feel better, but it merely needled the Unionists and had no more force than a child's nose-thumbing. Effective opposition to Unionist hegemony was still a decade and a half away.

Fortunately, Mary was able to do a great deal more than make counterproductive nationalist gestures. The socialist representative of the Smithfield voters had a huge task in front of her. Even though some Ulster linen still sold and big ships continued rolling down the slipways at Harland and Wolff, Northern Ireland was the most disadvantaged part of the United Kingdom. There were pockets of abject poverty – and Mary's ward was one of them. The population was mostly Catholic and suffered discrimination in employment and the allocation of public housing.

There were ninety-eight thousand officially homeless people in Belfast; Corporation houses were allocated on a 'points' basis. Mary describes the results: 'Endless queues came with pitiful tales of sickness, numerous children, bronchitis and no indoor toilets.' Public housing was not allocated fairly in Belfast, although not as unfairly as in some of Ulster's provincial cities and towns. 'Impropriety' had been confirmed by a public enquiry, which revealed that a prominent Unionist official had assisted 'a lady of doubtful reputation' to acquire accommodation out of turn. He acknowledged that he had visited her but that the pretext was to bring her 'a little chicken for roasting'. This story was a gift to the papers and caused much hilarity. So there was maldistribution of poor-quality houses which, anyway, were in short supply. The consequences were grim and painful for some of Mary's constituents. Heavily pregnant women, 'stressed and underfed', would come to Mary in search of a house. She would harry the housing department, but only occasionally succeeded in helping the applicants. They often came back, weeks later, and Mary would ask about the baby. 'In many instances it would have died, often of bronchitis.'

Mary was never able to help as much as she would have liked. But sometimes she succeeded. On 12 January 1953 Patrick Flynn wrote to her from 8 Collingtree Road with a simple request:

I wish to beg your assistance regarding a house. I am an ex-serviceman; I am married and have four youngsters. My service in the Navy was five years. I have got the full points for a house and still, with all, there doesn't seem to be a hope of getting one, ever. My wife contracted asthma from the two rooms in which I am now living. The Corporation has already condemned them but still, with all, they won't try to get me accommodated out of here. I have heard some very good reports about your ability regarding housing accommodation and that is the reason I am asking your help. I definitely have an air-tight case, if only I had someone to press it for me …

Three months later Mr Flynn writes from a new address, 4 Ballymurphy Drive:

Dear Cllr. O'Malley

I am deeply sorry for not having written you sooner. I am sure you thought I had forgot about you, once I had got the home. Well, I never forget good turns and I only wish I had some way to repay you. I know that it was your persistance [*sic*] that got me this house and my wife and I are more than grateful.

Yours very truly
Mr. P. Flynn

It's likely that Cllr O'Malley's intervention was decisive in pushing a man with full 'points', but the disadvantage of a Catholic name, to the top of the housing allocation list.

Housing remained Mary's chief preoccupation, but she also served on three other, very different, subcommittees: gas, museums and health. Gas, she admitted, was too 'technical' for her, although she did protest on behalf of her constituents when the price rose. Museums she found much more interesting and quite soon she became involved in an odd controversy surrounding the distinguished Ulster poet John Hewitt. He was assistant curator at the Belfast Museum where he had worked for twenty-two years and was in charge of the art gallery at the moment, in 1953, when the post of curator for the whole museum fell vacant. Hewitt applied for the job. Mary went to a subcommittee meeting, which was considering applications for the post. She detected 'considerable prejudice' against Hewitt. She decided to keep an eye on the selection process but was unable to attend the full committee meeting at which the candidates were to be interviewed. So she sent a letter to the chairman, apologizing for her absence and stating that, if proxy votes were permitted, she would cast hers for Hewitt. Soon Mary discovered that her letter was being bandied about City Hall and used to indicate 'the type of person that was backing Mr. Hewitt'. City Hall gossip made Hewitt part of 'the Tomelty gang'. 'Tomelty,' Mary says, 'was Joe Tomelty, the playwright and a Catholic like myself.' Mary was angry that her letter of support had been so counterproductive, and it seems likely that she began to campaign for Hewitt – even though, contrary to what was thought at City Hall, she hardly knew him at this stage. Eventually she was told that 'the best thing I could do was to say nothing in Mr Hewitt's favour'.

After interviews, the English candidate Wilfred A. Seaby, an expert on numismatics, was appointed curator on the casting vote of the chairman. Mary was furious that her letter of support may have weighed against Hewitt rather than for him. Afterwards she said so to the Committee: 'The suggestion that the support of a democratically elected Irish Labour member is likely to injure the prospects of a candidate is a very serious method of intimidation and one must condemn it in the strongest terms.'

This incident is difficult to read accurately seven decades later. Mary felt that Hewitt's lack of war service and his left-leaning political views, which were very far from orthodox Unionist values, had probably gone against him. Nevertheless, she thought the decision 'very wrong and unfair'. Fortunately, this career setback proved temporary for Hewitt. Soon he was appointed director of the Herbert Art Gallery in Coventry, which he ran successfully until 1972, when he retired and returned to Belfast to enjoy a fine late flowering in the suddenly luxuriant garden of Ulster poetry.

However, on another issue Mary found herself very much at odds with Hewitt. In the 1950s Hewitt was something of an advocate of Ulster regionalist writing, which Mary and other ILP councillors gleefully took to task when a PEN (Poets, Editors and Novelists) delegation came to Ireland around Coronation time in 1953. A big international gathering was taking place in Dublin and a one-day visit to Belfast was scheduled. The guests, celebrated writers from all over the world, were feted at a lunch in the City

Hall, with the Prime Minister, Lord Brookeborough, in attendance. The Irish Labour Party normally kept away from such junkets but Mary and the ILP member for the Falls constituency, Cronan Hughes, decided to attend, and to lob a small cultural grenade into this august assembly. They brought with them, and distributed, a carefully prepared and somewhat explosive statement from the ILP. It is dated 11 June 1953, comes from 'the City Hall, Belfast' and is addressed to the PEN delegates. It begins without ambiguity: 'It may interest delegates to know something of the political and economic situation in the Six Counties and to suggest reasons why writers of this area have so far found it difficult to produce work of real value.' The statement then derides the efforts to establish a cultural entity similar to the 'political and social entity known officially as Northern Ireland and unofficially as Ulster'. Writers of a 'distinctly Unionist outlook' are denigrated in the statement as having nothing more than 'a local reputation', although it's admitted that St John Ervine may be an exception. But even he is given short shrift: 'His reputation is, of course, greatly overvalued locally but he cannot seriously be compared with Yeats, Joyce, O'Connor and O'Faoláin. In recent years his main connection with "Ulster" has been as a political propagandist of indifferent merit and a writer of grocer's shop comedies.'

The statement then explores, without political inhibition, the dilemmas of the Unionist writer. 'He [there is no "she" in this document] ignores or plays down the larger background of Ireland' although some 'have tried an ingenious compromise of three loyalties, "Ulster", Ireland and Britain.' The result, the statement says, has been 'a spurious regionalism'. Then comes the real political meat:

> Why is it that an area which is so rich in tensions, political, social and religious, has failed to throw up work of importance? The explanation is in part the fact that many writers try to ignore their roots. The local market also creates difficulties. A quiet, but nonetheless powerful, censorship prevents the writer for radio or the theatre from dealing with the very tensions that are the most prominent feature of life in the area. The political and economic domination by the Unionist Party is taboo as a subject, as is the victimisation of political opponents. The nearest

approach that can be made is in the level of broad farce [a reference to the 'kitchen comedies' then popular in Belfast]. Treatment of historical questions, even of several centuries ago, is banned unless it is on an officially approved basis.

The statement concludes, 'Until Northern Ireland changes, the Ulster writer will continue to cultivate his garden and produce only a crop of literary weeds.'

Mary and four other councillors, including Jack Beattie, signed the statement. It was handed out to the PEN delegates as they arrived on the train from Dublin and headed off to Stormont for coffee. At the City Hall lunch which followed, the paper was keenly discussed. But normal political decorum prevailed until the speeches. The Lord Mayor, James Norritt, made an erudite contribution on the Brontës' connections, through their father, with Co. Down. Then came the dreaded loyal toast. Mary and Owen Sheehy-Skeffington (up from Dublin as an interpreter) and a few others remained seated. Further speeches and votes of thanks followed calmly, until the Lord Mayor wound up proceedings with the comment 'that Northern Ireland was part of the United Kingdom and proposed to stay that way. The pianist then struck up two verses of "God Save the Queen" – which led to a walkout from some of the delegates, followed by their absence from the rest of the day's functions.' There is a note of pride in Mary's account of these events. She concludes: 'The Regional Movement, well represented in NI PEN, suffered a severe blow. Those who may have hoped to use the occasion for a show of strength were disappointed.'

It is hard now to see Mary's political protest as any sort of victory, but it must have been a satisfying gesture of defiance. It is also interesting in that it shows how dismissive Mary is of much local writing, something which was to have unfortunate effects when she ran her theatres. (Young Ulster writers who had read her PEN statement were unlikely to bombard her theatre with plays.) The public defiance she and her nationalist colleagues showed on this occasion was not to be forgotten by her opponents. The word 'subversive' began to be attached to her name. Mary could acquire enemies almost as quickly as devoted friends.

Mary and the ILP were involved in more cultural clashes in the coronation year of 1953. According to an *Irish Times* report Mary publicly blamed the Unionists for 'making unscrupulous use of the British Royal family for party purposes' and suggested that 'public money could be spent to better advantage in helping the relief of unemployment'. This angered the Unionists, who issued an official statement saying that 'invitations to public functions would be withheld unless an unqualified prior assurance of "loyal" behaviour was given'. Whether Cllr O'Malley and her loyally nationalist colleagues stood, sat or were absent, for the many subsequent renderings of 'God Save the Queen' in that coronation year, is not recorded.

———————

The new house in Derryvolgie Avenue suited the expanding needs of Mary's family as well as providing more spacious accommodation for Pearse's practice. It was in the Malone Road area – the home of the mainly Protestant Belfast bourgeoisie. The house had four reception rooms and five bedrooms. Mary seems to have found time, from somewhere, to turn this impressive Victorian suburban residence into a comfortable home. But she turned it into something more: a house containing a theatre. From the start she saw the potential of the stable and hayloft which ran along the back of the building. It did not take her long to convert this space into a fifty-seater, upstairs theatre.

Mary had already been a councillor for six months when the move from Ulsterville House took place. A summer holiday in Ballyhalbert, accompanied by her two sons and their nurse, was a pleasant respite before the move. Mary says in the autobiography that Pearse stayed at home, 'keeping his nose to the grindstone – it all had to be paid for!' She had married an excellent provider.

Ballyhalbert, which is perhaps twenty miles from Belfast, was the O'Malleys' holiday destination for the three years she was a councillor. It is a pleasant but ostentatiously loyal village on the Co. Down coast. Its paving stones are still Union-Jacked; even today it is impossible to be unaware of its

Orange identity. When the O'Malleys were there in 1952 Mary thought they were the only Catholics around 'and locals tended to look at us askance'. Nevertheless, despite the Royal Ulster Constabulary's B Specials drilling noisily in a field nearby, the family enjoyed the usual seaside pleasures and visits from sundry Lyric players.

Summer holidays were a welcome relief from the admittedly self-imposed pressures of stage and council chamber. Cllr O'Malley waged two more welfare battles in 1953, which was by far her busiest year in the service of the Belfast Corporation. The first was a matter of animal welfare. Dublin had a fine zoo, which Mary used to enjoy visiting. The Belfast equivalent, on a windy site on the slopes of Cave Hill, was less impressive. So unimpressive in Mary's eyes that she, with the help of a zoologist from Queen's University, wrote a damning report on its shortcomings and presented it to the city council.

The report, dated 16 November 1953, criticises the range of animals on display. She suggests acquiring more varieties of monkey, gibbons for example. She wants extra parrots, a pets' corner for children, some penguins, a larger reptile house and an aquarium. She is unhappy about the size and state of the cages and suggests that the staff may be showing 'insufficient interest in the care of animals'. The report is not entirely negative and makes various helpful recommendations, suggesting, for example, the formation of a zoological society, cooperation with schools, which could 'adopt' animals, and short Saturday-morning talks by the keepers.

Mary's strictures on the zoo did not remain within the four walls of the council chamber. A *Belfast Telegraph* report of a corporation meeting quotes Cllr O'Malley as having seen 'rats in the monkey cages'. And she wondered whether the 'death-rate among animals was high enough to cause alarm'. According to Mary, her criticisms were ignored and very little changed. Bellevue Zoo is, nearly seventy years later, transformed, but its official history admits that 'in the 1950s and 60s the zoo went into decline'. As with so many things in Northern Ireland, change took a very long time.

Human welfare remained Mary's central concern as a councillor. She became alarmed about the state of the welfare hostel in Lisburn Road which provided temporary accommodation for the homeless and was managed by the corporation. After several visits Mary wrote a report – even though she was not a member of the committee in charge of the hostel. What she wrote makes painful reading. A single nurse looked after the three hundred inmates; two of the resident children had active TB; only one room had a proper floor covering; the heating was wholly inadequate, consisting of coal fires in very large rooms; outside the house, the grounds were neglected and overgrown; the children's swings were broken. In response to Mary's report, the staff attempted to defend the indefensible but admitted that the building was a legacy of the past, built originally as a workhouse. Mary said in council that conditions were 'below normal human standards'. The welfare officer in charge of the hostel admitted, 'The final remedy lies in complete evacuation – which I am optimistic enough to hope will be within five years.' Eventually the children were moved to a new welfare nursery. 'Maybe my interest did speed the process,' Mary wrote forty years later, 'the necessity for action had been made perfectly clear.'

Mary seems to have been much more active in the first two years of her three-year term on the council than in her final year. There were both personal and political reasons for this. In 1954 she was pregnant with her third child: Conor Plunkett's birth in July was difficult and Mary recovered slowly. Life got even more problematic when her mother had a stroke while on a holiday with Mary's brother Gerard. She and Pearse had to go down south where they found her 'still inarticulate but recovering'. The infant Conor tended to be wakeful and the month after his birth was difficult. They had lost their long-serving children's nurse, Philomena, but could not find another one, so more daily help was recruited. Luckily, they found a treasure in Sarah Hughes from the Ardoyne,

> a recently widowed woman with a family of nine. My problems seemed trivial in the face of hers. She was cheerful and hard-working, and we learnt to love her – the children, my mother and all those who passed through the house. She had a great big heart and showed a kindly toleration towards our various activities. Mrs Hughes was to remain with us for the next twenty-five years.

On such rocks are theatrical careers built.

Having a baby while serving as a councillor was unusual in 1950s Belfast. When Mary was able to rejoin the council in August 1954, she was congratulated by the Lord Mayor, Sir Cecil McKee. He added the arch comment that 'he hoped I would have the good sense to bring up the child a Unionist'. This piece of Unionist bonhomie was a rarity, although Mary does have a good word for some of the younger, more liberal Unionists, like Robin Kinahan. She had joined the Council with high hopes. She had believed that 'intelligent and forceful' public representatives *could* make a difference. But as time passed, she had come to feel that the Unionist monolith was too powerful to allow her and her fellow ILP councillors to achieve very much.

The Unionist hegemony was bad enough, but even more undermining for Mary was a feeling that her own side was falling well short of her expectations. In 1955, her final year in office, she remained active, but something close to disillusion set in. Her colleague Jack Beattie was flagging, and the suggestion came up that Mary should stand as a candidate for the Westminster parliament. This of course would have taken her away from her beloved theatre, so one suspects she had no trouble in refusing to take her political career any further.

The three years when Mary was a councillor were, despite all the social deprivation she encountered, a time of reasonable prosperity in Belfast. The traditional industries were still vigorous. Living standards were rising generally. The Attlee government's creation of a welfare state had reduced poverty. The historian Jonathan Bardon sees this rise in living standards as having offered another opportunity to the Unionist government. This was a moment when the majority had the chance 'to remedy obvious wrongs and soothe inter-communal resentment, still stubbornly alive, especially where pockets of disadvantage were dangerously concentrated'. But the Unionists made very little effort to 'draw Catholics into the institutions of state'. Lord Brookeborough never seems to have entertained the possibility 'that Catholics could become full, participating citizens of Northern Ireland'. Writing two decades later, Brookeborough's successor, Captain Terence O'Neill, regretted his predecessor's failure to use 'his tremendous charm and his deep Orange roots to try to persuade his devoted followers to accept some reforms'.

Down south, change was also slow to come. Early on in her term as a councillor, Mary had encountered in Dublin a shocking example of the restrictions on free speech in the Republic. In November 1952 she had been invited to speak at the inaugural meeting of the Rathmines Technical College's Literary and Debating society. 'Can the individual survive?' was the title of the debate. Mary was asked to second a vote of thanks proposed by the Irish Minister of Posts and Telegraphs, Erskine Childers. Another speaker billed to appear was her friend Owen Sheehy-Skeffington, now Reader in French at Trinity College Dublin and a socialist scourge of the Catholic Church as well as a doughty proponent of free speech.

Before the meeting, Mary had a note from the auditor of the society explaining that the vocational education committee had vetoed the appearance of Dr Sheehy-Skeffington, which it evidently had a legal right to do. There must have been concerns that this advocate of free speech would speak too freely. Mary and Pearse drove down from Belfast in a blizzard to find crowds outside Rathmines Town Hall. Sheehy-Skeffington had indeed been excluded by the committee; 'a nasty impasse had developed and the Gardaí were in attendance'. The meeting started and the auditor duly delivered his paper. The minister gave a lengthy vote of thanks, quite failing to make any mention of the exclusion of Dr Sheehy-Skeffington. There was palpable tension in the hall as Cllr O'Malley rose to speak. She commended the auditor's paper and the pertinence of its subject, then added wryly: 'I am sorry to see that one of our proposed speakers tonight did not survive to reach the platform!' and she went on to deplore the fact that 'a speaker, invited in the ordinary way, to the debate had been debarred without any reason given'. She then set out what was happening to some individuals in Northern Ireland. She denounced its 'sectarian and undemocratic government', inveighing against 'endemic discrimination' but also describing the benefits of the welfare state. 'I think we are very much in advance of you [in the Republic] in this matter.' The use of 'we' is interesting: Mary is now speaking almost as a northerner. She had been living in Northern Ireland for five years and had seen the benefits the welfare state had brought to the people – a sharp contrast to the Republic.

For three years Mary had tried to help her fellow citizens through political action. She had given her best as a councillor, but now, in 1955, she felt it was time to change her approach. As she puts it, 'I stepped into the wings to do my bit in another way.' She felt she could not make any political headway, so she transferred her energy and ingenuity into creating a theatre she could run and control without interference. She was now ready to turn the rooms above the stable into a theatrical powerhouse.

Even when she was fully occupied with Corporation business, her mind must have sometimes wandered away to her Studio stage. Housing problems and her production of *Hamlet* must have competed for space in her brain. Theatre and politics coalesce neatly in a single notebook, preserved in the O'Malley archive, which begins with ideas for Corporation speeches and memos and then becomes a fascinating set of notes for one of her most ambitious Derryvolgie Avenue productions, *King Lear*. During her three years as a councillor, she managed to put on eighteen plays in the Studio, directing most of them herself.

The Studio, as her theatre was sometimes called: two rooms ran across the whole breadth of the house at the back; they were divided by folding doors, which were soon removed to make a stage that was deeper than it was wide – twelve by ten feet – and an auditorium. The audience sat in the larger of the two rooms where there was just about enough space for fifty people. Access to the 'theatre' was gained through two doors leading from the landing of the main house. The invitees – for that is what they were – had to pass through the house first, but after a few years an external staircase was built to allow audiences to access the theatre directly. The stage had a serious limitation, as described by Conor O'Malley: 'On stage-left there was an exit leading to the rest of the house, but on stage-right there was no exit, only a small bay window.' When a new external staircase was added, it became possible for an actor to clamber out of the bay window onto the staircase, descend to the garden, gain access to the house through the kitchen, go upstairs and re-enter, if needed, by the more orthodox stage-left entrance.

Despite these limitations, Mary, being Mary, made her first production an ambitious one: *Icaro*, an Italian play she had helped to put on with the New Theatre in Dublin. She managed to move no fewer than twenty-two players around her tiny stage. She and her children's nurse had made the scenery; her mother had helped with the costumes. The production involved 'all the arts – music, dance, setting and costume'. The cast included many who had already stepped out on the Ulsterville bay window stage and some new names, including the precociously talented Norman Stevenson, who was still at school.

The press was invited to this first venture in her new playhouse and was complimentary about this 'unusual play in an unusual city theatre'. One paper said 'those … privileged to see last night's production must have felt grateful to these performers who call themselves the Lyric Players'. This initial outing convinced Mary that her stable could become a theatre even though it meant, for now, a weekend home invasion as the audience walked in through a side door, along the front hall, up the stairs, through a corridor and then down some stairs to get to their seats. It's worth noting that *Icaro* took place with the actors on the same level as the audience, although eventually a stage was built with two shallow steps leading up to it from the auditorium.

Having completed her house move by November, Mary pressed on with her now traditional Christmas presentation. This one was an eclectic mix, which the press liked. Prospects for the new theatrical year ahead were encouraging.

Mary often grumbled – perhaps always grumbled – about the lack of publicity for her enterprises. This was not invariable. Her New Year's party in Derryvolgie Avenue at the end of 1952 obviously had a striking effect on the *Social & Personal* reporter invited to attend: her account of the evening did not appear till February 1953. It begins with praise for Mary's production of plays, 'which might be thought impossible on a tiny stage with amateurs' and then goes on to describe the 'wholesale entertaining which she and her husband offered on New Year's Eve'. There were evidently 200 people in her new Derryvolgie Avenue home 'but everyone was most happily and comfortably settled in different rooms all over the house'. What the reporter found surprising was the variety of interests the guests represented:

There were medical men talking shop at intervals with Dr Pearse O'Malley; there were authors and actors and politicians and teachers;

some of Mrs O'Malley's colleagues from the Belfast Corporation [she had already begun her political career], not even of the same party as herself, and all quite happy together.

The writer obviously had a good time in 'the gayest and most comfortable melting pot' and marvels that 'at least one guest had come over from London specially for it'.

Mary writes happily about this moment in her life: 'We were coasting along and Pearse was introducing his patients to a new ambience. This was more pleasant and more private than Ulsterville House. God was in his heaven and all seemed right with the world.' Her domestic contentment was in sharp contrast to what she had experienced when she stepped outside her front door and went into battle against social deprivation.

There were five Studio productions in the 1953–54 season, pregnancy and council work notwithstanding. Poetic drama predominated: Yeats, Ronald Duncan, Austin Clarke, Christopher Fry and Federico García Lorca. The season had begun with what is now an almost-forgotten verse play, *This Way to the Tomb*, by Ronald Duncan. The Lyric production was chiefly notable for the striking El Greco-ish set painted by the rising young Ulster artist Terence Flanagan, one of many persuaded into giving generous quantities of time and talent to Mary's suburban theatre. There were other attractions for him in the stable loft: he had become friendly with Sheelagh Garvin, one of Mary's earliest recruits, and they were to marry, eventually. Garvin is interesting on her own and her husband's relationship with Mary. Pearse invited Flanagan to paint a portrait of Mary. Sheelagh explains what happened next: 'Mary couldn't sit still, she was reading scripts … and in the end Terry threw down his brushes and said, "I can't do this!" So, he gave it up – which is a great pity because he was very good at portraits.' Sheelagh, nevertheless, admired Mary's untrained theatrical imagination and her political activism. She had accompanied Mary to the dreadful welfare hostel and been witness to some of those embarrassing moments when Mary expressed her political convictions by staying seated for 'God Save the Queen'. Garvin's testimony suggests, however, that in her theatre Mary was, on political matters, restrained and undogmatic.

There was a family feel to productions at Derryvolgie Avenue. After the play the public would gather for coffee – and sometimes even meals – in the O'Malley's breakfast room and the actors would join them. The company at this stage had two main sources of male performers. One was the already mentioned Inst. Several teachers from the school joined the company, among them Keith Stevens whom Mary describes 'as a major asset to the theatre'. Probably the most talented Inst performer was Norman Stevenson, who was both a sensitive actor and a precocious director. The other source of male actors was, interestingly, the Northern Ireland Civil Service.

———————

1954 began with an ambitious series of productions, which included the first play by a local writer, *The Falcons in the Snare* by Elizabeth Boyle. This historical drama is about the relationship between the great sixteenth-century Ulster hero Hugh O'Neill and Mabel Bagenal, sister of the Queen's deputy in Ireland. Mary captured another talented local artist, the cartoonist Rowel Friers, to design the sets, which he was to do in several subsequent productions. Mary's first Shakespeare, *Hamlet*, was a little hampered by her having given birth to Conor three weeks before the first night. He arrived on 11 July, missing by a day the embarrassment, for a nationalist family, of having a birthday on 12 July, the Orange day of days. *Hamlet* drew high praise. Twenty-year-old Norman Stevenson, now studying English at Queen's University, played the prince. The ambitious choice of play was noted by the *Belfast News Letter* as was the 'artistic, clear and effective lighting'. The set was again by Terence Flanagan, who had not yet started his portrait of Mary. Also involved in this production was another Inst man, Kenneth Bloomfield, who played Horatio. Mary thought he looked 'a fine figure of a man in doublet and hose'.

Talking to him sixty years later, he says he can still remember most of Horatio's lines. Now Sir Kenneth Bloomfield, once the head of the Northern Ireland Civil Service and the survivor of an IRA bombing which blew up his house, he spoke to me about Mary.

She was a very striking individual … she was very beautiful in a traditional Irish way. There was also something very compelling about her … it was terribly difficult to say no to her … you were almost conscripted rather than volunteering.'

He remembers that, as Horatio was one of the few characters left standing at the end, he became 'a kind of layer-out of corpses'. (It was important on this miniscule stage for the living to be able to move and perform without stumbling over the dead.) Her directing style he described as 'not terribly directorial. If she tried you out and thought you were up to it, by and large she'd let you get on with it. She was quite a good spotter of talent; if you did something for her once, and weren't very good, you probably did not get invited again.' On the matter of discipline on stage and offstage, he says, 'It was taken seriously; we wanted to do it well; we didn't regard it as a bit of a lark.' Politically, he was aware of her strong feeling 'that there never should have been partition'. But at Derryvolgie Avenue she ran a largely apolitical ship. 'You had this extraordinary alliance of this nationalist [woman], really a Republican individual, and a cast, many of whom were involved in the Civil Service, including English people.' In the civil service category, he cites Arthur Brooke who was a high-quality leading man and was to play many important roles for the Lyric Players. Even though the other main source, Instonians, was mainly Protestant, 'nobody was put off for a moment at that stage … our political life didn't have the bitterness that it subsequently acquired. I never fretted, nor even remember anybody discussing their political activities. It didn't seem very relevant.'

In November 1954 the Lyric Players made their first excursion to Dublin, taking a revival of Christopher Fry's *The Firstborn* to the Bernadette Hall in Rathmines for one night only. Gabriel Fallon, writing in the *Evening Press*, noted the intelligence of the actors and the production and added: 'I have a feeling that we will hear more of the Lyric Players.'

Emboldened by the Dublin venture, and about to step out of politics, Mary made the 1955 season even more ambitious. They began with a Yeats version of *Oedipus* by Sophocles, in all-white costumes designed by Norman Stevenson, and with Arthur Brooke as Oedipus. The critics noted his 'compelling' quality and Mary mentions a rare theatrical occurrence: at the end of the dress rehearsal the company spontaneously applauded the leading actor. Writing to Mary many years later, Brooke remembers how she wanted speed in the performance:

> At first I could not believe what you wanted – it seemed beyond us. But at the end it dawned that it was exactly right – compelling urgently, faster and faster, the tragedy to move towards its awful crisis. And then the poignancy of the quiet when Oedipus, blinded, addressed front of stage, with the chorus at his feet, his two tiny daughters held either side of him. On one night – I think the third – I saw through my blinded eyes two   elderly women in the front row, crying copiously, the tears rolling in streams down their cheeks. And that, to an actor, one little bit of him icy cold and calm, assessing what he is doing, was very satisfying.

The chorus was led by the mellifluous Denys Hawthorne, soon to be another Belfast export to the English stage.

Mary did not have any more children after Conor. All the births had been difficult and it's likely that Pearse sensed the toll childbearing was taking on her health. He always had her best interests at heart and Conor believes that, although Mary would have liked to have a daughter, together they decided that their three boys were enough. Childbearing slid off into the past; motherhood and multiple cultural activities continued.

7

Flowering

OVER THE YEARS 1955–60 the Lyric Players Theatre became more than just an amateur playhouse. Mary began to build, incrementally, an impressive cultural enterprise. From their Studio theatre her players extended their reach – they took more productions to Dublin; talented new players like Sam McCready and Louis Rolston joined; and the stage facilities were improved by an extension. Beyond the theatre Mary started a drama school and, anxious for her playhouse to reach a wider audience, she and Pearse began a new 'little' magazine, *Threshold*. It did not boast about LPT productions, nor even advertised them very much; it was simply a literary journal with an all-Ireland perspective emanating from an unlikely Northern source. The downside of all this activity was that some valuable members of the company resigned, finding the pace too hot.

The 1955–56 season opened with *King Lear*, and Arthur Brooke in the title role. Mary did the lighting and felt that she and her company were 'learning ... how to cope with and utilise the small stage'. Norman Stevenson, in a letter to Mary, written just after graduating at Queen's – getting the best degree in English of his year – cheerfully admits he is 'luxuriating in despondency' because he can't get a job. But he also makes practical suggestions for some cuts in the text for the forthcoming *Lear* and puts forward ideas for the costumes.

Stevenson earned good notices for his Fool – one paper describing him as 'brilliant' – and *The Irish Times* was impressed by both Brooke in the title role and Keith Stevens. The paper summarized the production like this: 'Bare to its essentials, the sensitively lit stage, the economical curtains and the austerely decorated robing in greys and black, counterpointed the well-spoken verse.' The season continued on a high note with *Volpone*. Norman Stevenson, playing Mosca, was once again outstanding and Keith Stevens did the name part with dash and a sense of fun. According to Mary, 'people were now clamouring for seats in the little theatre and, as one reporter put it, "*Volpone* was the talk of the town."' The production was also notable for the arrival of a youthful Denis Tuohy, later to become a fixture in BBC current-affairs programmes, at this point playing 'a gentleman traveller'.

By 1956 Mary had put on thirty-two plays in five years. Irish works did not predominate. She did fourteen of them in those first five years but most were short Yeats plays, often done three at a time in a single evening. Sixteen plays came from the rest of the continent of Europe. Most of the authors were English, but there were also Italian, Spanish, Russian and Greek dramatists. Two plays were from further afield: *Princely Fortune* (China) and *Before Breakfast* (USA). Given how short most of the Irish plays were, the amount of stage time devoted to English and European drama was much greater. Yeats was becoming the dominant element in her repertoire, her resident dramatist in a sense, but full-length Irish plays were still rare.

To mark the first five years of production Mary and Pearse prepared a brochure, written by their friend John Boyle. He notes that in the first five not a single Irish (or Ulster) play with a twentieth-century setting had been featured. He knows that new Irish plays are needed, that creating 'an actors' forum' is not enough. He says that it is 'the responsibility of the new playwrights to develop the theatre's potentialities'. This amounts to an appeal for contributions from local playwrights, which raises a question that hangs awkwardly over Mary's stewardship of the Lyric Players Theatre. She was about to devote much time and energy to creating ancillary cultural activities on the margins of her theatre, so why did she not devote some of her formidable drive to seeking out local writers more vigorously?

The term 'workshop' did not have the currency then which it has now, but a more active approach to encouraging plays from local writers must have been possible. She should perhaps have done more than wait for the painstakingly produced typescripts to come through the letter box at Derryvolgie Avenue. Mary was an innovator, often ahead of her theatrical times: for example, she was just about to add an in-house choreographer to her team. But at this point she does not seem to have thought it possible to create a hub of local writers – a very high priority nowadays for artistic directors, especially those working in small theatres. By not seriously prospecting for writing talent, Mary left her theatre open to the charge of irrelevance to the local community. Some time was still to elapse before full-length, new Irish plays went into the repertory, and even longer before new, full-length, contemporary Ulster dramas were staged. Nevertheless, the Lyric's imaginative productions may have played a role in stimulating the poets and novelists, and playwrights, who were to emerge in the next decade in Northern Ireland. And it must be remembered that two larger professional theatres were still doing good work in the city; the Group and the Arts must have seemed a much more exciting market than the Lyric for an apprentice dramatist. Nevertheless, her stage, which did not depend on box-office returns, was an ideal space in which new Ulster writers could learn their craft. But at this point Mary preferred what had been tried and tested, often in Dublin.

In the mid-1950s the LPT still put on plays for just four or five nights, with a gap of several weeks before the next offering. But the 'down' time was often used for other cultural events. Over the years there had been poetry recitals – Norman Stevenson arranged one on sixteenth-century English poetry, John Hewitt another on 'the Irish mode in this century'. In the first five years there had been no fewer than twelve exhibitions of paintings, including the works of Basil Blackshaw, Rowel Friers, Terence Flanagan and Deborah Brown. And there were the traditional Christmas Eve events, with a specially painted crib, and plenty of singing – not to mention the elaborate St Patrick's Day presentations, which usually involved a short play and Davy Hammond singing Orange ballads, or someone doing a Dorothy Parker monologue.

In the autumn of 1956 Mary decided to add another item to her cultural portfolio. She and Pearse set up a drama school. She describes the motivation for this development: 'Many of our active members were married couples with young families. If we were to indulge our interests, why not incorporate the children? It might make us feel a little less guilty if they were there to share.' The school began with three reluctant pupils, including Mary's eldest son Kieran, but soon there were ten. Mary as usual swept aside any difficulties and teachers – mostly from the ranks of the LPT – began giving classes in music, dance, voice, speech and acting. By the end of the first term the pupils had enough expertise to present a Christmas play, *The Stolen Prince*. At this point all the pupils were under ten but in the next year a senior class for children from ten to fifteen was started. The sessions went on for an hour and a half at Derryvolgie Avenue on Monday and Friday afternoons. These soon began to create enough noise to threaten the already fragile mental health of the patients ensconced in Dr O'Malley's waiting room, so his consulting rooms were moved to a quieter part of the house. The staff of the drama school had a huge asset in the dancer and choreographer Helen Lewis, who had trained in modern dance in Czechoslovakia before the war and was now helping Mary with movement in most of her productions. Like everyone else she received only a tiny emolument for her teaching work.

Autumn of 1956 was busy in the theatre. First, another Shakespearean tragedy – *Macbeth*. Brian Baird, drama critic for the *Belfast Telegraph* and a teacher at Methodist College was courageous enough to take on the lead. He passed this demanding test, according to most of the reviewers but some critics felt that the difficulties of the tiny stage hobbled the production: 'For once this pint pot of a stage, which in the past has brimmed with so much light and feeling, proved inadequate for the swirls and tempests of so large a theme.' The size of the stage was a problem for every production. The author's experience there, some years later, was that fluid movement and clever grouping took one's attention away from the cheek-by-jowl closeness of the actors. Baird, the critic-turned actor, did not stay with the Lyric Players, but Louis Rolston, who played Lennox in this *Macbeth*, did. It was his first sizeable part and for more than twenty years he was to play many memorable roles for the Lyric. He was an actor of quiet intensity with a distinctive, gravelly voice.

After *Macbeth*, and before the children's Christmas production, came Lorca's *The House of Bernarda Alba*. This study of female oppression and utterly distorted 'family values' caused some heartache. Mary cast one of her regular players in the title role but the actress became anxious about the morality of the piece, consulted a priest and dropped out. A letter from 'Moya' is preserved in the Galway archive. Moya says that her priest, Father Brady, has read the play and found it 'very suggestive and crude'. He considered that 'any Catholics in the audience would be embarrassed and that I shouldn't leave myself in that position', so Moya 'regretfully' withdrew. Mary was disappointed, especially as she thought the actress had 'the right strength and passion for the role'. Other Catholics in the play also began to have qualms and Mary 'finally ended up with a cast of Protestants ...' Lucy Jamieson stepped in and made a formidable Bernarda. Mary comments: 'Some years later, when the play was done again, there were no such difficulties, times had changed.' This is almost the only time she records any sectarian division among her actors.

The sombre Lorca tragedy was followed by *The Children of Lir*, by Joy Rudd, a Cork-born woman, then living in England. A young actor called Sam McCready made his debut in this play. Mary had an exceptional talent for casting. She 'found' promising actors and then managed to keep them, often building up decades of loyalty. This was the case with McCready. He was to become a close associate of Mary over many years and later he wrote a lively memoir, *Baptism by Fire*, of his life in Belfast theatre and with the LPT. This book, perhaps more than any other, gives a picture of what Mary was like as a person and as a theatre-practitioner. McCready was a good enough performer to have already been offered a place at RADA in London but turned it down because he felt ill at ease with 'the posh accents and the affected manners of the others who were auditioning'. Sam was anxious to spread his wings nearer home and he liked the script of *The Children of Lir*. He warmed to the Irish names in the text: Aoife, Fionnula, Fiacra. He had been soundly educated in the Protestant tradition at Grosvenor High School, but at the Lyric he was about to make the exciting discovery that 'there was a body of Irish mythology comparable to the Greek and Roman cycles'. Here was a young, talented player ripe for conversion to Mary's brand of poetic drama. Appearing in *Lir* gave McCready his first experience of working on the LPT's tiny stage. He remembers the entrance/exit problem – 'running through the house and out by the front door and then climb the wooden stairs at the back and enter by the bay window – not the most pleasant experience in frosty December in a light tunic and tights …'

On stage Sam found it difficult to move freely and he had to have a lesson in specific actions and gestures from choreographer Helen Lewis before he could learn to be still and then make clear, limited movements. Perhaps because of Helen's tactful help at this point, Sam grew close to her; he says she became his 'mentor, teacher and confidante'. She was no ordinary person. She bore the indelible mark of an Auschwitz survivor on her forearm. She came from a German-speaking family in Bohemia, which had become part of Czechoslovakia in 1918. She had studied modern dance in Prague under the tutelage of one of Rudolf von Laban's disciples. She was Jewish and before the war had married another Czech-German Jew, Paul Herrmann. She was teaching dance and experimenting with choreography when her country was invaded by Hitler in March 1939. In 1942 she and her husband were sent to the Terezin (Theresienstadt) ghetto, then to Auschwitz. They were separated, and Paul died on a forced march at the end of the war. Helen was sent up to the Baltic coast to work as a slave labourer in another concentration camp, but after liberation by the Russians she made her way back on a terrible journey to Prague, helped more than once by the kindness of strangers. When she arrived she weighed only five stone and recovered her physical and mental health very slowly, not helped by the news that her mother had been murdered in Sobibor extermination camp. Then she began to correspond with an old school friend, Harry Lewis, who was now in Belfast. He was a Czech who had acquired British nationality in 1947 and they married in Prague later that year.

They came to live in Belfast and Helen took a while 'to understand that strange place, its language, customs and people'. For example, the significance of the tattoo on her arm was not obvious to people in Belfast.

Someone even thought that she had inscribed her telephone number in a convenient place as an aide-memoire. But after nearly a decade spent rearing her two sons, and getting accustomed to Ulster, she returned to dance and choreography. She began to work on amateur opera productions, and it was not long before she was recruited by Mary. Sam McCready describes how from 1956 onwards she choreographed all the Yeats plays and supervised movement in almost all the other productions. He explains that her role went beyond choreography:

> To the Lyric she brought many gifts, but chiefly she brought her own charming and beautiful self. Mary, in her day-to-day work for the theatre, was fighting for survival in a man's world but she needed female companionship, the kind of warmth and support which only another woman could give her. Helen was this support. Mary and she were real friends, and the rift, when it came, was devastating for all of us.

The 'rift' was still nearly a decade away – time for Helen to add to Mary's theatre a distinctiveness in movement, which it already had in voice. An undated letter gives an idea of the warmth and intimacy of her relationship with Mary: 'My dear Mary, please don't be angry with me for returning the cheque. I would have explained on Saturday, but I couldn't. You see working with you has given me great happiness and it seems wrong on my part to accept any payment for that. Love Helen.'

Sam provides interesting insights into the post-performance rituals at the LPT. The actors would go downstairs to the O'Malley kitchen where the audience was consuming coffee and biscuits:

> It was like walking into a lion's den. The audience, mainly from the Malone Road area, was knowledgeable and responsive, but it was a clique composed mainly of academics and teachers – and their wives. Over coffee, you quickly knew whether your performance had passed muster. If they liked you, they gathered round to congratulate you; if they didn't, they ignored you and you quickly left to catch the bus home. Those post-performance get-togethers were a tradition much appreciated by

the audience, and some of the actors … one of the strongest appeals of the old Lyric for many – but I was never convinced that it was a good thing to greet the audience when I was still raw and vulnerable.

There were five performances of *Lir* including one on a Sunday, which for Sam was uncomfortable. Sunday was always a day of rest in his 'good Protestant household'. Mary, on the other hand, thought Sundays were excellent days for rehearsals or performances – after Mass. She found it difficult to empathize with the swing-locking, Sabbatarian element in the Ulster psyche. However, Sam, like many other Protestants in her cast, managed to overcome his cultural prejudices and turn up on the Sabbath to rehearse or perform. The appeal of what was going on in the stable-theatre was too strong to resist and Mary was not an easy person to oppose.

Sam soon found warm acceptance from Mary and had no trouble in taking up the offer of 'another wee part'. This led to his 'baptism by fire' in Yeats's *Deirdre*. Mary had designed the sets herself and the music had been written by Havelock Nelson. Sam had found the idiom hard to master, but he soldiered on. On the opening night, playing the Dark-Faced Messenger, he had to place a burning torch in a holder and stand immobile beneath it, spear in hand, eyes gazing steadily ahead. 'On no account was I to move as much as a muscle.' Working props were rarely ready in the LPT before the first night, so this was the first time he had stood under the tall metal cone filled with paraffin-soaked cotton wool. 'During the scene in which Deirdre pleads with Conchubor for the life of her lover Naoise, the high point of the drama, I smelled burning. Paraffin had leaked through the cotton wool onto my head and my hair had caught fire. I smelled burning flesh – my own.' As Deirdre pulled a dagger from her bosom and took her own life, Sam felt as if he was being burnt alive, unable to do anything about it because of the strict injunction not to move. Eventually, 'throwing caution to the Navan winds, I ritualistically raised my arm and pressed down hard on my head – anything to ease the stabbing pain – while the others "cantillated" to the end of the scene.' Sam's baptism by fire went unremarked by audience and critics – one of whom praised Mary for a brilliant piece of direction –

giving the only physical reaction to the death of Deirdre to the Dark-Faced Messenger. Mary was delighted with her new player; he 'had passed the test … remained constant in the face of danger'.

Sam may not have realized what an unusual theatre he was joining. In a comprehensive study of the development of the Lyric, *The Evolution of the Lyric Players Theatre, Belfast* (2020) by Roy Connolly, there is a perceptive section on the Studio:

> The theatre's success had been established around a nexus in which actors and audience regularly exchanged roles: the audience of one show would frequently perform in the next … The effect of this was to heighten the social ambience of the theatre – to produce an aura of supportive rather than critical attitudes. It was precisely the environment where exploration was possible. An expression of dissatisfaction with the Lyric's programme was virtually unknown.

Connolly sees the Studio as a quite exceptional theatrical environment. 'It did not have wages to pay, nor did it have to face union problems. Its stage was cheap to run. Its performers were enthusiastic volunteers. Even the professionals involved in the scenic aspects of the show worked without pay.'

This environment allowed Mary the luxury of doing ambitious, big-cast plays like *Under Milk Wood*, her next production. Her ambition also ran in another direction; she wanted more, much more publicity:

> The press came and reviewed plays … but we could not advertise since we were performing in a private house. At times we sensed a certain hostility from local drama groups, because we were popular, could attract talent, were holding audiences and going from strength to strength. We did not want to function in a rarefied hothouse. We wanted writers to write for us, but if they didn't know of our existence, how were they to become interested? We were ambitious and felt we should let the world know what we were up to. A literary magazine, it was hoped, would do just that …

And so, *Threshold* was started, more Pearse's brainchild than Mary's, since 'he appreciated its importance more than I did'. It was to turn out to be one of Mary's more enduring achievements. In contrast to the high-visibility, neon 'Lyric' sign shining out above the Lagan today, the thirty-nine issues of *Threshold* sit modestly, rarely consulted, on library shelves.

The size of the task of creating *Threshold* should not be underestimated, nor should the O'Malleys' fitness for it be overestimated. A psychiatrist and a theatre director, with no prior experience in publishing or literary journalism, added this difficult managerial and creative task to the demands of running a theatre, a household, a drama school and a medical practice in a suburban home. Mary worked in her fast-moving undeviating mode to get the project started. The do-next-day lists, which she wrote in reporter's notebooks or children's exercise books, grew longer; she phoned persistently, sometimes while having a late breakfast in bed, and during the day typed her trained-typist's letters. One of these went to John Hewitt, shrewdly asking him to be poetry editor of the magazine. He accepted, contributed articles, and gave useful editorial advice from Coventry, where he had just moved. Early on he suggested that twice yearly would be a suitable frequency, but full-on Mary overruled him and went for quarterly issues.

The simple cover for the first edition of *Threshold* was designed by Rowel Friers. It showed a decorated Celtic doorway, done in beige and black, and with the contributors' names placed where a door should have been. The title came from the Yeats play *The King's Threshold* and every single issue over thirty-three years carried, inscribed inside the front cover, these mysterious lines from the play: '… cry out that not a man alive / Would ride among the arrows with high heart, / Or scatter with an open hand, had not / Our heady craft commended wasteful virtues.'

Threshold was small (octavo-sized) and over its history varied in length from roughly fifty to nearly 200 pages. For much of its early life it cost two-and-sixpence; by the end of its long run its price was two pounds.

The magazine did not appear in a blaze of publicity, but Isobel Henry, writing in her *Sunday Independent* column at the end of 1956, marked its arrival. She notes that Mrs O'Malley already 'looks after' a husband 'who is a busy doctor' and children 'as well as running a theatre which delivers unusual and ambitious productions in a tiny space'. Henry marvels at the fact that Mary has now taken on another obligation, explaining, 'she has started another ambitious venture, a literary magazine called *Threshold* …'

The early editions of *Threshold* announced, to the world in general and to thirty-two counties of Ireland in particular, the presence of the little theatre with big ambitions. But it did it in an oblique sort of way. It blew its own trumpet softly, simply providing, in the final pages of the first dozen issues, the growing and increasingly impressive list of Lyric productions since the start in 1951. Mary and Pearse knew about the chequered histories and short lifespans of Irish literary periodicals, especially those born in Belfast, like *Lagan* (1943–46) and *Rann* (1948–53). So, the O'Malleys' first editorial struck a modest note; the inexperienced begetters of the magazine admitted to 'a certain temerity' in starting it:

> The history of Irish periodicals is not encouraging. Despite high literary standards and imaginative presentation of general topics, few have survived. No one, however, would deny their contribution to creative writing and objective criticism. It is hoped that Threshold will provide a medium for a further contribution.

It did indeed provide 'a medium' which encouraged 'a contribution' from young writers. Some of the early editions were fairly described by the Dublin critic John Jordan as 'routine'. But whatever its youthful limitations, it was to prove surprisingly durable. Small literary magazines anywhere have a poor life expectancy; in that context *Threshold* survived to a ripe old age. It ran for thirty-nine issues, was published for thirty-three years and in doing so outlived almost every other Irish 'little magazine'. It did more than that: it provides a fascinating literary seismograph for the years when the flawed Northern Irish polity erupted in a long, painful explosion, which coincided with a remarkable flowering in poetry, prose and playwriting.

8

Pressure

THRESHOLD **WAS CREATED** at a time when Mary's domestic life was becoming even busier. Her mother, now in her early eighties and a permanent resident in Derryvolgie Avenue, was frail and in need of constant attention. The boys were growing up and becoming very active; and Pearse's practice was thriving. Large numbers of people waited every afternoon to see Dr O'Malley at Derryvolgie Avenue. Lengthy psychiatric interviews were not his style; he dealt quickly and decisively with patients. Conor says that although the LPT demanded a considerable amount of Pearse's time and money, it also served to advertise his practice. The nightly performances and the socializing afterwards may well have encouraged audience members and their friends and acquaintances to consult this gentle, thoughtful doctor; and some of those who had already consulted him were drawn to acting on the Lyric stage. Pearse seemed to cope calmly with the more frenetic moments at Beechbank and with the fallout from the activities of a wife-of-many-talents with a powerful will. An anecdote provided by Mary's niece, Gerard's daughter Mary, who regularly came up from Dublin to stay with her cousins, delightfully illustrates how theatre, family and Pearse's professional life sometimes interacted at Derryvolgie Avenue.

The neice remembered that once, during Uncle Pearse's consulting hours in the afternoon (which were important for the family income), Mary said she needed to go down to Donegall Square to get some hessian for costumes. She didn't drive at this stage, so Pearse just had to take her and, the niece's story goes on, 'I was detailed to go in and tell the patients that, Dr O'Malley had been called away on an emergency.' She did so. Reflecting, she says that her uncle 'was a very tolerant and patient man. She [her aunt] would sometimes go off the deep end and he would have to take the brunt of it.' Mary was fond of her niece – the daughter (which she never had) of her beloved brother, Gerard.

She also mentions another entertaining aspect of the arrangements in the Derryvolgie Avenue household. If her aunt's mother, Anne, was in residence she would often answer the phone and tell callers, 'What a wonderful psychiatrist Dr O'Malley is.' Mary junior also related that an unusual feature of the regime was that the three boys almost always had breakfast brought to them in bed. The domestic help had to arrive by 8 am to perform this function – although Mary remembers that not infrequent absences meant that the boys had to make their own arrangements.

Despite the demands Mary made on Pearse, the relationship was functional and contented. The love letter Pearse penned to Mary on 4 July 1957 from Dún Laoghaire (referred to earlier), where he is having a short holiday on his own, begins with some chatty news and then becomes a kind of inventory of their happiness: 'We have had ten good years together (despite my Melancholia and your Mania) Please God we will have many more. He has been generous to us. Look at the milestones:' [*What follows mimics the layout of the letter*]

Kieran Darragh
Donal Lysaght
Conor Plunkett

Ulsterville
Ballyhalbert
Psychiatric Clinic
Beechbank
O'Malley clan

Newman Soc.
Irish Labour Party

Belfast Corporation
The Lyric Players
Threshold
Drama School etc.

Pearse goes on: 'These are indeed nostalgic memories, so it's best not to think of what was negative ...' Then comes the apology, quoted earlier, for his behaviour when they were first married. After that Pearse goes on positively:

> How we live our lives in the future is the ultimate answer. After ten years I look back, not 'in anger' but with an increasing amount of affection and love for my 'Wild Romantic' and three dark-eyed sons.
>
> May God Bless you all, not overlooking Granny ...
>
> With all my love, a thousand times, and a warm embrace.
>
> Pearse

Mary had daily help with the household chores and there was now a receptionist in the surgery. But she did most of the cooking – and there was often at least one visitor for dinner, who frequently stayed the night. Pearse did not finish his clinics until after 6 pm and rehearsals would generally begin at 7.30 pm and run on till 11 pm. Performance days were even more demanding. The cast changed in the bedrooms and 'the spill over into the house was disruptive'. This latter problem was answered in typical O'Malley fashion: build an extension. This was soon done – giving a foyer, dressing-room accommodation and, underneath the auditorium, a large supper room and coffee-making area. The aim was to make the theatre completely self-contained. The construction was done rapidly and efficiently in the summer of 1956, so there was no pause in the play programme. But it involved yet another hard-cash contribution from the O'Malleys: the extension cost £1500. It needed planning permission, which required a degree of subtlety in the application; an extension 'to the private drama studio' had to become 'an extension to a private house'. It is a tribute to the O'Malleys' neighbours in Derryvolgie Avenue that they tolerated for seventeen years the regular arrival of an audience for an increasingly active theatre.

The 1957 season began with *The Seagull* and another stellar performance from Norman Stevenson, as Konstantin. The season rolled on with a rarity – an Irish play by an Ulster author – John Hewitt's eloquent verse drama, *The Bloody Brae*. As we have seen, Hewitt had by now shaken the sectarian dust of Belfast off his feet and was running the Herbert Art Gallery in Coventry. He wrote to Mary frequently, usually about the *Threshold* contributions she had sent him, but also indulging in witty social commentary, often reflecting ironically on the stance of the exile. In April 1957 he writes: 'Because I am from Ireland it is assumed here that I am a Catholic; a sobering thought because I thought my sash was visible.' Later in 1957 he refuses to cash a cheque Mary has sent him for his poetry editing: 'Anything I do for *Threshold* is because I like it and that's payment enough.' Mary's letters are more businesslike and more prosaic, but clearly Hewitt felt able to unburden himself to her. Just before Christmas he writes about his immigrant status in England. 'An immigrant here has three possible courses – A. Become anonymous in a crowd. B. Go native. C. Become a professional Taffy or Paddy. I alternate between B. and C.' After a year in residence across the water he thinks he may be developing 'a touch of the brogue' and reports seeing a notice saying, 'Regret, no Irish or coloured.' Eventually Hewitt becomes even more settled in Coventry and moves out to the suburbs. He is profiled in a local paper, which describes him as 'a stocky, progressive Irishman that the Almighty blessed with Celtic fire'. Hewitt responds: 'And me thinking I was a respectable, solid Belfastman from the Shankhill or Ballymacarrett.' Soon, however, the correspondence became more sporadic, as Hewitt found himself too busy to continue with the time-consuming task of being poetry editor.

In the studio, after *Deirdre*, in which the name part was powerfully played by Babs Mooney, came two huge new O'Malley productions: *Under Milk Wood* and *Peer Gynt*. The first was a big enough venture, the second positively gargantuan. The Ibsen play had never been done before in Belfast. Mary had the right man for the title role – the talented Keith Stevens, who had been a teacher at Inst. but had returned to England the previous year to take up another teaching post. He was now prepared to sacrifice much of his summer holiday to come back to rehearse and play Peer. Despite cutting hundreds of lines, the play ran for four hours and the cast was huge, but this was a triumph, not least for the sets by Rowel Friers. The *Plays and Players* reviewer (probably local critic Ray Rosenfield) was entranced by the production and fulsome in her praise of the director:

> With a set that was an artist's joy as well as a theatre-goers delight, she managed to sweep the audience across valleys and up mountains, over seas and into an oriental never-never land with almost the speed of light. It was the sheer size of the production that first compelled attention – the feeling not only of distance and space, but the variety and depth of content, comprising as it did the poetic and the bawdy, the terrifying and the funny, the ugly and the graceful, the archaic and the sophisticated – and the press of character, upwards of forty of them, manoeuvred with great skill and never a suggestion of jostling, on the tiny stage.

Tom Carson in the *Belfast Telegraph* was pithy and admiring: 'This is a tale to tease the mind and please the eye and ear.' *Peer Gynt* was a triumph for Mary and for Keith Stevens who was already back at work in Liverpool when his performance was cited on Radio Éireann as one of the two best in Ireland in 1957; the other being Micheál MacLiammóir's rather mature Robert Emmet in *The Old Lady Says "No!"* by Denis Johnston.

During the production the finishing touches were being put to the extension and its last night, on Sunday 15 September, was the cue for a whole week of celebration. The programme was far from modest: on Monday a lecture on Yeats; Tuesday night, three one-act plays; Wednesday night, opening of an exhibition of theatre memorabilia; on Thursday the full-length production of *The Seagull*, revived for one night; on Friday the opening of an exhibition of Irish periodicals; on Saturday, a reception followed by dancing. Mary, with marvellous understatement, says: 'The programme involved a good deal of effort, expertise and co-operation.' The intensity of effort involved in mounting in a single week five different plays, three talks and two exhibitions, not to mention holding a huge party at the

Mary's mother and father,
Anne and Daniel Hickey.
c. 1912. O'MFA

Mary's beloved brother,
Gerard, at work as a set
designer, Abbey Theatre.
Late 1930s. O'MFA

Mary with Brendan O'Sé
in a scene from Irish Film
Society's *Tibradden*. 1943.
NUIG

Mary Hickey marries Patrick Pearse O'Malley in Dublin. 1947. O'MFA

Mary, Pearse with their children – Kieran on left, Conor on Mary's lap, Donal on right. Late 1954. O'MFA

MUNICIPAL ELECTIONS

SMITHFIELD WARD

POLLING — 21st MAY, 1952

8-30 a.m. till 8-30 p.m.

Name (s)

Address

YOU VOTE AT

Your Numbers are

You MUST bring with you either your
MEDICAL CARD or RATION BOOK

Remember :- **WEST BELFAST**

Doric Printing Works, Belfast

Vote for :

T. McILMURRAY   T. CARRAGHER
(COUNCILLOR)   (COUNCILLOR)

Mrs. M. O'MALLEY   J. BEATTIE
(COUNCILLOR)   (ALDERMAN)

Belfast Corporation elections,
1952. Mary's campaign leaflet.
NUIG

Mary in the prompt corner
(located in a former toilet),
with Ursula Burns, harpist,
Christmas *pot pourri*. Early
1950s. O'MFA

Icaro by Lauro de Bosis, opening production at Derryvolgie Avenue Studio, 1952. A full cast on stage with Norman Stevenson as the dead Icaro. NUIG

A striking set for the verse play, *This Way to The Tomb* by Ronald Duncan. Set by Terence Flanagan, Marie and Edna Boyd. 1953. NUIG

The extension at 11 Derryvolgie Avenue Studio opened in 1956. In 1962 it was the setting of an outdoor production of *Romeo and Juliet*. NUIG

Interior of the fifty-seater studio theatre, 1950s. Cushions probably essential. Cinema seats were later substituted. NUIG

Sam McCready as Christy Mahon in *The Heart's a Wonder*, a musical version by
Mairin and Nuala O'Farrell of Synge's *The Playboy of the Western World*, 1965.
On Sam's right are Maeve McGibbon (front) and Kathleen Kelly. NUIG

Stalwart Lyric actor Liam O'Callaghan in Ibsen's *Brand*. 1961. NUIG

Greg Collins as Rashers Tierney in James Plunkett's *The Risen People*, directed by Mary. 1963. NUIG

Expressive Lyric actor Babs Mooney in Lorca's *The House of Bernarda Alba*. Studio 1964. Photograph by George Mooney. NUIG

Michael Duffy as The Bull McCabe in *The Field* by J.B. Keane. Studio 1966. NUIG

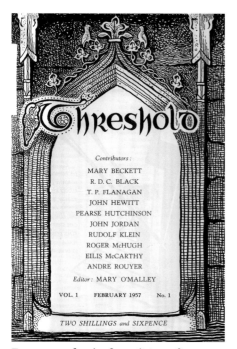

Front cover for the first edition of *Threshold* 1957, cover design by Rowel Friers. NUIG

Mary in Alice Berger Hammerschlag's New Gallery, located at 23 Grosvenor Road, Belfast. Mid-1960s. Photograph by George Mooney. O'MFA

The Lyric company, including the Brookes, the Lewises, the O'Malleys and their children, at Yeats's grave in Drumcliffe cemetery during their visit to the first Yeats Summer School. Sligo 1962. O'MFA

end of it, was meat and drink to Mary. But some of her players found it too much and it may be that, in an overcrowded programme, standards fell in some of the productions.

The demands of this schedule led some of Mary's regulars to reconsider their position as members of the company. She is frank in her autobiography, admitting that putting on a production of *The Seagull* for one night only may have been for some the last straw: 'Maybe I had asked too much of the company.' She had. Some of her founder members departed, among them Frances McShane, who had played Lady Macbeth, Edward McCarthy, who had been Gloucester in *Lear*, and, most painfully, Norman Stevenson. Mary pays tribute to their significant contribution. 'All had toured to Dublin with *The Firstborn*. They were the essence of *The Seagull*, the experts on Yeats. Above all they were dear friends – Frances and Edward were godparents to Conor. I think these players somehow feared the ambitious drift of the theatre …'

The loss of Norman Stevenson was a particular blow. Not only was he a skilled, imaginative and versatile actor but he could design sets and costumes and direct. He and Mary communicated very well. For example, the previous year he had written to her from his home in Orangefield Crescent, just before the production of *Macbeth*, in which he is to play the First Witch. He tells her he has been practising 'a wild Highland accent, but am not satisfied yet – it does not curdle the blood sufficiently … Your colour scheme for the play, incidentally, is beginning to grow on me and there are numerous instances in the text that seem to justify it.' He then ventures into Irish politics, speaking as a citizen of Northern Ireland: 'As for my feelings for your country [Éire] you will be no doubt delighted to hear that they have undergone a wonderful softening, that the shade of Robert Emmet has stirred, that the dark Rosaleen has not sighed in vain – last week I bought a green tie. A dark green, I admit, but nevertheless green.' Stevenson's mother had worked there with her son in the LPT's early days and he ends his letter with 'P.S. Mummy sends her love.'

It's clear from this and other letters that Stevenson had a fine literary intelligence and that he could collaborate effectively with Mary on questions of staging. But it's likely that his sense of theatrical proportion was affronted by having, in a single week, to play five roles in *Peer Gynt*, the lead in *The Seagull* and sundry smaller roles in the evening of one-acters. This workload would have daunted any actor, professional or amateur. Stevenson was a loss to Mary because his wide reading might have helped to broaden her choice of plays and he could have offered alternatives to Yeats which would have still fitted her concept of a poets' theatre.

Sam McCready admired Stevenson's qualities as an actor and thought 'he brought brilliance and intelligence to all he did at the Lyric'. He confirms that the resignation was 'a bitter blow' to Mary. But then he goes on to say something surprising:

> I had been part of the reason for his departure, she once explained, but she never told me why. Was it something I had detected at the first rehearsal of *The Children of Lir* when I saw Mary glancing at Norman uneasily? Was my coming to the Lyric a threat to Norman? If so, I could see no reason for it.

Stevenson later became a teacher at Inst and there he directed many of the pupils in ambitious productions. But McCready says that, to his knowledge, 'he never acted again'. Even sadder, he never returned to Derryvolgie Avenue. Twenty years later Sam tried to heal the breach by inviting both him and Mary to his production of *Spring Awakening*. 'They spoke cordially, avoiding each other's eyes, but said nothing – two proud people, neither of whom would give an inch.'

The New Year of 1958 was welcomed in traditional O'Malley fashion – with a party for 200 guests at Derryvolgie Avenue. It took four sittings for supper, served by a professional chef, to accommodate the crowd. Anne Hickey, Mary's mother, was still fit enough to contribute sculptural floral decorations as well as the traditional holly and ivy. Fires burned in almost every room and the new extension allowed dancing to an accordion. Dublin friends, Pearse's colleagues and of course the company, came. For Mary it meant a great deal of work, but she loved big parties and the tradition that they always meant a new dress for her. For Pearse it meant willingly footing another large bill. The scale of these parties was such that it's not altogether surprising that sometimes alcohol-induced euphoria broke out – unfortunately, in the case of one guest from Dublin who wrote a contrite letter to Mary some days after the event: 'I really behaved very badly. I didn't mean to and I can't really explain it, but I want to say how sorry I am if I was rude. I've never been to a party like that – Belfast intelligentsia are so different from Dublin ones. I'm still thinking over things people said and the whole atmosphere and attitudes ...' The apologetic letter-writer was Nuala O'Faolain.

In the new season came a venture close to Mary's heart, a production of the controversial O'Casey play, *The Silver Tassie*. Sam McCready was given the role of Harry Heegan, the footballer who goes off to the trenches and comes back disabled and bitter. The demanding, expressionist second act was carried off triumphantly. To create this huge panorama of misery in the trenches required exceptional design. It got it from a new recruit, Alice Berger Hammerschlag. She came from Austria, which she had left before the war, then lived in England and, after she married, Belfast. She was a talented painter who had come to the theatre and immediately written to offer her services. She was to become, like Helen Lewis, a valuable central European addition to the LPT and to Mary's other cultural enterprises.

The warmth of Alice's relationship with Mary is plain from their letters. After doing one of her first sets for Mary, the painter tells her how much she enjoys working in the theatre: '... it is wonderful to be able, once in a while, to work on a larger scale – and thank you for being you and giving so much pleasure to so many. Love, Alice.' There are further notes, in some of which Alice refuses to accept her 'honorarium'. At this stage the relationship was affectionate but, as with Helen Lewis, there were storms to come.

Before the summer break Mary had cast *Julius Caesar*. This production was to mark the debut of a big, powerful actor with a fine voice, Liam O'Callaghan. He played Brutus to Louis Rolston's Mark Anthony. Mary had the valued help of her brother Gerard, who came up from Dublin for the production. His work at the Peacock Theatre at the Abbey had become more sporadic because he now had a family, so he was happy to keep his hand in at the Lyric. In the past he had given her some simple, practical advice on design: for example, 'reduce sets to their simplest form, as a background for costume'. She paid close heed to this guidance when she visualized her productions. There were *Julius Caesar* rehearsals for four weeks, every second night at 8 pm. The critics were positive: Tom Carson in the *Telegraph* enjoyed 'the diamond clarity of the words' and summed up the production as 'clear and vigorous'.

Something less clear followed: *The Voice of Shem*. This project was difficult, even rash, and Mary knew that putting on a dramatization of *Finnegans Wake*, James Joyce's most obscure novel, would be risky. The text of the play is a collaboration between the Irish playwright Denis Johnston and the American writer Mary Manning. This was to be the first presentation of Joyce's work on the stage in Ireland. Mary had secured Johnston's permission to put on the play as well as a promise that he would come and help with the direction. She confesses that she found the script baffling, so when Johnston arrived, he and she and some actors began a tentative reading. Slowly the text began to make some sense and, remarkably, by the end of the session they had finalized casting. She had already twisted willing arms to work on the production: Rowel Friers was to do the sets and Helen Lewis the choreography. Things were looking promising, but then Johnston announced, a little alarmingly: 'You know this is a very blasphemous play, I hope you appreciate that ... Now I must return to Dublin.' He did so, promising to be back for the dress rehearsal. When the play went on the critics were indulgent. Betty Lowry played safe when she described the piece in the *Belfast Telegraph* as 'fascinating nonsense'.

Mary's big production in the summer of 1959 was an outdoor *Romeo and Juliet*. June does not always 'flame' in Belfast, so going out into the Derryvolgie garden was going to be a risk. But the exterior of the new extension provided a highly practical setting: a staircase and a balcony with a large, paved area underneath it. An ensemble played Elizabethan music before and during the performance. Lights were concealed in the shrubbery and the flowerbeds. The *Belfast News Letter*: 'It was a brave production, imaginative and daring in its use of an unusual "stage". The duelling scenes, the ball and the co-mingling of Montagues and Capulets in the streets of Verona had a fine sense of movement ...' The play finished in darkness, the floodlights went out and then myriad fairy lights appeared, followed by the lighting of a huge bonfire. Such was Mary's distrust of the weather that *Romeo and Juliet* ran for only two nights, but that was enough for nearly 800 people to see the play. The audience was still not being charged for admission, so once again the O'Malley exchequer would have had to foot a considerable bill.

After nearly a decade of activity Mary's theatre was by now getting more attention in the local press. And in Dublin too. In September 1959 there was a profile in *The Irish Times*, written by the respected Belfast journalist Martin Wallace – something much more substantial than the previous 'housewife who runs a theatre in her own home' stories. The profile assesses the LPT's record:

> Mary O'Malley's achievements are, paradoxically, both limited and substantial. They are limited because her auditorium is small and because the plays have had nothing to say of contemporary Ulster. (She is hardly to blame for the dearth of playwrights.) They are substantial because she has staged good plays well, and because these plays have sometimes reminded some Ulster people that they are also Irish and that they have a heritage of Irish literature.

The appearance of this profile in a Dublin paper at this moment was not coincidental. The LPT was about to make its way south to appear at the Dublin Theatre festival – attempting once more to convince local audiences that the Yeats plays were unduly neglected. As well as the Yeatsian version of *Oedipus at Colonus* (Terence Nonweiler was Oedipus), they put on *The Death of Cuchulain*, with Liam O'Callaghan in the leading role. These productions were new – with the notable addition of specially written music by Raymond Warren. He was an Englishman who worked in the music department at Queen's and over many subsequent years his compositions gave Mary's productions their musical distinction. Mary had heard – and liked – some music he had written in the Elizabethan idiom for a local production, so she asked him to do *Oedipus*. But she was uncertain if he would be able to do the very different Cuchulain play. However, he was not daunted and turned up with recorded versions of the music for both plays on the agreed date. He was both reliable and talented and Mary came to cherish his contributions – which in the following year were to include a children's opera, written especially for the drama school. He became Mary's main provider of music for her Yeats plays. In a letter written much later, when he had left Belfast and moved to Bristol, he told Mary why he had warmed to her project immediately. He knew that she thought the Cuchulain play might be too difficult for an Englishman, but then he says, 'Do you remember that day in 1959 when I turned up with the music on time and you greeted me with – "No wonder you English win all the wars!" I loved you from that moment onwards!'

Down in Dublin the Dagg Hall in Westland Row was not the most welcoming venue, but Mary had been forewarned by Gerard and took particular care with the lighting plot. Her lighting was deeply influenced by the Gate Theatre director, Hilton Edwards. She had seen, and admired, his productions during her Dublin decade and she took the trouble to acquire enough expertise to know what was possible and how to achieve it. At dress rehearsals she donned a white laboratory coat and patiently placed and tested her spots and floods. She often operated the control board herself, so she could get exactly the effects she wanted.

The LPT overcame the deficiencies in the Dagg Hall and the critical and audience response was 'heart-warming'. On Radio Éireann there was unstinted praise: 'They [the LPT] have become the guardians of the shrine the Abbey can no longer tend. They realise that the play, acting, design, directing and music make up theatre art … the use of lighting is an object lesson to our Dublin amateur groups and to some of our professional companies also.' Warren's simple, stark music – often involving just a single instrument – and the Alice Berger Hammerschlag sets were given accolades in the Festival's feedback *Survey*. This success in Dublin, Mary observes tartly, was not much noticed by the Belfast newspapers. She felt the performance of her theatre deserved more local press attention than it got.

However, some of this resentment may have been assuaged by a touching response from one member of the audience at the Dagg Hall, Rutherford Mayne. This was the pseudonym of Samuel Waddell, a veteran writer and actor, now in his eighties, who had been the driving force behind the Ulster Literary Theatre, which, fifty years earlier, had been set up with much the same artistic vision as the Lyric Players, except that, almost from the start its members had set about writing plays which they could perform themselves. They had done what Mary had yet to do – generate in contemporary Belfast, or at least Ulster, new dramatic work of high quality.

The ULT had prospered before World War One and for a while afterwards, but eventually it foundered, at least partly because it never managed to do what Mary *had* done; create a permanent, physical home for the theatre. Mayne wrote directly to Mary:

> Last night gave me the impression that you and your players had achieved all that had been dreamed of in those days of long ago … Rarely have I heard such a sensitive and beautiful rendering of the spoken word … You have brought a torch, lit with beauty, over the River Boyne. May God bless and keep you and your Company, for it has made glad the heart of old Rutherford Mayne.

Mary's enjoyment of this moment of triumph was savagely terminated a few days later by the death of her mother. Her health had been failing all summer and when it took a sudden turn for the worse during the Friday performance, Mary, Pearse and Gerard rushed up to Belfast in the early hours. Anne rallied, and Mary was able to return to Dublin for the final performance on the Saturday night. But her mother was mortally ill and the following week she died. Mary and Pearse sat with her on her final day, Pearse holding her hand, but Mary found herself 'completely overwhelmed'. Eventually Pearse sent her out of the room 'when he thought I was too distressed'. Later he came downstairs to tell her it was all over. Mary records that she felt angry with herself – that she hadn't had 'the courage to see this most important happening in my life to its finish'. But she has a vivid memory of her last, poignant moment with her mother: 'I will always remember her, shortly before she died, sitting bolt-upright in the bed, supported by pillows, looking around the room, seemingly taking in all the detail – the great big brown eyes focussing on each of us in turn as if to say "Goodbye".'

Gerard – perhaps even more deeply affected than Mary – came up for the funeral. The coffin went to Dublin for burial in Deansgrange Cemetery. Mary reflected on her mother: 'Difficult in many ways … we had disagreed frequently.' However, looking back, Mary was pleased that she and Pearse had managed to look after her and make her final years comfortable. As a child, her only parent had been 'her universe'. Mary's grief was intense: 'For many months after she died, I kept waking at night hearing the little bell ringing in her room and feeling she needed me and then realising, in desolation, that she was in fact gone and the bell would not ring again.'

After her mother's death Mary took a short rest from her theatre. But a complete break was impossible and during the pause she and Pearse did some strategic thinking. They had come a long way in almost ten years: productions now ran for a week, rather than just a weekend; audiences could total three- or four hundred for a single production. They now had a better-appointed theatre, a literary magazine and a drama school and they regularly put on lectures, one-off performances and art exhibitions at Derryvolgie Avenue. Not only were they endlessly busy but the whole operation was beginning to put a strain on the O'Malley purse. 'It was becoming increasingly obvious that we could not continue financing it for ever …' Others might have considered drawing in horns, pruning the rapidly growing list of LPT activities. Not Mary and Pearse. They were expansionists to the core. The answer lay, in Mary's mind, in a bigger, better, easier-to-publicize theatre – a public playhouse where her vision of a poets' theatre could be shared with the wider community.

Providentially, at this key moment she was provided with the means to plan and design a larger playhouse. Neil Downes, a young Dublin architect, was working temporarily in the North and he came to see the open-air *Romeo and Juliet*. Mary met him and may have filed him in her card index for future reference – as she tended to do with promising new acquaintances. A new playhouse needed a sympathetic architect with an interest in the theatre. She 'inveigled' (her word) him into appearing in her autumn production of the powerful Jewish drama *The Dybbuk*, playing the Third Scholar in the Synagogue. Not surprisingly, during the rehearsal process, conversation with Downes turned towards the possibility of a new theatre. She saw the purpose of a new playhouse like this:

> Our type of programme, with its mix of the work of Irish poets and playwrights, world classics and exciting new work of quality, would be safeguarded … Continuous theatre, six nights a week, fifty-two weeks a year, would demand even greater commitment from the Company … It would seem necessary to think in terms of a full-time professional theatre.

Downes started designing a 200-seater playhouse straight away. Once again Mary's ability to spot talent and then harness it had served her and the Lyric Players well.

Working on this exciting project must have helped to alleviate Mary's pressing grief. In any event she and Downes moved so quickly that within a matter of weeks they were able to go public with the project. They appeared on a programme on Ulster television and talked about their plans. There was considerable press coverage, rather more favourable in the South and in England than in Belfast. The local press asked the question: 'Is there room for a third theatre in Belfast?' In most cities of half a million people there would be ample capacity for a third, relatively small theatre, but cautious Belfast questioned whether an audience could be found. (It is also worth remembering that at this point a new building for the Arts Theatre was being constructed in a shopping centre; and the Group was still, though not for much longer, in fine form.)

Mary was not so naive as to think that a long-term plan to build a bigger theatre could, of itself, be a short-term solution to the current O'Malley overload at the LPT. So she and Pearse now took a radical step: they reorganized their enterprise by creating a small semi-professional company, setting up a board of trustees to administer it and making it possible to charge for admission. They felt the Studio had to stop being a private organization and become part of the community. Arranging all this took a while and the change did not happen until the following March (1960). Meanwhile there were more issues of *Threshold* to be edited and new productions to be mounted.

For her next choice Mary again selected from Dublin, going this time for something she had seen recently. *The Heart's a Wonder* had been an unlikely success – a musical adaptation by Mairin and Nuala O'Farrell of *The Playboy of the Western World*, which had been directed at the Gaiety Theatre by Micheál MacLiammóir. The LPT was a company of actors rather than singers, but Mary thought that 'the songs were tuneful enough not to present too many problems'. She had liked the colour and life of the Gaiety production, so Rowel Friers did an appropriately lively set. The production took off in Belfast, just as it had in Dublin, and it became one of the Lyric's biggest successes, being revived within the year in the Studio, later put on at the Grove Theatre and, later still, in Ridgeway Street. This production ran for an unprecedented fortnight over the Christmas period.

Sam McCready played Christy and Maeve McGibbon, Pegeen. A production notebook for the musical has survived, providing copious detail on moves and lighting. It is just one of many such notebooks and rehearsal charts in the archive. They indicate that Mary and her team, from the moment the first rehearsal started, went to great lengths to achieve exactly the effects the director desired. These productions would feature little of the haphazardness of the amateur tradition.

The moment had come for Mary to go public with the reorganization of her theatre, starting with a rather grand inaugural dinner. She chose Shrove Tuesday, 1 March 1960, for the formal announcement of the building plans and the naming of the trustees who were going to ensure the future of the O'Malleys' creation. The venue was the Crawfordsburn Inn, a comfortable hotel on the south coast of Belfast Lough. The food and wine were of high quality (presumably the O'Malleys had to foot the bill once again), the guests distinguished – and mostly from the South. Speeches were made and Mary replied to the various toasts, emphasizing the modesty of her plans, that they had set their sights on 'a small theatre consistent with our policy'. She said that she and Pearse had brought the private Lyric Theatre as far as they could and that 'it was now up to the people of Belfast to see that it continued to thrive and find a permanent home'. Then she handed over to the theatre's very literary solicitor, C.E.B. Brett, to announce the new administrative structure.

The LPT was to become a non-profit-making association or Trust (with the aim of presenting dramatic works 'of cultural or educational value' in a new theatre). The LPT would be bound to produce at least one Yeats play a year and the theatre would 'give special consideration to the work of Irish poets, writers and dramatists'. Seven trustees were named: two painters, Deborah Brown and Terence Flanagan (both of whom had done a fair share of unpaid set design and construction); a poet, John Hewitt; a dramatist, Denis Johnston; Gabriel Fallon, actor, drama critic and link with the Abbey in Dublin; and, of course, Pearse and Mary. There are numerous photographs of the occasion and they show a scene of some formality and style, with dinner-jacketed speakers and elegantly gowned women.

The occasion was big enough, and Mary's profile high enough, to draw in names like the novelist Kate O'Brien and Ria Mooney, the distinguished Abbey actor and director. The model of the new theatre showed Neil Downes's imaginative design, which was elegantly asymmetrical. *Threshold* copies were also on display and the achievements of the drama school were highlighted. No one was left in any doubt about the size, ambition and quality of the O'Malley cultural enterprise. Hands were probably poised to dig deep into pockets, but as Mary says, 'We made one big mistake; we didn't encourage our guests to fill up the [subscription] forms straight away … we did not want to spoil a memorable occasion by sending round "the begging bowl".' Commenting on the event she adds, a little ruefully: 'If only the story could have ended then.' She and Pearse had succeeded in moving their theatre onto more secure legal ground and, hopefully, were about to reduce the steady drain on their finances. They did not know then that they had stepped onto what was to become a site-finding and fundraising treadmill, which was to grind on for the next eight years.

9

Expansion

REPLACING HER STUDIO theatre with a fully-fledged professional 200-seater playhouse was to be a more complex, more demanding and more frustrating task than Mary could ever have imagined. A huge effort was needed to propel her proposal up the steep and bumpy sectarian hill. The difficulties were perhaps more keenly felt because she began to suffer from gall-bladder trouble, and experienced a sudden, unexpected bereavement.

In 1960, almost for the first time in the history of her theatre, Mary experienced a setback to her best-laid plans. She had decided on an American tour to show off the company's strength and originality, to spread the Yeats gospel and to raise money for the new theatre. An emissary was sent to North America to assess the terrain. Meanwhile, she began to prepare the company by rehearsing Yeats plays, *The Voice of Shem* and the second act of *The Silver Tassie*. She also set about fulfilling the onerous administrative requirements, visas and permissions for the many teachers in the company to have leave of absence. To secure this, Mary went to the Belfast City Hall to meet an assistant of Stuart Hawnt, the Director of Education (who knew Mary but who was, unfortunately, unavailable). She was kept waiting, then ushered into an office where an official was sitting with 'his chair pushed well back and his feet resting on the desk'. She handed over the list of teachers and their schools. The body language of the official was negative. 'I explained that the teachers already had the goodwill of their direct superiors; and they would be replaced by temporary substitutes.' Warming to her theme Mary then produced a letter from the US diplomatic representative in Belfast, Seymour Goodman, expressing the opinion that 'such a visit would be a good cultural gesture between the North of Ireland and the United States'. The official's retort was curt; he said that 'I may have the goodwill of some people in America who thought a lot of me, but that such goodwill did not exist here.' He turned the application down, indicating that although he would raise the matter with his education committee, 'he would not ask them to support the request'. Mary left abruptly and as she departed the official's feet remained firmly on his desk.

'Incandescent' would probably be an appropriate epithet for Mary's rage as she walked the two miles from the city centre to her home. She had already received dispiriting warnings from people who had direct experience of the costs and risks faced by Irish theatrical companies on US tours. Her can-do optimism made her keep these uncertainties to herself but quite soon it became clear the tour was impossible. The emissary (David Cronin, a friend of the architect Neil Downes) returned from the States with a pessimistic report. The financial guarantees offered were insufficient. The O'Malleys were just not prepared to take the huge risk of transporting a company of eighteen players across the Atlantic without guaranteeing themselves against financial loss. Mary's disappointment was keen; she felt intuitively that she had a company at the height of its powers: 'I knew in my heart that, maybe, I would never again have such a company together.' However, it did not take long for her and her deeply disappointed, but resilient, actors to go back into the-show-must-go-on mode. They continued to rehearse the Yeats plays in preparation for trips to Dublin and Sligo.

By the summer of 1960 the Lyric Players Trust had been set up and was functioning, although keeping track of the ancillaries was difficult from the start. The most urgent item on Mary's agenda was raising funds for the new theatre. So, an assault on the pockets of the Dublin theatre glitterati was launched on 7 June 1960, at the Shelbourne Hotel. The great, the good and the potentially useful were in attendance: Rutherford Mayne, Ernest Blythe, Denis Donoghue, Roger McHugh, John Montague, Professor T.W. Moody, Thomas Kinsella, Cathal O'Shannon, Sybil le Brocquy and Ray McAnally.

The press response was generous, but goodwill flowed more abundantly than cash – the takings were about £250. A second assault, at the Hibernian Hotel, on Dublin's captains of industry, fared no better; it was, in Mary's nicely understated phrase, 'financially rather unrewarding'. London was the next target. The Irish Club in Eaton Square hosted a wine-and-cheese event, which attracted only a modest number of guests and contributions. There was still a long way to go.

Mary comforted herself with intensive rehearsals of no fewer than six Yeats plays in preparation for the company's first appearance at the Yeats Festival in Sligo. The festival, which was making its debut, was an adventure for the Lyric company and the families associated with it. They travelled to Sligo by car; costumes, props and technical crew went by minibus. Pearse and Mary had decided to turn the event into a family holiday. They rented accommodation, as did Arthur Brooke and his wife, Florence, and Helen Lewis and her husband, Harry. The weather was good, the children from the three families played together on the beach, climbed Knocknarea and visited Yeats's grave in Drumcliffe churchyard. Meanwhile the cast was ensconced at Sligo Grammar School. Sam McCready remembers their time there very well, sleeping in damp dormitories on 'single iron beds with grey army blankets. There was no privacy; we were treated like school-kids and we behaved like school-kids.'

The daytimes were more serious. The plays were presented in Sligo Town Hall, which was packed with an audience of students, academics, locals and American Yeatsians. For McCready, performing Yeats in Sligo 'was like a homecoming'. He, like Mary, suggests that at that moment the company may have been at the height of its powers.

The origins of Mary's enthusiasm for Yeats are obscure, but she loved his dramas, as her intensively annotated Macmillan edition of the plays reveals. 'The limitations of space in her theatre made it essential that the director approached productions with simplicity and precision,' says Conor O'Malley. He goes on: 'More often than not one had to be content to suggest objects and locations. A keen imagination and a sense of pragmatism became essential artistic requirements.' Conor saw the Yeats productions in his mother's theatre, observed their planning and rehearsal and, eventually, put his description of them into his book *A Poets' Theatre*. He notes that the intimacy of the studio required (even in non-Yeatsian work) subtlety and restraint from the actor. Sam McCready, in a 1965 BBC radio programme on Yeats, says that on the tiny Lyric stage the actor must leave himself behind 'and allow the words, allow the poet, to speak to the audience ...' He emphasizes the importance of teamwork and how 'there aren't any stars in Yeats'.

Mary wanted the lines to be delivered clearly and unselfconsciously by a natural speaker of verse. In a *Threshold* article on Yeats she makes the point that 'an intense, highly emotional actor, no matter how good his professional competence, may not find it possible to subdue his personality to the necessary level of detachment and withdrawal'. Her success in finding and training good verse-speakers is attested by countless reviews of her Yeats productions. Recorded sound from those Studio days suggests how rich and strange the poetry must have sounded in those productions. The delivery has an element of chanting in it, something that did not always please Belfast critics or audiences. Movement was the other key element in Mary's Yeats productions. She required her players to be 'as proficient in movement as in speech'. Helen Lewis's choreography, simple and restrained, and sometimes featuring the choreographer herself on stage, was perhaps the most distinctive element.

Abstract design and simple music were also keynotes in her Yeats work. Conor again:

> Each Yeats play was designed to a narrow colour scheme, selected by consultation between director and designer and expressive of its particular atmosphere. *The King of the Great Clock Tower* was in red and black, *The Only Jealousy of Emer* was in varying shades of green, *Resurrection* used austere white and grey panels ... Where possible, the design was reduced to a finely painted abstract panel.

Over time Mary persuaded many distinguished Ulster artists to paint these panels. Generally these contributions were unpaid, but, as many of the artists freely admitted, the commissions provided them with unique opportunities to express themselves in a different, 'live' art form.

Music was sometimes difficult to integrate with Yeats's text, but the key was a less-is-more approach. Raymond Warren, Mary's composer-in-chief for Yeats, suggests what is needed is 'monody, a single melodic line with perhaps percussion accompaniment'. In the Cuchulain plays he identified each of the characters with an instrument: Cuchulain was a horn; the Hawk a cor anglais, for example. In *On Baile's Strand* Aoife is a harp, Emer a violin. Mary's Yeats productions were closely based on Yeats's own ideas and those of his brother Jack: an emphasis on the 'unity of presentation, with the words as "sovereign"'. The O'Malley achievement was recognized by a German Yeats scholar, Professor Kleinstock of Hamburg University, who found in the mid-1960s that the Abbey Theatre's actors 'have almost no experience in verse-speaking' but that 'unexpectedly' the Lyric Players in Belfast 'play especially Yeats and know how to play him. Thus, Yeats's dream hasn't remained unfulfilled.'

Derryvolgie Avenue contained one less resident from that autumn of 1960. Kieran went to Clongowes Wood, perhaps the most distinguished boarding school in the Republic of Ireland and once attended, briefly, by James Joyce. This was another strain on the already overstretched O'Malley purse and the decision to send their eldest son away to boarding school was not taken lightly. Mary knew what boarding schools were like and how painful the break from home could be. But she and Pearse did not like what she called 'the Englishness of the Northern Ireland system of education'. Kieran was consulted and it was established that there were other northern boys at the school.

When the day came, Mary, Pearse and eleven-year-old Kieran set off for Co. Kildare in a reasonably positive frame of mind. Mary was dreading the loss, but Kieran was settled, apparently satisfactorily, into a huge dormitory, made friends with the boy in the next bed and with Hilary Iremonger, son of Mary's old friend Val. Mary cried after she had said goodbye. But Kieran was not to be left there for the whole term: Pearse and Mary agreed to come and see him after four weeks. When they came back it was clear that the boy was not happy. Later he explained that he had been bullied: 'I had a very strong Northern accent and every time I stood up and spoke people would mock me. It was very shaming. I was an outsider.' Pearse and Mary resolved to visit fortnightly, which they did, completing the 250-mile journey in a day over the variable roads of the Republic. Kieran was given the option of coming home if he couldn't stand it anymore, but by the end of term he was settled.

At Christmas, with Kieran now relatively happy, Mary looked forward to 1961. The autumn had been reasonably satisfactory in the Studio. She had done another *King Lear* with Terence Nonweiler, a lecturer in aeronautical engineering at Queen's, in the title role, which he accomplished with skill. Mary then took a rest by inviting Louis Lentin, a young Dublin director, to stage Donagh McDonagh's lively verse play *Lady Spider*. Lentin registered some anxiety about the size of the stage but seems to have made an accommodation with the tiny space. The critics liked the way he persuaded the company not to speak the verse in 'a slow, chanting manner', which delivered a much 'crisper and speedier approach' (Mary's 'Yeats method' may not have been appropriate in a play classified as a tragedy but containing many comic moments). At this point, plays usually ran for eight days in the Studio, with the seats priced at four and five shillings, so the O'Malleys were beginning to defray some of their costs. Theoretically they were able to take up to £12 night and perhaps close to £100 over the whole run, but the accounts indicate that production costs would eat up most of that sum. A sparkling revival of *The Heart's a Wonder* spread Christmas joy and good cheer and replenished the coffers.

———

1961 was to be dominated by a savage blow when Mary's beloved brother Gerard died suddenly on 23 April. She was resting before a Sunday rehearsal when the phone rang in Derryvolgie Avenue. It was her niece Anne, Gerard's daughter. She told Mary her father was dead. Disbelief, shock and then, 'very gradually', realization, were her reactions. She had been prepared, over many years, for her mother's death, but Gerard was still 'in my estimation, quite young. He had a lot of living to do'. She had noticed that he seemed frail when he had come up for the traditional New Year's Eve party. She had spoken to him a few days earlier on the telephone and he'd mentioned that he hadn't been well. She had suggested that he took a train to Belfast and Pearse would arrange for him to be checked over. But he was dead two days later.

Mary and Pearse drove to Dublin that day. When she saw Gerard's body, still in the drawing room where he had died, she felt that, as a great practical joker, he might jump up and gleefully surprise them. She was shocked by his appearance in death: 'He was so unlike himself, so different.'

Gerard was a huge loss to Mary. He had paid her school fees, provided her with little luxuries during her childhood and he had helped her in the theatre. He had gone a long way towards filling the role of the father she never had. She missed deeply 'his gentle nature and sense of fun'.

The theatre helped to distract Mary from her grief and so did a welcome domestic development. The male/female imbalance in the household was now marked and on a recommendation from a friend, the O'Malleys engaged a Danish au pair, Elsebeth Orntoft, who quickly became 'like a daughter to me and an elder sister to the boys'. An earlier attempt with a French girl had not worked out, but Elsebeth already spoke good English and had relatives in Belfast, so she was able to adapt to O'Malley modes very quickly. First, she had to get used to the endless comings and goings in the house – Pearse's patients, actors, Birgit Kirkpatrick with costumes, stage carpenters and three different domestic helpers – the doors were opening and closing all day.

Central heating was the norm in Denmark, but at Beechbank Pearse would open the windows early in the day and the coal fires would not be lit till 5 pm. Fifty years later Elsebeth says, 'I have never been so cold in my life.' She even took to wearing an Aran sweater in bed. Productions in the theatre dictated the rhythm of the household. Actors would use her bedroom to make themselves up. And there were money-making 'theatre suppers' to be prepared ('always Beef Stroganoff and Lemon Mousse'), after which there were mountains of washing-up to be done, often by a very weary Elsebeth. And, of course, Mary would have invited numerous visitors to stay overnight after seeing the play.

Normal family meals involved Mary dolloping out huge portions ('You're a growing girl,' she would say) and Pearse telling her at length about the disgraceful gerrymandering in Northern Ireland. Elsebeth saw Mary's temper in action and how Pearse could calm her down and how, despite her feisty truculence, Mary depended on him. Elsebeth also noted how fiercely Mary demanded loyalty and observed how close she was to Helen Lewis. They talked on the phone almost daily – about plays, dance and much else besides Sadly, that strong female friendship was to encounter severe turbulence later.

This au pair arrangement had worked so well that, when Elsebeth went home, more delightful young Danish women followed. First came Gitte, who was 'artistic, helpful and gay' and willing to take part in Lyric activities, even dancing in a late-night entertainment. Gitte caused a stir whenever she accompanied the O'Malleys to Clongowes. Visits from this 'gorgeous creature' made Kieran the envy of his classmates. A third au pair, Lise, was quite formidable, and Mary gives a revealing account of her effect on the household:

[She] got into her stride straight away and for one year my home was managed as never before ... She even succeeded in getting a housekeeping allowance. My household management consisted of ordering groceries and other requirements by phone ... I was [now] encouraged to organise myself, so that when special guests were expected I would have to sit down and arrange a menu. This was unheard-of. My slipshod method of quick-thinking and quicker action was discouraged. Here she was, organising me and doing it well. She had authority and knew when to put her foot down. We all benefited. After her departure life was never the same.

Mary's account of 1961 in the theatre is quite cursory. The programme included Ibsen's *Brand*, which ran for ten nights and was later to go to

the Dublin Theatre Festival; some one-acters, including Lady Gregory's
The Rising of the Moon; *The Dreaming Dust* by Denis Johnston (with Louis
Rolston as Dean Swift); and the rather insipid – by Lorca's standards – *Doña
Rosita la Soltera.*

The administration of her theatre now began to cause Mary stress.
There were signs that the commitment of some of the trustees – particularly
the long-distance ones – was wavering. The national anthem question arose
again. There was now the possibility of doing plays outside the theatre in
various halls in Belfast, so the trustees had to agree a policy. They came up
with a reasonable formula: 'The Lyric Players should continue its policy of
having no National Anthem at productions on the premises, but it may
be played at the discretion of the Trustees, at any outside function.' So
Mary's least favourite tune would never be heard in Derryvolgie Avenue
but the necessary token loyalty could be provided elsewhere. 'No anthem
on the premises' became an over-my-dead-body article of faith for Mary, a
conviction which, when she acted on it later, had explosive results.

Threshold and fundraising were still taking a lot of Mary's time and she
admitted to feeling 'exhausted'. She soldiered on and in October 1961
succeeded in establishing a more solid organizational base for her company.
She rewarded those who had worked 'faithfully and well' over the years. She
named a First Eleven – a list that included designers and a choreographer
as well as actors. The actors were Joan Carslake (soon to marry Sam
McCready), Sheelagh Garvin, Kathleen Kelly, George and Babs Mooney,
Sam McCready, Olga McKeown and Louis Rolston. The choreographer was
Helen Lewis and the two designers Alice Berger Hammerschlag and Birgit
Kirkpatrick. Their obligations were to take part in at least two productions
a year, for which they were to receive tiny payments. Because admission
was now being charged at the Studio, the drain on the O'Malley purse
had been slightly alleviated, but they continued to subsidize their theatre.
Pearse mentions spending $3000 to $5000 annually on the Lyric in a letter

to an American correspondent. In present-day terms that would amount to a considerable sum. Fortunately, his private psychiatric practice was prospering.

Yeats took over again in the summer of 1961, with another visit to the Summer School in Sligo. Two plays they had not done before were added to the repertoire: the tense, philosophical *The Hour Glass* and the lively *Player Queen*. These plays, along with *At the Hawk's Well* and *The Dreaming of the Bones* were taken south in September for another visit to the Dublin Theatre Festival. Laurels were dispensed by the critics to the Yeats offerings: John Jordan in *Hibernia* was delighted with *The Player Queen* – 'continuously enchanting as theatre, full of surprises and epiphanies and what is more, at times, funny'. Yeats was not the only Dublin offering, however. *Brand* was brought south as well. This was not so popular, although there was praise for Liam O'Callaghan's 'majestic' performance as the preacher.

Back in Belfast Mary was still frustrated by not being able to find a site for the new theatre. Deals kept falling through at the last moment, with strong hints that sectarian disapproval of Mary's politics and her whole enterprise were the cause. Thwarted on this front, Mary satisfied her desire for expansion with not one but three new projects. First, she decided to go commercial and raise money for the theatre by setting up an Irish handcrafts shop. Never one to do things by halves, Mary and Pearse rented sizeable commercial premises in the Grosvenor Road, not very far from the Opera House and the centre of the city. The rent was low – only £5 10s. a week – perhaps because the area around it was slightly depressed. There was plenty of space, but not much passing trade.

At this point in the early 1960s Irish crafts were beginning to be revived and thrive. With more disposable income around, it became fashionable to acquire certain high-quality brands. So Mary sold Avoca and Donegal tweed, Crock of Gold fabrics, Shanagarry pottery, Carrickmacross lace, Gael-Linn records and Dolmen Press books, as well as Irish linen and handmade silver and copper jewellery. With the help of Neil Downes, the premises were made as attractive as possible, although when I visited in 1964 the building was bare enough to be described as spartan. Just in case Mary's shop venture might seem unduly rash, it's worth noting that she had tested the market beforehand, successfully selling Irish handcrafts from a stall in the Green Room in Derryvolgie Avenue.

The new building had the big advantage that the theatre's administration and box office moved there and that there was space upstairs for other developments. For nearly a decade Mary had been hosting painting exhibitions at Derryvolgie Avenue. But here was a chance to create an art gallery. Two big rooms were renovated, and suitable lighting installed to set up what Mary called the New Gallery. Alice Berger Hammerschlag arranged the first exhibition of work by the Greek Cypriot, Michael Anthony Michaelides, which was opened in April 1963 by Mary's good friend the novelist Kate O'Brien. For six years the New Gallery, run by Mrs Hammerschlag, was to host fine exhibitions by artists from England and continental Europe while giving due place to locals – in all there were twenty-nine exhibitions by Irish painters and sculptors. The New Gallery's critical success owed a great deal to the European perspective and the hard work of Alice Berger Hammerschlag: but it did not make a profit.

So Mary had added two new ships to her cultural fleet. Seeing the possibilities which the spacious Grosvenor Road offered, she now added a third. There was in the early 1960s no music academy in Belfast. For years there had been talk of creating one. Mary saw an educational need and a gap in the market and within months, on a shoestring, she created the Belfast Academy of Music, which opened with a roll of eighteen pupils. Her method was quite simple. She knew musicians who had contributed to LPT productions, including Raymond Warren who taught music at Queen's. He responded positively to the idea of an academy and advised Mary on tutors. Soon they had nine potential teachers on the books and a prospectus was written, making clear that the academy's intentions were to provide a wider and more comprehensive musical education than was then available in Belfast. It would not be a diploma factory – and a key element was that the whole curriculum would be 'enriched by close association with the Lyric Players and the New Gallery'. This connection was to become controversial.

There are vivid vignettes by Sam McCready of life in the hyperactive world of Grosvenor Road. He would spend his Sunday afternoons doing the window displays for the shop, making something out of theatre props, leaves, bamboo, 'anything I could get my hands on to showcase the beautiful objects within'. Upstairs he would find a new exhibition, by painters like Gillian Ayres, Patrick Scott, Jack Yeats or Deborah Brown, to name but a few; the music academy students would come every night and the drama school pupils on Mondays and Fridays. As if this wasn't enough, an art class, led by promising young Ulster painters like Ivan Armstrong and Neil Shawcross, took place on Saturday mornings. In his book about the LPT, Conor O'Malley makes an interesting point: that Grosvenor Road, although not called an arts centre, was in effect a very successful one, in which there was a rare fusion, a true cross-fertilization of the arts.

1963 was notable for a major production outside the Studio. *The Risen People*, by James Plunkett, dealt with the 1913 Dublin dock strike and subsequent lockout. Plunkett had come to Mary's attention as a contributor of short stories to *Threshold*. When she put on his play (which had already been done by the Abbey) at Derryvolgie Avenue, the large cast was supplemented by real-life local dockers. The production was successful, and it became clear that a two-week run at the Studio (seen by perhaps 600 people) was inadequate, so Mary rapidly hired the King George VI Hall in May Street and put it on there. James Larkin Junior came up from Dublin for the big-theatre production and in a letter to Mary expressed the opinion that it was better than the original in the Abbey; even more usefully, he enclosed a subscription to the Lyric Players Trust.

Spotting that there were more opportunities on the big stage of the George VI Hall, Mary quickly put together a programme of four one-act plays. She seized the opportunity to create on a larger scale the kind of visual effects that had always been part of her directorial signature. For *Riders to the Sea*, Alice Hammerschlag created 'a huge canvas triangle, painted white, flecked with large brushstrokes of black and grey, to give the impression of the gable end of a cottage'. The programme finished with Yeats's sombre *Calvary*, about which Mary waxed lyrical: 'In *Calvary* we had total theatre in twenty minutes of extraordinary beauty. We had, I think, captured the coldness, the loneliness and bleakness of the magnificent text – "Why hast thou forsaken me," giving way to that never-ending single note on the oboe.' As usual Raymond Warren and Helen Lewis had made their vital contributions to the whole.

Clearly the chance to use a bigger stage meant a great deal to Mary and so did the fact that the venue was in the centre of Belfast; she felt that 'appearing there might help to dispel the notion that we were a secret society operating in Derryvolgie Avenue'.

––––––––––

In the period between 1962 and 1965 Mary broadened the repertory at the Studio with some unusual choices. She did *The Carmelites* by Georges Bernanos. It was Mary's kind of play, but audiences stayed away, and the critics were ambivalent. *A Man for All Seasons* was a box office success – making a profit of £33 2s. 5d. There was Chekhov (*Uncle Vanya* and *The Cherry Orchard*); Beckett (*Endgame*) and *Next Time I'll Sing to You*, a play by James Saunders whose work was then somewhat in vogue in London.

Then there was *Richard III*. This young *Belfast Telegraph* reporter was sent to review it:

> Most of us thought it would be like doing Swan Lake on the dining room table. However, Mrs O'Malley's ingenuity has matched her audacity in mounting Richard III in her garage-theatre [*sic*] at Derryvolgie Avenue, and she has created a dexterous, mobile, sensible production. She has overcome the limitations of her stage – although not those of [all] her actors – and her use of the slightly enlarged acting area is most imaginative. Different levels are cleverly employed on a stage the depth of which is greater than its width.
>
> There is discipline in the handling of the historical trappings: pages manoeuvred banners in and out of the four exits with confident expertise on the first night. The lights often enlarged the stage; the martial music led our imaginations to huge chambers and open battlefields; the costumes were simple and quietly colourful – clumsy suits of armour were sensibly avoided.

The review goes on to say how the second half generated 'an exhilarating momentum' and assesses Sam McCready's interpretation of Richard like this: 'He started uncertainly but gradually a fluent, studied performance emerged. There was no attempt at rant and histrionics; this was a light, almost caricatured Richard whose malevolence was clothed in a delightfully macabre wit. It was a performance just right for an unpretentious production.' The piece ends with a few plaudits for some other fine individual performances and summed up the production with a slightly glib: 'Altogether a courageous contribution to the centenary celebrations.'

In the spring Mary farmed out the direction of the Brian Friel play, *The Enemy Within*, to Ronald Mason who was later to become Head of Drama at BBC Northern Ireland. In the programme he wrote: 'Friel, who has just returned from a year's study under Sir Tyrone Guthrie in Minneapolis, is one of the most successful of our young Irish writers. It is not surprising that this theme [the story of Colmcille] attracted him, for his native Co. Derry is steeped in Columban tradition.' Sam McCready played an ancient scribe, Caornan, while George Mooney was the earthy Columba. This play, with a set by Rowel Friers, was done in September 1963, just a few months after its premiere in the Abbey in Dublin. Mary knew Friel quite well by this stage (through *Threshold* contacts) and we have to presume that she would have liked him to premiere his play in her theatre, but probably both she and Friel were realistic enough to know that the Abbey was the way to larger audiences, larger fees and more press attention.

By now the Lyric's publicity machine was becoming much more professional. The press release for an Ionesco double bill refers back to an earlier production of Beckett's *Endgame* and says that the Lyric Players are continuing 'their exploration of ... the French *avant-garde*. Dublin-born Beckett; Romanian-born Ionesco. Both major international playwrights whose influence on modern drama, welcome it or not, cannot be denied.' In his memoir, McCready makes a nice comic scene out of the Ionesco double bill. *Jacques* and *The Future Is in Eggs* were directed by the promising Denis Smyth. Sam played Jacques who, in the first play wants to marry a woman with three noses, and in the second has to lay a large number of eggs:

We made hundreds of papier-mâché eggs for the production and while I laid them I was cackling and crowing, while the rest of the cast carried them off stage, chorusing 'Production, Production.' One evening the ridiculousness of the situation overwhelmed me and as I got to the final lines, I started to laugh. Bernadette Keenan (my wife in the play) began laughing as well. Then others on the stage began to laugh and before we knew it, the whole theatre audience was laughing uproariously, and it became impossible to continue. We abandoned the play and the laughing could still be heard as the audience made its way down the wooden stairs ...

This broad-ranging and imaginative selection of plays from all over the world once again raises the question: could the Lyric, which was already educating Belfast children in speech, movement, acting and music, have done more for local writing? Back in 1961 the thoughtful Martin Wallace of the *Belfast Telegraph* had wondered if there had been too little effort to foster native playwrights. Mary took up the theme in an undated newspaper piece:

> If the main function of a local theatre is – as I believe it to be – to stimulate the Irish poet and writer, in this area, we have failed. I believe that the old Group Theatre did cope adequately for the Northern writer – but we have not received one decent play from the North. We have received plays – let me make that plain – but they have not been of a calibre to warrant a production.

She goes on to say that she has received new plays from the South and that three of them were 'well worthwhile' pieces. It seems reasonable to ask why Mary did not contact the local writers who had submitted plays, however bad. In an interview with John Fairleigh in the *Belfast Telegraph*, talking about policy in the new theatre (when it is built) she says: 'As far as possible the theatre will try to put on plays by local writers who may not have fully developed but need the encouragement and the chance to see their work in production.' We don't know whether plays by Ulster writers were coming into the LPT in any number at this stage, but for now she continued to rely primarily on world classics and more modern Irish plays, many of which had already been seen in Dublin.

In 1964 the insurance company Irish Life instituted a playwriting competition. Mary became involved in its administration and seems to have had an informal arrangement that she would stage the winning plays in her theatre. This was an all-Ireland event and the winners of the first three competitions were all dramatists from the South. The winning plays Mary put on were *King of the Castle* (Eugene McCabe), *The Green Desert* (Patrick Hughes) and *The Last Eleven* (Jack White). At least they were new plays, but over the next three years their production tilted her programme still further away from representing new Belfast writing.

If directing – or getting others to direct – interesting plays had been Mary's sole occupation in the mid-1960s then she would have been much happier. But the rapid expansion of the Lyric's ancillary activities took up a lot of her time. The minutes of the trustees' meetings show, for example, how difficult it was to manage the Irish handcrafts shop. In October 1962 the trustees had been told that business and management were 'unsatisfactory'. There was only one full-time member of staff at the Grosvenor Road Centre. The manager's job was to run the shop and do the bookings for the theatre. There were constant resignations; it was hard to find suitable candidates for what could be a demanding and lonely job. Even the theatre faced administrative difficulties. The Studio mostly lost money, but 1961–62 had been an encouraging year: the loss was less than £60, compared with £477 for the previous twelve months. The New Gallery had prestigious exhibitions but did not make money. It was responsible for £300 of the £400 loss in 1963–64. There is a strong sense of crisis management in the minutes of many trustee meetings, but no feeling that any of the leaky ships should be docked. Optimism rules impressively. Interestingly, the Arts Council's first tranche of subsidy arrived in 1965, the sum of £1000, aimed at helping with a transition to full professional status. It was divided among four company members only: Sam McCready got £350; Louis Rolston £250,

Peter Adair £250; and Liam O'Callaghan £150. The division seems to have been based primarily on number of appearances as well as merit. What the other, unrewarded, members of the company thought about the share-out is not recorded.

10

Loyalty

MANAGING HER THEATRE and its offshoots, while having to persist doggedly with the long, frustrating search for a theatre site, stressed Mary. Sam McCready suggests that the stresses and frustration she was experiencing sometimes made her 'irascible and paranoid, identifying enemies and subversives in all kinds of unlikely places. And a major cause of her paranoia was what she perceived as disloyalty from the resident company – the enemy within.' Company members had to acknowledge their association with the LPT when they did outside work. There may have been some carelessness by the players who perhaps did not always take Mary's *diktat* entirely seriously. Sam himself directed for the Studio Opera group and worked as an actor for other companies, as well as professionally for the BBC. He always tried to acknowledge his connection with the Lyric but explains that 'formal recognition in publicity was not always possible'. Mary, however, was uncompromising about this. If a company member failed to publicly acknowledge a close association with the Lyric Players, it was 'a sign of disloyalty'.

This led to a painful conflict with Helen Lewis, Mary's trusted and talented choreographer. Helen had set up her own Belfast Modern Dance group, which she ran in tandem with choreographing almost all the shows at the Lyric. Havelock Nelson, Ulster's composer-in-chief, did a setting of Christina Rossetti's poem *Goblin Market* and invited Helen to create a ballet based on his music. Helen did so, and *Goblin Market* was premiered at a hall in Rosemary Street along with *The King's Threshold*, done by the Lyric Players. The evening was successful, apart from Mary having to skulk out of earshot while Havelock Nelson played the national anthem. Some months later Helen's Modern Dance group repeated the performance at a fundraiser for Purdysburn Hospital. Mary attended and, according to McCready – who was doing the make-up for the dancers – was in good spirits at the interval. After the performance Helen phoned Mary, who refused to speak to her. Helen's crime? There had been no mention of her connection with the Lyric in the *Goblin Market* programme. Helen later justified her omission by saying that her Modern Dance group was entirely separate from the Lyric and thus there was no reason for an acknowledgment. But Mary knew that many of Helen's dancers were Lyric players, even if not official members of the company, and thought that her theatre should have some credit for this. And, after all, hadn't *Goblin Market* shared the evening with the LPT's *The King's Threshold*? Mary thought that Helen, at the very least, should have acknowledged that she herself was a foundation member of the Lyric Players Theatre. Mary was so angry that she cut off all connection with Helen for a time; Helen wanted to talk it over, but Mary was obdurate.

John Hewitt, in a tribute poem to Mary (quoted at the front of this book), mentions 'that dark woman's mood'. She undoubtedly had a violent temper but, as McCready says, 'she was also a generous and wonderful friend'. But, he says, she demanded total loyalty: 'She gave you the moon and demanded the stars, and she became jealous if you showed favours elsewhere ... she wanted to own you.' As the years went by, the rift with Helen began to heal over and they worked together again, but later another conflict blew up over something rather different.

A year or two later there was a row with Alice Berger Hammerschlag. Alice had started by doing the sets for *Red Roses for Me* back in 1959. In 1961 she had accepted a role in the 'First Eleven'. By 1963 she was running the New Gallery and wrote with admirable realism to Mary soon after it opened: 'First two exhibitions artistically first rate and the reaction of the public was as foreseen – lots of controversy and, so far, no sales.' She goes on: 'If this high standard is maintained, a financial success cannot be expected before a run of two or three years' time and even after that the Gallery will probably, at best, keep itself, like the Theatre which, rightly does not play to box office, but aims at quality.'

Two years after this, when Mary had, at last, managed to make a start on building her new theatre, she gave an interview to the *Observer* journalist Mary Holland. The resulting piece seemed to suggest that the whole cultural flotilla, including the New Gallery, was run largely, or even entirely, by Mary. Holland says, 'Mary O'Malley bestrides the Belfast scene like a latter-day Lady Gregory. She even looks like a figure out of Yeats – dark and comely with the passion of the political women he described.' Holland then pays homage to the quality of plays Mary puts on and adds: 'She recently laid the foundation stone for a 300-seater, also runs an art gallery … edits a literary magazine and has a school for music and drama.' The article provoked an explosive response from Alice:

> You have always been stressing the great team-work – well why not mention it? It is true of course that the idea of a Music and Drama School and that of a gallery was yours, but certainly not the running of either. It would have sufficed to say, even without the mention of names, that you had experts (or whatever you may choose to call it) running these enterprises for you – surely it is quite a credit to you to run a 55-seater [*sic*] theatre and be heart and soul behind building a new 300-seater, and being the editor of a literary magazine, without adding the enterprises you are not running.

Towards the end of the letter, she suggests that Mary's 'slip' might help her to understand why her team don't always credit the Lyric when doing outside work. And she finishes in uncompromising style, asking Mary in future to 'bear in mind the teamwork you are rightly proud of when it comes to public notices … now let's forget this incident without further comment'. It appears that the breach was not healed quickly. A few weeks later Alice asks, in a letter written to Pearse, 'What a pity that neither you nor Mary can use the words "I'm sorry" occasionally.' However, time – and their deep artistic connections in the theatre and the New Gallery – helped them to make up.

It is easy to lose sight of Mary, Pearse and the boys in this long recital of her professional struggles. Kieran admits it was strange, growing up in a house 'with a psychiatrist's consulting room at the front and a theatrical environment at the back – it's ridiculous'. The theatre was intrusive, 'people would charge down the main staircase. You became de-sensitized – you learnt not to be seen. It was equally intrusive to have psychiatric patients in the house – you were not allowed to interact with them.' These patients were more likely to be Protestant than Catholic but also included a good many nuns and priests. 'Dad did some ECT in the house – controversial I know, but it does work with intractable mood disorders. Anaesthetists would come to the house to help with ECT.' Conor says one day the inevitable happened: 'Two people arrived and were shown into the doctor's waiting room and when they came in to see Dad as a pair, it took him a few minutes to realize that they were actors who had come for an audition.' Kieran sees Pearse as a good father, 'always fair and always there', and applauds him for 'quietly facilitating [Mary's] creative genes'. But Pearse had interesting quirks. 'He was not tactile; he didn't shake hands with patients – he was phobic about germs.' And he was much more religious than Mary: 'He would get holy water every New Year's Eve.'

Mary's second son, Donal, was less involved with the theatre than his two brothers. He remembers doing a small part, 'an executioner' in one play, and much later he served briefly as a stage manager, but rugby was perhaps a higher priority for him than what was happening on the Derryvolgie stage. He sometimes found the invasion of the house by theatricals uncomfortable. 'One day I came back from Clongowes, went into the house and there, in the TV room, two people were sitting on the sofa. I told them: "You can't come in here; this room isn't for the audience. You have to go round the back."' Asked who he was, he said, 'Well actually I live here.'

Conor found the theatre less intrusive: for him it was 'normal to have a theatre in the house'. He remembers a happy childhood, 'running around the house with the dog Grainne and trying to outpace it'; or re-enacting World War One in trenches in the back garden in the snowy winter of 1963; and the children's parties, involving chess competitions, military whist and plates piled high with sweets and toast. Conor says he did not resent his mother's preoccupation with the theatre. He didn't like having to learn the violin at the Music Academy, but he did enjoy the drama school where Helen Lewis taught him 'how to open up like a flower.' He was one of the princes in the tower in *Richard III* and remembers there being questions about whether he would be allowed to come back at the end as a ghost – because it would be past his ten-year-old bedtime. He could see the theatre from his bedroom and would sometimes slip down backstage but be sent back to bed by his mother who would be doing the lights on the other side of the stage. But he did manage to see a lot of performances. 'That's where I learned about Yeats's plays – a lot of it went over my head and a lot of it must not have been age-appropriate, but that was normal.' Once, when audiences were sparse, he was offered 6d. to attend a Yeats offering and make up the numbers. 'There were three short plays, so I got smart and said, "Should that not be sixpence per play?"' Conor found talking to Pearse easier than to his mother:

> One of my favourite things as a child was that every Sunday afternoon we would go for a walk in Barnett's Park, just Dad and me. (Mum was not a great person for exercise.) We would talk politics – I remember him telling me about John F. Kennedy. I remember him saying, 'This was the most hopeful time there had ever been.' He was always an optimist.

Was he closer to his father? 'Yes. That's not a criticism of her; she was quite hands off in a lot of ways. She just let you get on with it …' His parents' relationship was so close Conor says, 'you couldn't separate them with a razor'. Although they would sometimes argue and rage, Kieran has an abiding memory of them sitting together on the sofa watching television and holding hands.

Not surprisingly the theatre was never far away from Pearse and Mary's thoughts and holidays were used for the pleasant task of thinking up the next season's programme. They usually had plenty of time for staying indoors and reading because each year their vacations tended to attract the worst summer weather Ireland could offer. It didn't matter where they went: after the Ballyhalbert years, they tried Bray in Co. Wicklow, then Cranfield in Co. Down. Mary says ruefully: 'We were more or less confined to July [they needed August to start rehearsals for the season's productions] and it always seemed to rain. Achill in a downpour has to be seen to be believed. We covered the whole country, from Parknasilla to Donegal and we were nearly always unlucky. With a sigh of relief, we would make for home and hope for better the following year.'

In the autumn of 1964 Mary and Pearse decided to take a long trip to the United States. Mary had hoped to get a cultural bursary from the American government, but she needed a British passport to qualify – and she was not about to acquire one. So Pearse's stretched resources were once again put to the test as they booked their sea passage to New York – Mary had a fear of flying (and cycling and driving). The older boys were at boarding school and Conor was in the safe hands of the latest Danish au pair, Ellen. The expenses of the journey were mitigated a little by staying with some of Pearse's numerous relatives who had frequently invited them to visit. Mary's huge production of *The Possessed* had just opened and she managed to tear herself away from the run, leaving George Mooney in charge of the autumn programme. To show that she was going to be missed, the company presented her with 'two beautiful silk scarves' before they left.

Once in America, naturally the O'Malleys gravitated towards the theatres. They saw *Blood Knot* by Athol Fugard, which Mary later tried to do in Belfast but could not find a black actor for the main part. The next play they went to was Frank D. Gilroy's Pulitzer prize-winning *The Subject Was Roses*, with the young Martin Sheen starring in the coming-of-age drama. Mary liked it enough to put it on in her theatre not long after they returned, but it played to very small audiences.

They drove through the autumnal colours of Connecticut to Boston, where Mary felt nervous: their visit had coincided with the moment when the Boston Strangler was at the height of his ill fame. In their hotel she refused to use the bathroom 'until it had been checked for interlopers'. The task of confronting the mass murderer in the toilet would have fallen to the gentle psychiatrist, Pearse. They spent an invigorating final week in New York, brunching at Stouffer's, visiting art galleries, going to mass at St Patrick's Cathedral and shopping at Macy's, where they phoned home from a coin box in the store. Mary sums up: 'The very energy of the place stimulated us and we felt rejuvenated.'

Back at home all was reasonably well at the theatre. *The Possessed* had finished its run and been followed by Friel's *The Blind Mice*. Alun Owen's *The Rough and Ready Lot* was playing when they returned. George Mooney, who had acted as artistic director in the O'Malleys' absence, had managed to keep the momentum going but, although he was prepared to contribute in the future to individual productions, he was about to resign as a trustee. Keeping a set of trustees on board for any length of time was proving hazardous. And the familiar, and still unsolved, problems of site-finding and fundraising were going to require all the new energy Mary had acquired on her transatlantic foray. They had come back with their pockets empty; it had not been possible to persuade Americans to part with money for the new theatre. As Mary puts it, 'Many had expressed interest, but that was the end of the matter.'

At this point in 1964 Mary's contribution to culture in Northern Ireland was recognized by the BBC. She was asked by Robert McCall, Controller of BBC Northern Ireland, to join their advisory panel. She accepted, a touch conditionally: 'As you are no doubt aware co-operation between individuals with different points of view in this part of the world is not easy, but I will be very pleased to make whatever contribution I can under the prevailing circumstances.'

The matter of finding a site and raising funds now became Mary's preoccupation. A piece of land had to be found if donors were to be convinced that Neil Downes's design would ever put down its foundations in Belfast soil. Early on there had been a promising option of a Lagan-side site at Shaw's Bridge, but at the last moment this had been mysteriously withdrawn from sale. This happened more than once and it's difficult not to attribute these failures to what Downes called 'political factors'. Mary, the former firebrand nationalist councillor, now running a playhouse putting on a great many plays from the South of Ireland and a socialist to boot, would not have made an ideal purchaser for vendors of a more conservative and Unionist persuasion.

These setbacks just made the O'Malleys more determined. In 1965 they tried a new approach: keeping the identity of the Lyric as purchaser secret until the last moment. They found another site by the Lagan, a former bakery on the Annadale Embankment. It was smaller than they wanted but in the light of all the previous difficulties the trustees saw it as a reasonable option. The £2000 needed to buy it came courtesy of a friendly manager from the Falls Road branch of Munster and Leinster Bank. The sum was guaranteed by eight 'old friends' of the Lyric. The policy of keeping the purchaser's identity secret till the last moment worked: there was no last-minute withdrawal, so at her end-of-season Strawberry Party (which involved strawberries for 500), Mary was able to announce that her theatre would be built at the Lagan end of Ridgeway Street, a modest thoroughfare of red-brick houses.

Mary took a typically bold decision: now she had a site, she would kick-start fundraising by a public event – the ceremonial laying of a foundation stone for the new theatre. A date was chosen (12 June 1965, Yeats's birthday minus one – it should have been Sunday 13 June, but Mary decided that Ulster's Sabbatarians would prefer a Saturday event); a huge block of Mourne granite was purchased; a Dublin sculptor was engaged to carve a legend on it; six poets, including Seamus Heaney, were invited to commemorate the occasion with a new poem; an exhibition of Jack Yeats's paintings was arranged to coincide with the stone-laying; and a display of his brother's first editions organized. Mary set herself another modest target, putting on no fewer than seven Yeats plays in the Studio at the time of the stone-laying.

When audiences filed into the Studio in the early summer of 1965, they would have seen an artist at work in Mary's garden. The amiable Dublin sculptor Michael Briggs was shaping a piece of granite that weighed three-quarters of a ton and chiselling out an inscription from a Yeats poem, 'Look up in the sun's eye'. The day dawned, cloudy but not wet; a silver band played as the guests arrived and took their places in seating neatly arranged on the building site. Neil Downes, architect of the whole plan, was an informal master of ceremonies and welcomed, among others, Senator Michael Yeats, Ernest Blythe and Gabriel Fallon, all up from Dublin, and two Ulster playwrights, Joseph Tomelty and Brian Friel. John Boyle, a founder member of the LPT spoke for the theatre. He described Yeats as 'a myriad-minded man' and went on to say: 'I think that it is a tribute to him that the theatre which is being built has so many diverse activities.' He then introduced Austin Clarke – once sceptical of Mary's plans for expansion but now prepared to take on the task of stone-laying. Clarke spoke briefly, partly because he said he was anxious 'that this stone be laid as soon as possible'. His central message was that at last here was a theatre 'catering especially for the poet', something unique because 'there is no other verse theatre in these isles'. Then the white-haired bard was handed a silver trowel, a crane lifted the huge stone above the two pillars of Tyrone brick, mortar was applied and once the stone was in place, the poet tapped the four corners with a wooden mallet. There was a fanfare from the pupils of the Academy of Music and the poets read their verses. Seamus Heaney wrote:

> I dedicate to speech, to pomp and show,
> This house that I erect for poets, actors.
> I set my saw and chisel in the wood
> To joint and panel solid metaphors:
> The walls a circle, the stage under a hood.
> I fit the players thus with cowl and halo.

The stone was now well and truly laid; the first building block of Mary's new theatre was in place. There were more speeches; the most significant from Captain Peter Montgomery, chairman of the Arts Council, who gave the LPT a generous tribute, describing it as 'a pearl of great price'. As she sipped her champagne with the guests in the patchy Ulster sunshine, Mary was confident that the event would generate welcome publicity, but she still wondered where the tens of thousands of pounds needed to actually build Neil Downes's theatre would come from.

11

Struggle

WHEN MARY LAID the foundation stone of the new theatre, the
political weather was changing and, as an Ulster resident in the mid-
1960s, I did feel, at that moment, a strong sense that Heaney's 'thaw' was
happening already. In March 1963 Lord Brookeborough had resigned (at
last) as prime minister and been replaced by Captain Terence O'Neill. His
inheritance was unpromising. The Ulster economy was by now stagnant,
shipbuilding was in decline, and it was clear that something needed to be
done, about the undemocratic, discriminatory franchise. 'Transformation'
and 'bridge-building' became keywords for the O'Neill administration.
Foreign companies were encouraged to come to Northern Ireland and did
so, but such was the decline in the traditional industries that unemployment
continued high – much higher in Catholic West Belfast and western parts of
the province than elsewhere.

O'Neill knew that he needed to improve the lot of the Catholics in
Northern Ireland. His government set about this task in a rather odd way. A
huge blunder had been committed in the early 1960s, when the new University
of Ulster was located in the Protestant seaside town of Coleraine rather than
in Ulster's second city Derry, with its sizeable and vocal Catholic population.
O'Neill had, however, managed to end the long stand-off in relations with
the Republic of Ireland when the Taoiseach, Seán Lemass, was invited to
come up from Dublin for talks in Belfast. This sent a certain influential

preacher, Dr Ian Paisley, into paroxysms of not-an-inch Unionist rhetoric and, as O'Neill and others sought to lessen division in the community, the demagogue gleefully greeted the announcement of the death of Pope John XXIII with the words: 'This Romish man of sin is now in hell.'

O'Neill tried to break through the political stalemate with timid reforms. He even won an election, despite the concerns about his contact with Lemass, but the Ulster polity was now more fragile than it looked. The Campaign for Social Justice had been launched in Belfast in January 1964. One of its founders, Conn McCluskey, later wrote of its very reasonable aims: 'Our idea was, since we lived in a part of the United Kingdom where the British remit ran, we should seek the ordinary rights of British citizens which were so obviously denied us.' The march towards civil rights for Catholics in Northern Ireland had begun. It started slowly but gathered momentum as the 1960s went on. Ulster was sleepwalking towards a horrible crisis.

At this point Mary seems to have been aware of the need for plays which came to grips with the flawed polity. But she still felt that the submissions she got from local writers were not good enough. There was, however, one she believed in: Brian Friel. She asked him to write a political satire on Northern Ireland. His response, on 18 November 1964, was an impassioned refusal:

> To write a good satire one must (1) be able to see things from a remove and (2) have great charity and compassion and (3) a sense of justice. Where the Unionist is concerned, I have none of these three. At times I don't give a damn about the whole thing. At other times I'm at boiling point. It's no way to live. Good luck with the new theatre. It could be great – and that's entirely up to you. All good wishes. Brian (Friel).

It was to be more than a decade before Mary eventually got the satire she wanted – from an outsider, a man from Cork, Patrick Galvin.

Money weighed on Mary's mind as she prepared for her summer break in 1965: tens of thousands of pounds were still needed if her theatre by the Lagan was to be built. And then a new problem appeared – for once not financial. The residents of Ridgeway Street were unhappy with the idea of having, at the end of their road, a theatre, which might make noise late at night, would certainly create parking problems and, furthermore, was being built by someone who did not stand for the national anthem. The *Belfast Telegraph* had researched and prepared a piece about the Lyric and was on the verge of running it when a friend on the reporting staff told Mary about it. The marching season was fast approaching, and Mary knew that the political inflammation that often came with it might give some residents the opportunity to make life difficult for her project. Clearly strings would have to be pulled behind the scenes and the story killed.

Mary knew the editor of the *Belfast Telegraph*, Jack Sayers, and eventually got through to him ('a clever, subtle man' is how she describes Sayers). He asked her if she was telling him how to run his newspaper. She stood her ground. He made no promises, but the story did not appear. Sayers probably thought the protesters could manage without his paper articulating their grievances for them. If he did spike the story, it was a generous action: he had long been an advocate of an alternative plan to build an Ulster Civic Theatre. However, he later made it clear that he was not a wholehearted supporter of Mary's venture. On the day of the opening ceremony, he bombarded her with fifty copies of his paper, which contained a leading article congratulating her on the stone-laying but suggesting that a National Theatre project would have much wider backing: 'If the personal initiative of one woman could lead to today's ceremony, the efforts of a representative committee should yield much more.' The proposals for a Civic/National Theatre had been pushed by, among others, John Hewitt, but Mary, with her high-quality company plus her sense of focus, was always more likely to create a new theatre for Belfast than a committee, no matter how 'representative'.

Both Mary and Pearse now decided that professional help with fundraising was essential, and they found it in the shape of the Wells Organisation, based in London. It did a feasibility study, which suggested that a target of £110,000 was reasonable. A fee of £5000 was agreed with Wells for them to mount a four-month campaign beginning in January 1966. It was led by Geoffrey Bostock, a 'jolly' man who 'cajoled us into action'. The members of the existing Finance committee found themselves contributing £500 each and some sizeable private donations were secured. But the business community, as a whole, did not respond generously, although Bostock managed to secure the participation of one of the captains of industry in Northern Ireland, Cyril Lord, the carpet manufacturer, who agreed to be chairman of a capital development trust. This delivered a useful £13,000, with Lord giving £5000 himself, Gallaher's providing the same amount and J. Arthur Guinness contributing £3000. But generally Bostock found fundraising difficult, reporting that the obstacle seemed to be 'the erroneous belief that the theatre was in some way linked with politics'. The LPT of course was apolitical, but when it came to fundraising it did have certain disadvantages, aptly summed up by Roy Connolly who saw the dichotomy between the theatre's ideology, 'a complex of left-wing and republican politics and southern-Irish culture', and its location in a 'Northern Irish, conservative and Unionist city'.

At the end of the four months the total raised stood at £73,000. This included £20,000 guaranteed from the Arts Council which came with an important proviso – that the theatre should seat at least 300 if it was to be financially viable. Neil Downes set to work to meet this requirement, adding a balcony to his design and having to struggle to get an extra hundred spectators into a theatre on a tiny site. Progress had been made but uncertainty still reigned.

Meanwhile, of course, there was the Studio – and much else besides – to run. Luckily at this point in 1965 an opportunity came up for the LPT to spread its wings and try out a larger space. The Grove Theatre, a former cinema with a capacity of more than a thousand seats, had been refurbished by the Arts Council at a cost of £41,000. The Council was offering modest subsidies to productions using the theatre. Mary saw an opportunity for the Lyric to reach a wider audience. However, the refurbished cinema was a challenge. Mary and Sam McCready happened to be at the Grove when Micheál MacLiammóir came to put on his show *The Importance of Being Oscar*. He greeted Mary and Sam with an ironic, 'Isn't this theatre divine?', and he rolled his eyes towards the ceiling and swept a hand through his henna-enhanced hair. McCready goes on to list the Grove's disadvantages: apart from the poor acoustics, 'the stalls smelled of disinfectant and stale sweat. There were posters for X-rated movies on the way to the Gents.' It was also inconveniently placed for public transport, so it was hard work to attract audiences. But it was an opportunity – a chance to reach a wider public in a thousand-seater playhouse.

The Lyric made light of the old cinema's deficiencies and successfully presented plays there over three years, beginning with the ever-popular *Heart's a Wonder*. As Mary had hoped, this had wide appeal. Rowel Friers did the design, Mary directed and there was a small orchestra. Almost inevitably a row was threatened over the national anthem, but Mary wisely decided to leave the decision to the theatre's management, who duly played a gramophone record. The press greatly enjoyed the musical: 'From start to finish this was sheer entertainment, full of colour, splendid dialogue and equally splendid music – the show was a delight.' The Grove had provided Mary with an opportunity to try out her skills on a larger stage.

Over the next three years there were fifty-one productions at the Lyric and the Grove. Mary directed thirty-six of them. She lists the productions which interested her, especially *Marching Song* by Peter Whiting, *The Fantasticks* (directed by Denis Smyth), which made a very entertaining piece for Christmas, Eugene McCabe's *King of the Castle*, Webster's *Duchess of Malfi*, *The Promise*, a contemporary Russian play by Aleksei Arbuzov, and Pirandello's *Henry IV*. The Lyric also played in the Belfast Festival, scaring theatregoers with Joseph Tomelty's Halloween drama *All Souls' Night* in early November (the play was voted 'best drama' of the festival). She also did Eugene O'Neill's *A Touch of the Poet*, which she and Pearse had seen in America. A poster for the play has been preserved in the Galway archive. It obviously had a later, secondary use; handwritten on the back of the cardboard are these CAST RULES: 'Cast to be in theatre not later than 7.45 nightly. Curtain up at 8.00 p.m. Please hang costume on rack and check personal props. If you must come up stairs, do so quietly. Interval after Act 2, when tea will be provided. NO TALKING BACKSTAGE. Mary O'Malley.'

Other directors also made high-quality contributions. Denis Smyth, for example, did a version of Sam Hanna Bell's *That Woman at Rathard*, a tense and powerful domestic drama, which was highly praised by Suzanne Lowry in the *Belfast Telegraph*. This distinguished Ulster play was exactly the kind of piece Mary was looking for, but which she says was in short supply.

Mary now needed an experienced fundraising helper. He appeared in the form of Lt Colonel Archibald Johnson who had been recruited by the Capital Development Trust. He was appointed in April 1966 at a salary of £850 p.a. He was to manage Mary's diverse and demanding enterprises as well as raising money for the new theatre. The colonel had an initial effect: by 4 April 1967 the Treasurer was noting 'with satisfaction that the Music Academy, the New Gallery, the Drama School and Irish Handcrafts were all self-supporting'. This was to turn out to be no more than a short lull in the Lyric's almost continuous financial storm. For a while the colonel was a bustling tower of strength, particularly in negotiations with City Hall, which was now cautiously in favour of the new Lyric. It is difficult to keep track of the rapidly developing financial situation at this time. A key element was the £20,000 promised by the Arts Council, which eventually materialized. Peter Montgomery wrote to Mary, 'We are quite unanimous in our wish to help the Lyric and it would have been horrible if we hadn't been able to do this for you.'

There were some other positive signs that the campaign was enjoying a following breeze. Cyril Lord, for example, stressed publicly that the arts needed subsidy; and the Irish Congress of Trade Unions said that while raising the general standard of living was important, 'the quality of living is just as important – and there is real need for a theatre like the New Lyric in Belfast'.

The autumn of 1966 was difficult for Mary. First, she had to go into hospital for a gall-bladder operation, which kept her away from her desk and telephone for some weeks. Then, suddenly, the Academy of Music became troublesome. It had expanded slowly during its first two years, but when Daphne Bell, a music teacher of high repute, was appointed organizer, her drive and enthusiasm led to rapid expansion to the point where she employed twenty-five tutors. By the summer of 1966 this success was causing problems – there just wasn't enough room at Grosvenor Road for all the students. Colonel Johnson and Mary searched for overflow premises, without success. Daphne Bell grew impatient and expected expanded premises to be available for the start of the new academic year in the autumn. When they were not, she grew even more uneasy. The Lyric Trustees then stepped in and tried to reassert control over the Academy which, despite its expansion, was still in deficit. Bell became so frustrated with the *impasse* that she indicated that she would resign as Director at the end of the year. Many of the parents of the students at the Academy took her side, perhaps feeling that the dynamic Bell was not getting the support she needed. Havelock Nelson was certainly unhappy with the way things were going and wrote to Mary in uncompromising terms.

Things probably went wrong because Mary and others were just too busy to provide the close management the Academy required. Managerial intervention should have come earlier; expansion should not have been allowed to get out of hand. Mary alleges that the Academy's close link with the LPT, and the nationalist overtones which ultra-sensitive Unionist parents might have detected in the Irish dancing classes and Irish harp lessons also happening at the music school, were factors in the defections. Mismanagement sounds like a more likely cause of the trouble. Mary supplies the end of the story: 'Daphne [Bell] I liked. She worked for the love of the thing, but different counsels prevailed on her side, and we parted ways.' Daphne Bell bore no animosity towards Mary; indeed, she wrote to her and Pearse to say 'privately to you both, how greatly I appreciate ALL [underlined several times] your many kindnesses, official and unofficial, to me during the last year. Everybody has been utterly and completely wrong about us not being able to work together. Very sincerely and affectionately, Daphne.' The breakaway Ulster College of Music, which she founded, still survives.

Of the other ancillaries, the Lyric's drama school still prospered at Grosvenor Road and now subsumed the remnants of the music academy. Irish handcrafts and the New Gallery were a different story; neither did more than break even, at best. And administrative costs were rising all the time. For a start there was the £850-a-year salary paid to Colonel Johnson, who also had a part-time assistant. By 1967 the overdraft was mounting, and the trustees decided to take an audacious initiative. Conor O'Malley describes their proposal: 'The Trustees took the unprecedented step of offering the entire theatre organisation and all its assets to the Arts Council, if they undertook to build the theatre.' This desperate measure failed; the Arts Council responded by explaining that 'its function was primarily the distribution of funds, not the instigation of activities'. The trustees then moved in a different direction, which involved abandoning the Ridgeway Street site and converting an existing building into a theatre rather than building an expensive new one. The Friends Meeting House in Frederick Street was for sale and could be turned into a playhouse. Negotiations began, and an offer of £17,500 was made but, Conor explains, 'as so often in the past, the building was inexplicably withdrawn from sale at the last moment'.

Part of the cause of the escalation in the overdraft was the cost of paying some actors something near to official Equity rates. Mary 'saw this merry-go-round' out of the corner of her eye. 'What had been successful and simple was now so complicated, I was no longer in touch.' This uncertainty and the haemorrhage of money could not go on. Finally, the trustees came up with a practical scheme: build the new theatre, but a cheaper version, which would be closer in price to the resources raised so far. In November 1967 they agreed to proceed with plans 'on the basis of the resources available, with an opening night target date of September 1968'. This meant a redesign of the theatre and, ultimately, the resignation of the architect Neil Downes. He had already modified his design to fit it into the limited Ridgeway Street site, but now a very different theatre was to be built for half the money his design would have cost.

In January 1968 Sir Alfred McAlpine's building firm entered the scene. They agreed to build for the modest sum of £32,000 the bare shell of the theatre and, remarkably, to have it finished by the autumn deadline less than nine months away. One of the Lyric trustees, Frank Wright, principal architectural adviser to the Ministry of Health, agreed to act as liaison with McAlpine's who would, basically, design the new theatre. Wright saw Downes's original design like this: 'The architect has been over-enthusiastic in attempting to cram many desirable theatrical quarts into a very small pint-sized site.' He suggests that the audiences are better served in Downes's design than the actors and technicians. He notes the 'pleasant' bar overlooking the river but considers that 'backstage space is at a premium'. By now Neil Downes had quit. In his resignation letter he says that he hopes the new design will 'work out as well as possible', but he is adamant that he would be 'unhappy to be associated with this building'. Mary was deeply upset at his going.

A deal was duly signed with McAlpine's and, when it was announced on 11 March 1968, there was widespread disbelief that the theatre would be completed, as stated in the contract, by October in the same year. The specification required an auditorium that could seat 300 people, a large foyer, a stage flexible enough to allow 'a wide variety of presentations' and adequate dressing rooms and storage space. These were the basic needs of any theatre, but the difficult part was that they had to be fitted into a space, which Conor O'Malley describes as 'little more than that required for two large houses'. The site also had a steep gradient, and the foundations could be secured only by driving in piles to a depth of 30 feet. McAlpine's had taken on an intensely demanding project.

Work started immediately, catching Mary on the hop. She was busy at the Grove Theatre when her attention was drawn to the proscenium arch in the new plans. She protested to the contractors: all she had wanted for the £35,000 was 'four walls and a roof, giving a raised auditorium and an acting space about two feet from floor level'. McAlpine's at first said it was too late – the relevant steel beam was already on order and anyway the tight schedule would be disrupted by a change. Mary dug in her heels and the contractors, who were to prove extraordinarily flexible and helpful throughout, agreed to increase the space between the two stanchions on either side of the stage. What emerged eventually was a vestigial proscenium arch, a very wide stage, slightly curved at the front and jutting out beyond the vertical stanchions. It was to be the large flexible space of which Mary and her company had dreamed.

The spring and summer of 1968 were poignant times for Mary. A seventeen-year odyssey was coming to an end as the new theatre emerged on the Annadale Embankment. She and Pearse had made the major decision that they were going to say goodbye not only to the Studio theatre but also to their home, to sell Beechbank in Derryvolgie Avenue and move to something smaller in the same area. Selling proved harder than expected: one potential buyer looked over the studio theatre and enquired a little anxiously, 'What could one do with this?' The slow sale of Beechbank was a worry for a time because the O'Malleys had already bought a smaller house a few streets away in Deramore Park and were now having to finance a bridging loan. But, after a few anxious months had passed, Derryvolgie Avenue was sold and became a veterinary practice.

Mary had to consider how to end in the Studio: with Yeats, of course, but which of the twenty-six in her beloved volume? The choice was *The Dreaming of the Bones* and *Oedipus at Colonus* on one night, and on the next *The King of the Great Clock Tower*, *Purgatory*, *Calvary* and *Resurrection*. Liam O'Callaghan was to play Oedipus, as well as Christ in *Calvary* and the Old Man in *Purgatory*. The familiar team of Raymond Warren, Birgit Kirkpatrick (costumes) and Helen Lewis made their contributions. On the last night Sam McCready spoke the final lines of *Resurrection*:

> Everything that man esteems
> Endures a moment or a day:
> Love's pleasure drives his love away,
> The painter's brush consumes his dreams;
> The herald's cry, the soldier's tread
> Exhaust his glory and his might:
> Whatever flames upon the night
> Man's own resinous heart has fed.

McCready's plangent, mellifluous rendering of these lines has been recorded and so has much of what followed on that last, emotional night in the

Studio. We hear Mary asking her whole team to step forward – backstage people like Sandra Fusco, long-term contributors like Helen Lewis, Alice Hammerschlag and Birgit Kirkpatrick and, of course, her actors. Soon there is no curtain as Mary cuts the cords and it falls to the ground. After Mary has been presented with some Waterford glass, we hear the measured Belfast tones of George Mooney, paying tribute to Mary. He lists the astonishing range of plays performed on the tiny stage, adding, 'For half its history this was a free theatre – it must have cost Dr and Mrs O'Malley a fortune.' He praises Mary's ability to do 'absolutely impossible' plays on her stage: 'She has suffered pressures of all kinds and. I might add, created one of two of her own. She has suffered from apathy, hostility and ignorance, from lack of money and lack of talent, but she has carried on and earned the title of That Bloody Woman.' He explains that this is the sort of 'exasperated utterance you make when Mary rings you up and drags you from your fireside and your television set and says, "Would you do a wee part for me?"'

His peroration is eloquent:

I hope the people of Belfast and this province now realize there is a theatre in their midst – organized, large, comfortable, requiring no club membership, having no association of any kind, religious, social or political – dedicated to preserving the best drama of this country and of the world at large, and having what I believe to be the greatest collection of theatrical talent in this province, ever …

As the cast took off their make-up for the last time, a huge bonfire was lit in the garden, lights came on in the trees, a cake with an image of a harp on it was presented to the main begetter of the Studio, who graciously replied with brooches and tiepins for her company. Sam McCready knew it was final when, at the end of the evening, he saw young Conor removing the theatre sign put up outside the house before each performance, leaving the estate agent's FOR SALE notice to stand on its own.

Around this time Sam McCready found himself drifting away from Mary: the fact of being paid had somehow altered their relationship, so he knew very little of her plans for the new theatre. But, reflecting later, he felt that 'so intensely was she involved with the problems she encountered with the building of the theatre, I don't think she gave sufficient time to how it might be run'. He believes that 'she thought it would be the same as running Derryvolgie Avenue but on a larger scale and she expected to use all the members of the company as before, supplemented by professional actors'. As for leadership, Sam believes she knew she could not make all the decisions herself in the new theatre and that she would have to hand over responsibility to others, but 'she had not thought deeply about what that might mean'.

In summer 1968 Mary took a big step towards delegation and decided to appoint a 'productions director'. She had the money to do this because of the annual Arts Council grant designed to ease the progression towards fully professional status. Her eyes turned southwards – in the direction of Christopher Fitz-Simon. He was a Radio Teilifís Éireann producer who had already directed for Mary in the Studio (*Uncle Vanya*) and had the advantage of northern family connections. He was a good candidate, but Mary sought reassurance about his qualities from Micheál MacLiammóir, who assessed Fitz-Simon in these terms:

> He is a quiet, fastidious, but I think extremely competent young man with excellent taste which leans, however, rather to the Jane Austen school of thought – if you follow me – than to the shall we say, Dostoevsky. I mean that he at his best in a slightly artificial, rather polished and precise world and, given the right material, makes an excellent director.

He goes on to describe Fitz-Simon as 'industrious, patient, painstaking', so with this recommendation and her prior knowledge of his work, Mary and the trustees took him on at a salary of £2160 a year. The LPT made it clear that Fitz-Simon did not have any direct responsibility for the ancillary operations but, on the vital matter of choosing plays, 'in the event of opposing viewpoints the trustees' attitude would have to be accepted'. He agreed to these terms but, perhaps wisely, took leave of absence from Teilifís Éireann rather than resigning. And some sixth sense prevented him from signing his contract.

Why did Mary choose someone who was, in company terms, almost a stranger to the Lyric Players? Why did she not consider, and perhaps approach, two big local talents? Sam McCready was master of many arts and he had directed plays for her; he knew how the Lyric worked; he had bought into Mary's vision of a poets' theatre. Much the same applied to Denis Smyth, a director with a striking track record and someone already displaying management potential. Smyth evidently did apply for the post and was interviewed by Arthur Brooke, star Lyric actor, now a senior civil servant, but it was felt that too much of Smyth's experience had been gained at the Lyric and not enough elsewhere. One can only assume that Mary thought a quite widely experienced Dublin theatre professional was the man for the job and that an outsider was usually preferable to an insider. Conor O'Malley provides an interesting grace note to Fitz-Simon's appointment. 'Mam was hopeless at interviewing people because she would talk all the time,' he says. 'Dad told me later [Conor was only fourteen at the time] that in the Fitz-Simon interview she asked very few questions and talked about what *she* had been doing for most of the exchange.'

On 24 July the foundation stone was repositioned above the entrance. It was a warm summer and McAlpine's were, Mary says, 'proving the model of efficiency'. They had reduced their price by taking into account the gifts in kind which the Lyric's Building Committee had already received: all the necessary bricks from Tyrone Brick; the bar from Irish Bonding; the wood for the stage from the Ulster Timber Company; all mirrors and glazing from Harold Clokey and Co. Later McAlpine's themselves were to provide the ceiling free of charge. Goodwill seemed to be flowing.

McAlpine's was not only flexible but fast. It was clear by late summer that an opening on 26 October was feasible. Conor O'Malley emphasizes the value of the building firm's contribution: 'The generous contract terms, the rigid, self-imposed time limit and McAlpine's architectural resources placed at the theatre's disposal all demonstrated that McAlpine's could not have undertaken the project for purely commercial reasons.' This was the first time this large firm of builders had built a theatre, and senior management in London took great interest in the project. It seems likely that building the Lyric was a useful rehearsal for McAlpine's; a few years later the company was to get the contract for constructing the iconic National Theatre on the South Bank in London.

Expansionist Mary had time for one more coup before her theatre opened. The drama school needed more space for its activities. So why not buy a church to house it? This is what the trustees did when one became available in September 1968, in Cromwell Road, not far from Grosvenor Road. Funds? The church was on the market at the bargain price of £5000, which of course the trustees did not have. Enter the Irish Life Assurance Company, which ran an annual play-writing competition, for which Mary occasionally read the scripts which had been entered. (This competition was already providing Mary with useful play-fodder.) A loan at a favourable rate of interest was secured and the church was bought, so the trustees now had very adequate teaching premises – and another financial commitment.

How deep these commitments were is made plain by a letter to Pearse from Arthur Brooke, who had been asked to survey the financial position. Writing on 18 September 1968, he puts the 'present' cost of building the theatre as £66,500. Then come fairly hopeful figures for current resources available to pay the bill: £34,000 in gifts, £20,000 from the Arts Council and further gifts 'to be obtained' (presumably promised), £6000. This means a shortfall of only £6500 on the capital cost. Brooke comments: 'The rise in the cost of the theatre, through extras etc. is not exceptional. The theatre is still comparatively an economical job. It would not be unusual, or excessive, for the theatre to open with a capital debt of £12,500.'

But then he lists the current 'difficulties': 'We have exhausted our credit' is the theme. He mentions a bank overdraft facility of £25,000, which is being used to pay bills; he says that this overdraft was originally required to cover the £8000 overdraft already accumulated on other activities. 'Other activities' is almost certainly the ancillaries and he notes darkly that 'these sorts of expenses have been continuing and there are outstanding accounts on them'. He ends with the warning that 'if nothing is done ... sometime in October or November the Bank credit runs out and our cheques (e.g. for salaries) will not be met'. He puts the ball firmly back in the trustees' court: 'Steps can be taken about this, or at least attempted, but the Trustees must decide what they are to be.' Brooke's conclusions suggested that Mary's beloved ancillaries were threatening to drag down the flagship. It seemed that at least one of them would have to go. Final decisions on these painful cuts took many months to make because other, potent, distractions were to intervene.

12

Launch

BY EARLY OCTOBER Mary was rehearsing her first Yeats productions for the new theatre. She had a list of plays she wanted for this first season, but now the new productions director also had his choices to offer. Christopher Fitz-Simon chose, with the trustees' approval, *The Seagull*, *Tarry Flynn* (the novel by Patrick Kavanagh adapted by P.J. O'Connor) and he liked Mary's suggestion of John Whiting's charming *Penny for a Song*. But Fitz-Simon was not happy with Mary's decision to begin with Yeats. On 1 August he wrote to Pearse saying that he had told Mary that he thought it 'somewhat self-indulgent of us to mount yet another Yeats programme at this time: I would like to make it clear to the Trustees that while I would do everything possible to make such a programme a success, I have immense reservations about the desirability of the project ...' He goes on to suggest that a change of programme is still possible at this early stage, that members of the company, while prepared to loyally fulfil their Yeats obligations, would have preferred to start with something else. Fitz-Simon and some of the company thought that the Yeats plays would not be of interest to potential audiences because 'they had seen so much of it so recently'. He concludes:

> I have many reservations, but I want the Trustees to know that if they feel they must proceed with the Cuchulain plays so soon, I will naturally support their decision. I do think that these plays could be presented

with pleasurable support from the company and the public alike, later in the season.

Fitz-Simon failed to change Mary's mind and rehearsals duly began in the early days of a warm Belfast October – ironically in the old Studio, still available to the O'Malleys until contracts were exchanged on Derryvolgie Avenue.

During that autumn of 1968 Mary was involved on many fronts: directing, keeping track on building costs, interviewing new front-of-house and administrative staff and keeping an eye on the ancillaries, which had now spread into the new premises at Cromwell Road. And, of course, there was *Threshold* which, at intervals, grabbed time and energy. Now, suddenly, an old problem in the O'Malley narrative re-emerged: the national anthem. At a trustees' meeting on 8 october 1968 a firm proposal to play the anthem was put forward. The minutes read:

> The question of the Anthem at performances in the new Lyric was considered. It was accepted as a part of the Ceremonial involved on special, official public occasions. It was suggested that the procedure at Covent Garden [playing it on the first and last performances each season], should be adopted, but no vote was taken.

Had a vote been taken, Pearse and Mary would have been outvoted. The other trustees present were Molly McNeill, Arthur Brooke and Kenneth Darwin. Darwin and the other two, who were of broadly Unionist persuasion, would probably have voted for the anthem. Mary and Pearse protested. Mary did not like the idea of giving 'a fixed imprimatur to the ritual' of playing 'The Queen'. There seems to have been no question of playing it at the grand opening on Saturday 26 October, so the decision was taken to play it on the first public performance of the season, Monday 28 October. Mary felt that sounding out the anthem in the theatre when the occasion was not a ceremonial one would 'affect artistic independence'. She was emphatic that all the private donations were given unconditionally and that the innovation of playing the anthem in the theatre 'would do less than justice to the Lyric subscribers'.

At another trustee meeting on 15 October, Frank Wright, the architect who had contributed to the design of the new theatre, was welcomed as a new member of the board. Since the previous meeting, Brooke and McNeill had written to Pearse suggesting that the minute of the previous meeting was incomplete. So a new version was agreed; it said that Darwin had proposed the Covent Garden arrangement and been seconded by Miss McNeill. And another line was added: 'Mrs. O'Malley disassociated herself from this decision and Dr O'Malley asked that no vote be taken.'

'I was out from this moment,' says Mary in her autobiography. And so, surprisingly, was Pearse, probably out of loyalty to Mary. A split in the board as the theatre opened would not make good publicity, so these conflicts and decisions were kept from the cast and the rest of the team at Ridgeway Street. Mary and Pearse held back their official resignation until the offensive tune had been sounded out. Surprisingly the press took some weeks to find out about the conflict.

On opening night the theatre was not yet finished, with lighting and sound systems still to operate at full capacity. However, these worries were kept backstage as the audience filed into the floodlit theatre. Mary waxes lyrical about her creation:

> On the outside of the building, in copper, was the theatre motif, Cuchulain – the raven on his shoulder – all mounted on the harp, symbolising the lyrical, heroic and tragic aspects of the human condition … I wonder if many people appreciated its significance – Cuchulain at last reflected in the Lagan.

Already there was a good press. The *Belfast Telegraph* had published a leader welcoming the theatre and describing its opening as 'a milestone in the history of drama in Northern Ireland'. It goes on to deliver a ringing personal tribute to Mary herself:

The lion's share of the achievement belongs to Mary O'Malley whose fierce love of drama and pioneer spirit is one of the most formidable influences which the cultural life of this place has known ... Success of this nature can only be commanded by a rare personality and Mrs O'Malley stands with those like Annie Horniman and Lilian Baylis who helped to shape theatre in this country.

The guests were a distinguished gathering. From Dublin came Ernest Blythe, Austin Clarke and Anne Yeats. Among the poets attending were Seamus Heaney, Tom Kinsella and Eavan Boland. From Belfast came Hubert Wilmot of the Arts Theatre and the dramatist Joseph Tomelty. Captain Peter Montgomery and Michael Whewell were there for the Arts Council. Nearly all the stalwarts from Mary's teams attended, although Neil Downes was an absentee.

The host, Arthur Brooke, introduced Captain Peter Montgomery, President of the Arts Council, who spoke of the responsibility which the community had to the theatre and the theatre's responsibility, in turn, to the community. The speeches were long, but at last the plays began.

Mary had no concerns about the cast, but both the crew and the theatre's equipment were largely unknown quantities. The unexpected, of course, happened: Sam McCready, leading the chorus, spoke the first words in the new theatre. The designer had placed him fourteen feet above the stage and Sam soon became aware that the weather had turned rainy and the roof was leaking, which gave him another stage baptism, this time by water. Huge gold-coloured metal screens, designed by Edward Delaney from Dublin, provided the background for all four plays. Mary was pleased with the colours of the costumes: greys and blacks in *At the Hawk's Well*, orange and bronze in *On Baile's Strand*, silver and green in *The Only Jealousy of Emer* and blue and gold in *The Death of Cuchulain*. Sam felt it was a 'satisfying performance' from the acting point of view. The Helen Lewis choreography and Raymond Warren's music emphasized the ritualistic elements in the plays. Mary was particularly delighted with Sam McCready's Fool and Louis Rolston's Blind Man in *On Baile's Strand*. She felt her productions were both good and original, but this was a new theatre with a new audience, and she was concerned, for example, about how Unionists would respond to *The Death of Cuchulain*, in which Yeats suggests that, spiritually, Cuchulain stood with Pearse and Connolly in the post office in 1916: 'Who thought Cuchulain till it seemed / He stood where they had stood.'

The opening-night notices covered the full spectrum of opinion. First, the antis – for example, local critic Ian Hill in *The Guardian:* 'It is an irony that William Butler Yeats, the enshrining of whose dramatic image has been the principal spur for the creation of the new 304 seat, £50,000 Lyric Players Theatre in Belfast, should provide it with its first disaster ... The Yeats shrine, on the evidence of this performance is too much of a mausoleum – though it is painful to comment so adversely.' Hill admits that 'the beauty of Yeats's words shines brightly in the choruses of the four plays which chronicle the life and hard times of Ulster's legendary warrior Cuchulain, but where, Mrs O'Malley was the drama?' He sees no unity of style in the productions and criticizes the costumes and lighting. This was one of a number of negative reviews Ian Hill was to write about Lyric productions. (His fierce criticism drew blood: eventually the trustees decided that he should be crossed off the invitation list for first nights, but then thought better of it.) John D. Stewart is similarly irreverent: '"Recitations in fancy dress," snorted my neighbour at the lovely new Players Theatre. I must admit I did not get much more out of the four plays of the Cuchulain cycle myself. Philistines we may be, but all the same it is widely held that to succeed a play must involve some of the emotions of the audience. Most plays are surely written with that end in view, but the great Yeats was a law unto himself with his own private theatre and privileged circle of admirers.' Stewart graciously admits to having admired the performers but is very glad that 'Yeats comes only once a year'.

Ray Rosenfield felt that the occasion was perhaps too much for some of the players and that she had seen better Yeats productions by them in the past. But in the *Belfast Telegraph*, Betty Lowry, usually something of a Yeats sceptic, was won over:

Saturday night's audience must have included some, like myself, for whom poetic symbolism and fantasy on the stage instantly create a barrier between them and the players. It says much for the skilled direction of Mary O'Malley and the talent of her cast that they enabled me to cross the barrier, accepting and enjoying an absorbing, impressive performance.

A few days later, in a review on BBC radio, Seamus Heaney displayed his gifts as a critic. He began with the 'mysterious resonance' which the plays set up:

> Yeats's drama aimed for this effect; he wanted performances on the stage that were remote, spiritual, ideal; he did not aim to compete with the kind of ready manipulation of an audience's emotions and the deployment of fashionable conventions that occurred in the commercial theatre. Nor did he want to be judged by the hurried pen of the professional reviewer. I imagine he wouldn't have been disturbed by an audience who said, 'We don't understand,' as long as they were prepared to surrender themselves to the performance and to leave opinions and preconceptions about what a play should be at the doors. His drama is a solemn ritual of word and movement where speech approaches incantation and the stage directions have the weight of rubrics. So, I'd rather not single out any aspect of the production for separate comment since the performance is so remote in content and intention from an ordinary theatrical experience. I hope I can dispense with ordinary theatrical reviewing techniques …

Nevertheless, he did praise the direction, the sets and the music: 'all combine into a harmonious, unified world of illusion where Yeats's explicit desires were fulfilled'. He finished with this tribute to Mary's theatre: 'We are privileged to have the Lyric Players in this city; perhaps nowhere else in the world is the work of a great writer served with such affection and dedication.'

'The hurried pen of the professional reviewer' (Heaney's phrase) delivered another notice that must have been deeply satisfying to Mary and Pearse. Writing in *The Observer*, the London critic Ronald Bryden described the plays as 'a revelation'. He found in them 'a superb and timeless theatricality'. And he marvelled at the company: 'Though only partly professional, [they] know the plays so intimately and are sufficiently trained as dancers, that they impose both pace and abstraction as music does. A treasure of the English-speaking world has been overlooked.'

The national anthem was duly sounded out on the following Monday, the first public performance of the season. According to Christopher Fitz-Simon, Arthur Brooke was insistent that the productions director should stand over the gramophone to make sure 'the Queen' was heard. That first playing triggered Mary and Pearse's formal letter of resignation the next day. Their joint note to the chairman of trustees, Kenneth Darwin, dated 29 October 1968, expressed 'sincere regret that we find ourselves in a position which leaves no alternative but to retire from management of the theatre'. This was because 'the new policy concerning the playing of the Anthem at performances in the theatre will affect, in our view, artistic independence and vision. We are therefore submitting our resignation as Trustees – and from the posts of Artistic Adviser and Secretary.' The letter ends with 'cordial good wishes' for the 'growth and prosperity' of the new theatre.

The resignation was probably the most important decision of Mary's professional life. Her experience would have told her that her that stepping out at this juncture would cause dismay among her company and, when her action became known, it did. Sam McCready was speechless. Mary told him that 'people had made contributions to this theatre unconditionally. It was the people who built the theatre and to impose conditions now would only betray their trust. I can't do that.' Sam felt that she was making a mountain out of a molehill: 'I argued with her and told her not to be so hasty. I pleaded with her to reconsider, but the intensity of the dark eyes and the firm set of her mouth told me she would not be reasoned with.' There was a political gulf between them. '"I don't expect you to understand," she said as she left.'

Mary's resignation was a practical demonstration of her mantra, 'Compromise is the prince of lies.' As McCready puts it, 'She would either run her theatre on her terms or she would abdicate all responsibility.' Considering the issue, it would be reasonable to ask: had not the Arts Council of Northern Ireland been courageous in supporting the building of a new theatre for a group led by someone who consistently promoted an all-Ireland culture? Did the council and its paymasters, Stormont and Westminster, not deserve a modest quid pro quo, in the form of playing 'God Save the Queen' twice a year?

In the light of years of subsequent peace-processing, in which compromise became the way forward, it is easy to criticize Mary's stand. But we should remember that in 1968 Northern Ireland was still an unreconstructed, undemocratic state in which Unionists practised gerrymandering and discrimination against Catholics. Legislation removing these abuses was still years away. The issue over the anthem was first and foremost a political matter, however much Mary claimed that playing it would compromise artistic independence.

Mary's justification in her autobiography focuses on loyalty to the subscribers whose donations built the theatre. However, it seems dubious that Catholic or nationalist donors, long inured to 'God Save the Queen', would have felt betrayed by it being played twice a year. Justifiable political anger probably motivated Mary's decision, but viewed nearly fifty years later, her tactical judgment feels faulty, especially as Pearse was soon to undo his resignation and rejoin the trustees.

There is another explanation: Mary's exhaustion. By her own admission, building the theatre and keeping some sort of control of the ancillaries had become an almost impossible task, even for a person with her energy. Had her anxiety risen to a point where she could not see clearly anymore? Kieran, who was close to her at the time, says she was 'overwhelmed'. Her resignation decision is perfectly of a piece with her temperament and her political views, but it might also have been partly due to a loss of nerve and perhaps a feeling of anxious alienation from this strange new professional organization she had been trying to construct.

Pearse was prepared to take a longer view: to Mary the trustees' vote for the national anthem was a personal betrayal (she does not seem to have registered that there were two senior civil servants on the board, Brooke and Darwin, and that for them there had to be, for professional reasons, at least the essential-minimum of anthem-playing). But Pearse 'the unflappable', as Conor calls him, saw that this new theatre already had value as a cultural institution, and he was determined to do everything in his power to keep it alive.

13

Crisis 1

OCTOBER 1968 WAS not a good month to open in Belfast a playhouse promoting an all-Ireland culture, and where mythological Irish heroes bestrode the stage and homage was continuously paid to William Butler Yeats, a great Protestant nationalist (although also a Unionist). In fact, it was probably the worst possible moment in the whole of Northern Ireland's recent history for a new theatre, whatever its agenda, to try to make its mark. The fissures in a divided society were opening; violence was in the air. A few weeks before the opening, in the city of Derry, which had endured some of the most blatant discrimination in housing and jobs, a protest march morphed into rioting, which was brutally suppressed when the RUC became the target of petrol bombs. Shops were looted in two days of chaos; local news crews captured the ruthless baton-work of the RUC and broadcast it to the outside world.

Then in January 1969 a People's Democracy march set out from Belfast for Derry, aiming to show that O'Neill's modest concessions were not sufficient. The march was badly managed by the police and, in what amounted to an ambush at the village of Burntollet, the RUC and the B Specials lost any semblance of impartiality and dealt fiercely with the marchers. To some extent this allowed the protesters to achieve their aim; they knew confrontation and police retaliation were likely and news pictures of it happening would destabilize Northern Ireland further.

Threshold magazine did not normally comment very directly on current politics. But as the situation worsened in 1969, and showed no sign of abating in 1970, Mary commissioned John Montague to edit a 'Northern Crisis' issue. He wrote an interesting letter to her about its gestation:

> To begin with, I struck a monstrous block; people don't for what reasons you can imagine, want to write about the situation in the North. The excuses range from aesthetic detachment – surely this is a question for journalists? – to the impotence of rage. I care so much I can say nothing … Only the young responded immediately; I am using them to lever the others into action.

Montague gave his writer's licence to comment freely on the escalating emergency, and some remarkable contributions emerged. One was a fine piece of first-hand reporting by Eoin Sweeney on the ambushed People's Democracy march to Derry.

John Hewitt provided a resonant reflection on the current situation, a sharp political polemic in verse. His poem 'The Coasters' became widely known for its skewering of the pre-Troubles complacency of comfortably off middle-class Protestants. It hits hard and unrelentingly with its constant refrain, 'You coasted along', which changes shockingly in the last line. There is a local reference in the title: 'Coasters' are those who live along the shores of Belfast Lough, particularly on the affluent southern side. The first stanza sets the tone:

> You coasted along
> to larger houses, gadgets, more machines,
> to golf and weekend bungalows,
> caravans when the children were small,
> the Mediterranean, later, with the wife.

Hewitt mordantly catalogues the norms of the Coasters' lifestyle and attitudes. They of course enjoyed broad-minded friendships with 'the other sort', '… decent folk with a sense of humour'. And 'relations were improving', the annual processions had come to look like 'folk festivals', so

> When that noisy preacher started,
> He seemed old-fashioned, a survival …

To the Coaster the political status quo seemed permanent and comfortable:

> You coasted along
> And the sores suppurated and spread.
> But now the fever is high and raging
> The cloud of infection hangs over the city,
> A quick change of wind and it
> Might spill over the leafy suburbs.
> You coasted too long.

———————

By March 1969 O'Neill was struggling to survive, by end of April he was gone. His resignation was greeted with gleeful bonfires on the Shankhill Road. But his successor, James Chichester-Clark, could do no better. The summer marching season inevitably caused combustion and by now the police, after nine months of holding the line, were exhausted. In a few areas mobs ruled; no fewer than sixty burned-out Belfast Corporation buses were now part of barricades on the Falls Road. In August 1969, when the Derry rioters fought the RUC to a standstill in the Battle of the Bogside, the British army was called in. Rioting spread to Belfast, six people were killed, over a hundred houses destroyed and more than a thousand families in mixed-religion areas fled their homes. More troops arrived and a brief pause ensued. Westminster was by now trying to reassure both communities. The Downing Street declaration, made in August 1969, said unequivocally: 'Every citizen of Northern Ireland is entitled to the same equality of treatment and freedom from discrimination as obtains in the rest of the UK.' There was comparable reassurance for the Protestant community that 'the border is not an issue' – thereby ruling out any short- or medium-term possibility of a United Ireland.

From the start the violent uncertainty gripping Belfast, and indeed the whole of Ulster, created internal difficulties for the Lyric: in finance, administration and governance. Management came under unprecedented political scrutiny. Clear demonstrations of loyalty to the Northern Irish state, symbolized by the playing of the national anthem, took on an importance which they would not have had in more peaceful, less polarized times. Rioting and later bombing and shooting made the day-to-day management of the theatre harder: actors could not get to the playhouse on time when explosions closed off whole areas of the city; uncertainty affected advance bookings and an anxious public often preferred to stay safely at home. So, audiences became variable and sparse. Running any theatre at this moment in Belfast would have been difficult.

This progressive slide into near chaos was, however, still some distance away when Pearse and Mary resigned. After receiving their letter, the trustees wrote to ask them to reconsider. Kenneth Darwin suggested to them that 'no indication was given after the decision of 15 October that either of you regarded the playing of the Anthem on 28 October as a resigning issue'. The letter goes on to suggest that the trustees would 'not have proceeded in the way decided upon if they had known it would lead to the resignations'. The letter is remarkably conciliatory, praising Mary's achievement and asserting that she 'must remain completely identified with the theatre'. Darwin even offers to resign along with the other trustees – Molly McNeill, Frank Wright, Arthur Brooke and himself – if it 'will allow you to return to full participation in the management of the theatre'. But Mary, at least, was not for turning.

The resignations did not become public knowledge for some time, but almost immediately there were intense reverberations within the theatre. Astonishment and incredulity were paramount reactions. Arthur Brooke had been strongly for playing the anthem. He and Pearse fell out over this and on 4 November, a few days after the theatre's opening, Pearse responds firmly to a letter from Brooke. 'When you questioned the Minutes, I knew "the chips were down." And had I not endeavoured to keep a form of unity, resignation would have taken place before the opening. We were scrupulously fair by waiting until the actual event …' He reiterates his and Mary's position: 'I made it quite clear [at the trustees' meeting where the decision was taken] that the Anthem was acceptable to Mary and myself where the decision was imposed upon the management, as e.g. in "ceremonial protocol" but not as a decision voluntarily arrived at by the management.' Pearse believes that

> in the future it is possible for Mary and myself to move away from a central position without, as you say, the news breaking. There is a full-time professional staff and the necessary changes for efficiency can be gradually made … Mary has made it clear that she will be "about" until the theatre is functioning well.

He sees himself and Mary as withdrawing 'not from the Lyric but from management'. He believes that 'our action at this stage will in the long term be beneficial … It is better for the Lyric to flourish in its community than to be tied too much to the viewpoint of one or two people.'

Conor characterized his mother's argument like this: 'If the Lyric was not going to be an independent theatre, forging ahead with its own ideals, I'd be better off not there.' He regarded her reaction to what she saw as the imposition of the anthem by the trustees as 'not entirely rational – an emotional, visceral response. Dad was much more measured, more calculating – in the best sense of the word; he was looking at the longer-term. He was showing more understanding of the North and the character of the people and the politics and the forces impelling people to behave in a certain way.'

Pearse returned to the board a fortnight after his resignation. He was sure that an O'Malley was needed in this hour of need to help to keep the theatre afloat. He managed his re-entry cleverly, telling the other trustees in a letter written on 11 November that because there had not been an adequate definition of the term 'ceremonial protocol' that it would be 'unfair' to hold to the viewpoint that the [anthem] policy had been changed and 'I am, therefore, withdrawing my resignation.' One half of the O'Malley team was now back in harness but almost immediately he faced problems with Christopher Fitz-Simon. Pearse was beginning to have severe doubts about the productions director who, in turn, was not happy with the way the new theatre was working. He felt he had been given a false prospectus of the job at his interview. He found the limited availability of the actors in the old Lyric company unacceptable. He did not want to cast teachers who could rehearse only the late afternoons and at weekends; he objected to the instructions he received from the board on casting; and he seems to have run into problems over stage design and the delivery of sets. The trustees wrote him admonitory memos. He had been asked before the opening Yeats night to help with 'staging problems and the indiscipline of staff'. He met the trustees and told them that he 'was perfectly satisfied with the backstage staff'. Later he is upbraided for giving contracts to the actors in *The Seagull* 'without approval of the trustees'. Then, in *Penny for a Song*, the trustees (probably at Pearse's suggestion) did not want Fitz-Simon to cast a particular actor. Fitz-Simon refused – merely apologizing to the board on 5 December for not producing the cast list earlier. This was seen as insubordination by Pearse and the board; the outcome was to push the already unhappy Fitz-Simon nearer to a resigning edge.

Although her help was needed, Mary stayed away from the theatre. She says, 'I attended the opening of *The Seagull* [a week after the Yeats plays]. There was a good cast, but the overall production left much to be desired.' After the performance she was advised by Colonel Johnson 'that in the best interests of the theatre I should disappear from the scene'. This must have hurt but, in the autobiography, she just says that she had 'hoped for a more decorous exit!' She records feeling oddly distant at this juncture from what was going on down in Ridgeway Street. She busied herself with making alterations to her new house and consulting the Lyric actor and horticulturalist Jack McQuoid about the garden. Domesticity had to suffice for the moment. Leaving Derryvolgie Avenue had been a huge physical and emotional task. 'It was a sad business, dismantling a life,' is how she puts it. However, the new house seemed more comfortable than the old and the garden 'a joy', although it needed a lot of work to keep it in order. Indoors the two daily helps, Mrs Hughes and Mrs McDermott, were pleased: 'there was less house to clean, and no theatre'. From now on Mary would be able to close her front gate at night. The transplant from Derryvolgie was complete, although one of their two cats had taken offence at the move and disappeared. Physically, though not mentally, Mary had left the Studio behind. She managed to keep her promise to keep out of the new theatre: 'I felt that I might be tempted either to interfere or say something which could be embarrassing for all concerned.' The New Year's Party to welcome 1969 was quieter than usual.

Back in Ridgeway Street the board tried to regroup and implement the report Arthur Brooke had written for the trustees in September – with the help of Colonel Johnson. Brooke had questioned the 'continuance of Irish Handcrafts and the New Gallery until details of their finances have been studied'. Financial and administrative problems were affecting morale at the theatre and Mary's as yet unpublicized departure was causing concern. A further blow came on 8 January: Brooke resigned as a trustee. In a letter to Pearse he explains that he has been appointed as one of a three-man civil service team tasked with preparing a NI development programme for 1970–75. He says, 'I simply have no time for the Lyric as well.' He stresses that his trusteeship was always temporary; he had only taken on the role when 'it became evident that Kenneth Darwin could not continue'. (Darwin had by now resigned because of ill health.) Then he makes suggestions for a new chairman: Frank Benner would be 'a most suitable choice – a staunch supporter of Mary, a man respected by all, and one with a wealth of experience to be able to perform the functions attaching to the role'. Brooke suggests, in his letter to Pearse, that Colonel Johnson may be about to resign because he felt that under the new administrative order proposed by Brooke, his role would be 'diminished'. Pearse was frustrated by Brooke's resignation because he liked and respected him. He had hoped that he would be a positive force in the board but now he would have to do without him. Sadly, after this an estrangement developed between the Brooke and O'Malley families, who had been close.

There is an interesting coda to the Brooke resignation. In a long letter he wrote in 1990, on receipt of Mary's memoirs, he says that his resignation came about partly because of pressure from his wife, Florence, and was 'one of the worst moments of my life':

> I remembered how Pearse, in such circumstances, tried if possible to do as you [Mary] wished, not to cause you more distress. But I don't wish to place the blame at Florence's door. She was in a sense right: if the sailing from then on was not to become easier, with less controversy and conflicts, I was placed most vulnerably with my position – being about to take over one of the Government Departments.

Brooke then strikes a personal note with Mary – regretting the rift between their families: '... our world came to an end in one important regard. To Florence and me, you and Pearse were our best friends. And we said so, high and wide, in all circles. So much so, that I heard (it's probably not true!) some stupid people in the Civil Service were saying I must be a Roman Catholic'. Then, for Pearse's benefit, he makes a retrospective political point about the Northern Ireland Civil Service: 'Most people don't believe it but, knowing me, you might – in all the Selection Boards I was a member of, or chairman, not one discriminated against a Catholic. On the contrary we were desperately looking for talent to promote, but Catholics of talent were simply not joining the N.I. Civil Service – and who would blame them.'

By January 1969, only two months after its opening, the Lyric was truly in crisis. Christopher Fitz-Simon was continuing to displease the trustees but not audiences. Mary had found both his productions in the autumn season substandard, but reviews of *The Seagull* and *Penny for a Song* suggest that they had more quality than she discerned. The *Belfast News Letter* saw the choice of the Chekhov play as 'unadventurous', but thought it was 'competently staged'. 'Outstanding' performances by Louis Rolston and Aileen Harte were noted.

Penny for a Song did poor business over Christmas. It is possible that this delightful play, which carries within it the seed of the immensely successful TV series *Dad's Army*, was perhaps too English for Belfast audiences. The critics found merit in it: Ray Rosenfield, writing in *Ulster Theatre*, regarded it as 'the first complete success of the new theatre'. She praises Fitz-Simon's direction as 'being firm in every part and the whole moving briskly and pertly and every incident, every character, attuned to the spirit of the play'. *The Irish Times* enthuses in a similar vein and is keen on 'the gay set designed by Jim O'Hare of Teilifís Éireann'. These views contrast starkly with Mary's: *Penny for a Song* 'seemed to be outside the capabilities of both director and designer… We had seen this play in London and felt it was a good choice. It was a pity that the opportunity was lost.'

Looking back, Fitz-Simon expresses clear views on Mary. He admires her leadership qualities and he liked her sense of humour. 'She wasn't witty but she saw the funny side of things.' But he says unequivocally that 'she didn't have the skills for running a [professional] theatre' and that she was 'a gifted amateur'. And he did not share the general high opinion of the quality of her Yeats productions; nor did he think she was good at spotting new plays. He would like to have seen her do 'more trawling for interesting new work'. Before Christmas he had rung Ken Jamison at the Arts Council and told him of the difficulties. (Fitz-Simon refers to him as 'a tower of strength'.) He was counselled to stay a bit longer, but the overwhelming amount of administrative work and the demands made by the board pushed him over the edge. He resigned on the same day as Arthur Brooke and a few days later another trustee, Molly McNeill, left as well, resigning on 10 January 1969.

The board was now down to four (Pearse, Frank Wright and the absentees, Roger McHugh and John Hewitt), so Brooke's proposed chairman Frank Benner, a prominent Belfast businessman, was persuaded to join and brought in two more local trustees: James Fitzpatrick, a solicitor, and Terence Mack, a businessman.

With events spiralling out of control and Colonel Johnson about to walk out, Pearse took decisive action, supported by at least one trustee,

John Hewitt. On 16 January he issued a press release detailing the theatre's difficulties: 'A new structure had been proposed by the trustees, but because no agreement had been reached with staff, all contracts will be terminated.' The theatre would close in early February and re-open on the 25th.

News of the trustee resignations was leaked, causing confused speculation in the press. The *News Letter* sniffed anthem trouble but quotes Pearse as saying that the 'question of the anthem has no connection with the subject'. Colonel Johnson says he knows 'nothing about the matter' and Louis Rolston admits that the company 'really know nothing of what is going on'. The next day the *Belfast Telegraph* confirmed that the theatre 'was having production difficulties'. The paper says Colonel Johnson had been absent from his office 'but denies he has left the organisation'. Mary is then quoted as saying that Johnson had left; but Frank Wright states that he had not, 'but is not operating at the moment'. On 22 January *The Irish News* carried a clear statement from Frank Benner, chairman of the trustees. He says that 'because of administration and management problems it is essential to re-assess the running of the theatre and make certain changes. Difficulties have arisen in the ... transition from the tiny theatre in Derryvolgie Avenue to the new modern building ...' He says 'a short breathing space is necessary for the changes to be made'. But the story bubbled on for a few more days.

Ray Rosenfield in *The Irish Times* said that staff had been given salaries for three to six months in lieu of notice and that Colonel Johnson had received 'a letter of dismissal'. *The Irish News* on 23 January had an accurate headline above a short news item: 'LYRIC: "THINGS IN A MESS AT THE MOMENT," MRS O'MALLEY'. The piece mentions a visit from 'Mr John Berkley, an official of Equity ... [who] will be in Belfast tomorrow to discuss the closure ... with members of the company and the management'. Mary explains Pearse's return to the board very neatly: 'It was put to us that we owed it to the theatre to remain. For that reason, my husband went back.' She adds that 'she had resigned for personal reasons'.

One of the Trustees, at least, remained completely loyal to Pearse and Mary. In letters, Roger McHugh noted 'the confusion between capital and revenue accounts' at the Lyric and suggested that Johnson 'certainly left things in a mess and it will take some time to clear up'.

Belfast's rumour mill reached a dangerous speed when, two months later, Colonel Archie G. Johnson wrote to the *Belfast Telegraph* on 1 April 1969. He had decided not to go quietly. He rejects the imputation that his 'mismanagement' was responsible for 'the present troubles'. He complains that his task was greatly affected by 'constant change and internecine strife among the Trustees'. And he makes clear that 'all the staff in the theatre, from the productions director down to the cleaners, were selected by Mary O'Malley at salaries and conditions of employment dictated by her'. He then makes a ringing declaration: 'The theatre should be run for the people of Ulster and by the people of Ulster, not as a private concern for the edification of a small coterie of so-called intellectuals.' He amplifies this with what amounts to a pro-Fitz-Simon, anti-Yeats PS: 'After all Belfast is not any easy place in which to put on pure theatre and we might have done better with different productions in the early days ...' The sentiments expressed in these final sentences were to lie at the core of the critique of Mary's stewardship of the 'new' Lyric.

The arts commentators, predictably, took a grim view of events at the theatre. John D. Stewart, fundamentally a supporter of Mary, lamented the fact that Fitz-Simon couldn't do his job properly because 'the selection, even the casting of plays, remained with the trustees'. This was perhaps an overstatement, but Stewart felt keenly that the resignation was a blow to the city's reputation: 'I am deeply saddened at the departure of the civilised Christopher Fitz-Simon who will carry back to Dublin no flattering impression of Belfast.' Fitz-Simon did not go immediately, because it took a while for the trustees to organize a replacement. He had been faced with an almost impossible situation, with a heavy-handed board undermined by internal conflicts and an administration that was unfit for purpose. He also might have found the bare-knuckle frankness of Belfast rather a long way from his Dublin civility. This was a sad ending to Mary's first attempt at major delegation. She had failed to realize that Fitz-Simon was a good deal less enthused by Yeats than she was and to notice that he was, managerially, relatively inexperienced. For his part Fitz-Simon erroneously believed that he was coming into a fully professional set-up where, as director of productions, he would have considerable freedom to choose and cast plays as he wanted. But when he had directed at the theatre previously he had enjoyed contact and discussion with Mary. He found her absence disturbing: 'In fact we didn't even have an argument, she simply withdrew.' The worn phrase 'irreconcilable differences' would do to explain this divorce.

Despite all this turmoil the theatre produced, in its hour of crisis, a truly remarkable *The Royal Hunt of the Sun*, praised even by out-of-sorts Mary. It was directed jointly by Sam McCready and Denis Smyth and starred Liam O'Callaghan as Pizarro and Jeremy Jones as Atahualpa. It had help from the National Theatre in London, which loaned costumes, but it was still astonishing that it came in £3000 under budget. John D. Stewart was entranced by it: 'The most impressive and glamorous theatrical event since Sir Laurence Olivier brought his company to our Opera House.' He praised Trevor Scott's 'simple, spacious and convincing setting'. He was delighted that 'Liam O'Callaghan, as General Pizarro, at last finds himself in a role worthy of his great powers' and concluded, 'I would recommend this play to everyone, young and old'.

Although the theatre officially closed on 8 February 1969, rehearsals for the next play, *The Quare Fellow*, continued and the Lyric reopened with George Mooney's production of the Behan work on 25 February. The *Belfast Telegraph* welcomed the reopening of the theatre but thought the production didn't quite succeed, noting a cast of twenty-three but no leading role. *The Irish News* said that the director succeeded in capturing the major element in the play, humour. Both *The Quare Fellow* and *The Royal Hunt of the Sun* were productions directed by members of the 'old' company and both casts contained large numbers of the 'amateurs' to which Fitz-Simon had objected. Somehow the directors managed in both plays to rehearse, costume and design them successfully while working around the limited availability of some of the actors, and to stay reasonably on budget. However, in the longer term this model was unlikely to be sustainable.

This was hardly the moment for Mary to step forward to receive an honorary degree, along with such notables as Philip Larkin, but she did so in July 1969 at Queen's University. J.C. Beckett's citation praises her resistance to the constant danger of provincialism: 'For her the world of theatre has also been the theatre of the world.' He says, with a nice touch of realism: 'The future historian of the Ulster Theatre will no doubt find Mary O'Malley at the centre of some controversies but also, and far more significantly, he will find her at the source of many achievements.' The degree was a pleasing recognition that she had by now laboured successfully in the unpromising vineyard of Ulster theatre for eighteen years. However, as always with Mary, there were controversies. Kieran O'Malley thinks that a mere MA was an insult, that it should have been a doctorate. And it took heroic efforts by the Vice Chancellor of the university to make sure that Mary would *not* be in the hall when God was asked to Save the Queen, but *would* be there, in her place, and ready, when her name was called.

In the spring and summer of 1969, the financial weather at the Lyric did not improve. There were grumbles from the Arts Council about the lack of audited accounts and it seems to have taken an inordinate length of time to get proper financial controls working in the new theatre. The deficit was by now more than £20,000 and Equity was not at all disposed to help with economies. In 1967 the Lyric had agreed to pay union rates to actors who were members of Equity, but still retained the option of using non-Equity actors in productions. This half-way house remained until the new theatre was built. But once the subsidized, semi-professional Lyric opened, Equity became steadily more vociferous in its demands for full professionalization.

There is a lively letter from Equity, in November 1969, to Mary which indicates the roots of the conflict. The writer merely signs himself 'Michael', but is clearly an Equity official. 'Michael' has obviously disagreed with Mary, earlier, on the telephone. Now he is mildly accommodating but adamant: 'I sincerely hope all the theatre's problems resolve themselves, but until the always present dispute between the amateur and professional is recognised, I personally cannot see a solution to this underlying friction.' He ends the letter in a conciliatory way; he says that he 'admires her and is only sorry that we have had this conflict'.

The union's problem was that in the past in the UK it had become too easy to secure an Equity card, with the result that there were thousands of unemployed professional actors in England. In Ulster there weren't many. As Conor O'Malley puts it: 'An aspiring actor could only be given a contract by a theatre management once he had a union card, but he could not obtain a card until he had a contract.' Equity was determined to avoid creating a glut of actors in Ulster and allowed Lyric players only two new cards per year. This meant that quite soon there were not enough Ulster actors stepping onto the Lyric stage.

There were some stalwart members of Mary's amateur Derryvolgie company, like Bernadette Keenan, who declined to apply for an Equity card. She describes herself as 'a happy amateur … I couldn't do full-time professional theatre'. She had played with the Lyric since 1963 – a Yeats sceptic but excellent at doing Dubliners in O'Casey – who nevertheless stayed long enough in the new theatre to do well as a Belfast woman in plays like Boyd's *The Flats*. Other members of the old company remained active but never became full-time professional actors: Patrick Brannigan, for example held onto his job as a schoolteacher until his retirement, but continued to play leading roles and direct as a part-timer at the Lyric throughout the 1970s. Equity did not like part-timers although they had been a key ingredient in Irish theatre companies, North and South, since the beginning of the century.

Just to indicate how strongly professional actors felt about the presence of amateurs in the Belfast theatre, it's worth quoting from a piece in *Fortnight* magazine, written in late 1970 by Seamus McKee. Its main theme is the inadequacy of the new Equity minimum of £20 a week. Then the piece goes into a diatribe against amateur actors: 'The profession is crowded with so many dilettantes, people who already have perfectly good jobs and who are attracted to the stage through vanity. Managers are keen to use them, rather than professionals because they will accept a lot less money for a chance of appearing on stage. Standards inevitably decline, until you have no standards left at all.'

This description of the amateur does not fit most of Mary's actors: simple vanity seems rather far down the line as a motivation for going onstage with professionals and taking on difficult parts in demanding plays, as well as doing 'a perfectly good job' elsewhere. And many of Mary's 'amateurs' had acquired remarkable skills in long apprenticeships at the Studio; they were often 'professional' in all but name.

It seems likely that there was some professional jealousy of the subsidized, brand-new Lyric on the part of the other less-fortunate Belfast theatres. Actors from the defunct Group Theatre were involved in the management of the local Equity branch. There was also probably envy at the size of the subsidy the Lyric was receiving, and the union must have wanted a good proportion of that subsidy to go towards helping Equity cardholders make a living. They must also have objected to large-scale productions going on at what was effectively a cut price because of the number of 'amateurs' involved.

Equity also continually made life difficult for the Lyric by insisting on demarcation between stage management and the actors. Rigid enforcement of the principle that actors did not move scenery created more jobs for stage staff, leading to overmanning, which was not compatible with the relatively low budgets. The Lyric's costs were also increased by the need – as a result of the miserly rationing of Equity cards in Northern Ireland – to employ actors from the Irish Republic and from England. This brought in good English and Irish actors, but these imports cost the Lyric more because they had to be paid subsistence as well as wages. The Equity problem ran on and on at the Lyric for most of the 1970s and so exasperated Mary that she was driven to publicly protest at the way the actors' union was, as she saw it, holding back the development of high-quality theatre in Ulster by ratcheting up the overall cost of productions and restricting the development of local actors.

According to Conor O'Malley, 'fifteen or so' actors from the original company stayed on in the new theatre, but with all the troubles – both within and without – this group did not have the longevity or the cohesion of the old one. And it became increasingly difficult to develop a new company because the Lyric's parlous finances just did not run to long-term contracts for full-time actors. Now that Mary was no longer directing productions it was hard to achieve the consistency that had been possible in the Studio. New directors came and went, and they did not – or could not, because of Equity – always cast the experienced Lyric players Mary had nurtured and favoured. Finding an artistic director who could oversee productions was also to be a continuing problem, although for now the gap left by Christopher Fitz-Simon had been filled by the talented Denis Smyth.

The financial situation got no better in the summer of '69 but encouragement came from an unlikely quarter in a letter written to Pearse on 5 June by Purvis Bruce, who worked for the Lyric's accountants, Atkinson & Boyd. He began by suggesting that capital and revenue accounts, which had always been kept apart in the past, were now merging 'so as to render pointless a separate fund designated for building'. Bruce then praises the Arts Council for its contribution towards the building and for subsidizing productions. Then comes the encouragement:

> The trustees now stand possessed of a company worth some £30,000 and have a well-equipped theatre backed, I understand by promised contributions ... I am optimistic that, properly managed, the theatre should be capable of surviving. This is a view I have not held in considering previous years' accounts. Up to the present I have regarded the theatre as being hopelessly under-capitalised, but it now appears to have a margin of capital to a degree that holds prospects.

Nevertheless, Frank Benner, as chairman, was determined that his new broom was going to do some sweeping. Study of the accounts of the Irish Handcrafts shop and the New Gallery convinced him that they were a drain on resources. He decided to close both and indeed the whole Grosvenor Road operation, with the approval of his loyal local-resident trustees. Pearse, naturally backed by Mary, protested, but to no avail.

Shutting the New Gallery was a painful business. Alice Berger Hammerschlag protested fiercely. She, Pearse and Mary saw it as an integral part of the Lyric's cultural enterprise, with the theatre at the centre. In March 1969 Alice wrote to Benner, citing the gallery's achievements: 'The Tate Gallery has asked for catalogues for almost every exhibition for their library; the Arts Council has bought paintings from almost every exhibition for their public collection; the Ulster Museum has done so too ...' She finished with a sharp rejoinder directed at those local trustees who had been in post for only a few months: 'I recall these facts for the information of those trustees who have joined the Board only recently and who have not had time to find out.' But Benner's cuts were implemented and from June 1969 the gallery and Irish Handcrafts were no more.

Mary was very upset at the closure of the gallery, and it had a sad coda. Alice Hammerschlag had been diagnosed with cancer in the spring; her last days were clouded by the closure of 'her' gallery. Mary visited her in hospital, where Alice drew and painted to the end. She died, aged fifty-two, within a month of the gallery closing.

Mary's cultural flotilla was now diminished, but *Threshold* had managed to survive, although its appearances became more erratically spaced. Mary got Seamus Heaney to edit Number 22, which came out in the summer of 1969 under the heading of 'New Theatre'. In his editorial Heaney said that the theme was 'Springboard' and added, 'I had thought that "Harvesting" would have been a suitable theme, now that the Lyric Players are coming into their right, but typically Mrs O'Malley refused to let any such self-satisfied connotation enter, even at this point.'

This account of the Ridgeway Street theatre's troubled early days has featured process more than product, finance and administration rather than art. After the closure, Dublin plays predominated for a while. *The Quare Fellow* was followed by a revival of Mairin O'Farrell's *Smock Alley*; then came a dramatization of Seán O'Casey's autobiographical *Pictures in the Hallway*. Sam McCready directed *School for Scandal* next, and this was a big success, deemed suitable by chairman Benner for a visit from the Governor of Northern Ireland, Lord Grey. The dreaded anthem was played on this truly 'ceremonial' occasion without repercussions. It was never played again at the theatre.

After *The Prime of Miss Jean Brodie* came another play from the Republic, John B. Keane's *Sive* (McCready directing again). This provoked one of Ian Hill's more caustic reviews: the piece was a case of 'melodrama with everything, schmaltz, stage Irishness'. Less acerbic critics like Judith Rosenfield found the play 'had the power to grip and hold the attention of the large first-night audience'. It is notable that this first season in the new theatre had not featured a single play with any direct connection with Belfast, or even Northern Ireland – although Cuchulain counts as an Ulster character.

Alice Berger Hammerschlag was not the only friend of Mary's to die of cancer that summer. The disease also killed Babs Mooney, George Mooney's wife, who had performed at the Studio from the very start. Dark-haired and dark-eyed, she had been a striking Bernarda Alba. Then came more pain: Maeve McGibbon, Pegeen in the first production of *The Heart's a Wonder*, a 'vivacious, always happy' person was taken by the disease as well and died shortly after the other two. These deaths 'shocked and bewildered' Mary and those who had shared the Studio experience with these lively women.

To make matters worse, one of these deaths was to open a new rift with Helen Lewis whose relationship with Mary had been patched up since the *Goblin Market* conflict. The loss of Alice Hammerschlag affected Helen deeply (as it did Mary). According to Robin and her other son Michael, 'her distress was immeasurable; the two women [Alice and Helen] were inseparable'. The following year Helen organized a commemorative event in honour of Alice. It was called 'There Is a Time' and it included poetry, dance, music and drama. It was held in the Lyric Theatre where Mary, at that moment, was suffering the travails of her large-scale *Peer Gynt* production – which, alarmingly had lost its lead actor early on. Robin Lewis remembers some conflicts over the use of Mary's stage, with its complex set, for rehearsals for Helen's quite ambitious commemorative event. It is likely that the two stressed women clashed, certainly that communication broke down. Afterwards Helen felt that Mary distanced herself from this event. This was, in Helen's eyes, 'unforgivable, so Helen wouldn't and couldn't repair it', according to Robin and his brother Michael. Happily, much later there was a reconciliation. When Helen's husband, Harry, died in 1991, Mary and Pearse came to Belfast for the funeral and went to the Lewis house afterwards. 'If it was not a complete reconciliation, it was enough for both women.' Further meetings between the widowed Helen and the O'Malleys followed.

Out in the streets tension mounted. In late summer of 1969 the Home Secretary, James Callaghan, arrived from Westminster to see for himself. In Derry he was jostled and retired, with John Hume, to a tiny terraced house. There, from a bedroom window, he made a 'compelling speech with the aid of a megaphone, recognising past wrongs and promising justice in the future'. The Home Secretary was upbeat about the situation, almost jaunty, but it got no better. There were riots on the Shankhill Road, the army fired twenty-six shots and two men were killed. At this stage the IRA was almost weaponless and also split. But soon the sectarian Provisional wing became dominant and began to arm, buying Armalites in the USA. 'The long war' was about to begin.

14

Crisis 2

MATTERS GOT NO better in the autumn, both inside the theatre
and outside on the streets. The board now consisted of Pearse, two mostly
absent trustees, John Hewitt and Roger McHugh, and the recently recruited
locals. The trustees were polarized: Benner and his supporters wanted more
financial stringency; Pearse and his wanted to keep as much of the Lyric's
cultural convoy afloat as possible. There was now more, serious, trouble
ahead. Benner had strong business connections in Belfast and, responding
to the theatre's dire financial situation, encouraged an apparently well-
intentioned fundraising body to assist with the job of restoring the Lyric's
finances.

Patrick Shea, a respected senior civil servant, decided to lend a hand. He
wrote to Benner referring to a 'recent meeting' of potential fundraisers. He
then lists a dozen names of those who have agreed to serve on a committee
and raises a key question:

> The Lyric is still politically suspect in some business circles and its
> attitude to the Constitution etc. must be clarified if the goodwill of
> the business world is to be won. Michael Curran [property developer
> and a director of McAlpine's], who has particularly strong business
> connections, was very firm on this; he said he could not help us unless
> the matter was cleared, in writing, by the trustees. I asked whether it

was not well-known that a reasonable arrangement about the national anthem had been made but was told by all present that there are still considerable murmurings about the Lyric being anti-Government. It was pointed out that this could be a very serious barrier to fundraising.

Patrick Shea, the prime mover in this attempt to help the theatre, was that rare bird, a senior civil servant who was also a Catholic. His support might be difficult to turn down.

The motivations behind this sudden helpfulness from the business community are obscure. It's possible that there is sympathy for a theatre struggling to make ends meet in desperate times, or perhaps a little guilt that such a venture has not previously had the support it deserved from Belfast's businessmen. But the premium put on demonstrations of loyalty suggests there may have been some political motivation as well as benevolent intentions behind the ad hoc committee's actions.

Mary and Pearse were, to put it mildly, not pleased with this development, even though the potential sums the 'committee' might raise were desperately needed. Mary describes the letter as 'unfortunate and heavy-handed'. The O'Malleys made their feelings plain to the committee although it seems their fellow trustees were more positive about the intervention. 'Heavy-handed' would be a good description of the fundraisers' next move. They decided that, if the Lyric was to benefit from their work, each trustee would have to sign a document prepared by the committee. This was presented twice to trustee meetings in October. Pearse and the absentee trustee, Roger McHugh, refused to sign what McHugh called 'a loyalty test'.

It is not clear whether John Hewitt, the other absentee trustee, was prepared to sign the pledge, but he may have done so. He had written to Pearse on 14 November in a state of some alarm. 'What has gone wrong? What kind of houses are we getting? This bickering is bound to give the place a dubious name. What about the loyalty of the players with these abrupt switches in management? If the fundraising effort is not accepted, what are we going to do for money?' A few days later Pearse wrote back saying that 'the theatre's financial position is not as bad as the papers are saying'. But more, anxious letters from Hewitt followed. On 30 November 1969 he wrote a little testily to Pearse asking, 'What is the position? Do we owe £23,000 or £42,000? The discrepancy appears to be in the widely differing amounts ascribed to Bank Overdraft ...' Pearse sent a moderately reassuring reply on 4 December. He clarifies the position, saying that roughly £10,000 is owed for the construction of the theatre, but that the overdraft on running the theatre has 'skyrocketed'. Hewitt seems to have been quite in favour of the fundraising initiative, but Pearse would not sign. At this point, the four local trustees, Benner, Wright, Fitzpatrick and Mack, all recent appointees and all willing to sign, decided to resign.

The press was already asking what was going on. On 11 November 1969 the *Belfast Telegraph* asserted that the fundraisers had a right to ask 'for an assurance on the theatre's pro-constitutional policy'. Betty Lowry and Brian Boyd took Pearse to task in an article for refusing to sign what amounted to no more than an extract from the trustee minutes defining the practice for playing the national anthem.

Pearse called a press conference at the theatre on 13 November 1969. What he said in his statement provides a core document in the Lyric's history. He addresses the current crisis caused by the resignations. He justifies the roles of the long-distance trustees by making plain that when the board was constituted in 1960 'it was decided that two or three trustees from outside Northern Ireland should be appointed to ensure a reasonable level of objectivity should the trustees become involved in "local controversies"'. Then he rehearses the fundraisers' anxieties about the theatre being 'anti-government'. In the light of this, he says, he sought advice from the Arts Council, and quotes from a letter he wrote them, suggesting 'that monetary freedom must not be bought at the expense of artistic freedom'. He sees being indebted to the fundraisers as the thin end of a political wedge: 'There is also the danger that political conditions might be imposed on management, selection of plays and the employment of personnel.' Pearse suggests that employing professional fundraisers – as had been done in the past – would be more 'prudent'. He then makes a pledge of his own: 'I will take all possible steps so that the capital debt of the theatre is honourably discharged – without endangering its artistic policy and self-respect.' He stresses the need to ensure a realistic Arts Council grant – £24,000 a year rather than £13,000. He fears that the fundraisers' intervention might lead to a level of financial and political control that would be incompatible with running an independent organization.

It would be difficult to find anything subversive in the way Mary and Pearse were running either the theatre or *Threshold*. They were not putting on dramas challenging the status quo; indeed, their choice of plays and most editions of *Threshold* were strikingly apolitical at this point. They merely wanted to assert that there was an Irish and an international culture, which could broaden Ulster attitudes as well as providing educative entertainment. And the trustees had even agreed to play the national anthem. If the trustees were behaving constitutionally in the theatre, which they were, its attitude to the constitution was an irrelevance. The O'Malleys avowed nationalism and their desire for a united Ireland were well-known but hardly relevant considerations when it came to managing a theatre. They were, like hundreds of thousands of Catholics, and some Protestants, 'anti-government': their 'attitude to the constitution etc.' was clear – they wanted change. It was impossible for them to sign the 'pledge'.

This press conference resulted in more coverage. John D. Stewart was fairly positive. 'What can be done to save a fine theatre'?' is the headline of a piece in *The Sunday Press*. He sees trouble ahead for the three remaining trustees – the articles of association require 'a minimum of five …' He asks who can help the surviving trustees, adding that the Lyric project has 'a considerable fund of goodwill in Belfast'. He acknowledges that putting on serious plays in a fully professional environment was always going to be costly, and that the theatre began with a £9000 debt 'carried over from its little forerunner'. More income is urgently needed, but Stewart trashes one of the suggested options for achieving solvency: putting on trousers-down farces. He believes that 'informed opinion' in Belfast wants the theatre to survive. 'Everyone who matters agrees that we were in desperate need of a real theatre and everyone who cares and can pay is paying to keep it going.'

An administrative nightmare now ensued; Pearse, McHugh and Hewitt were theoretically in charge of the theatre. 'Theoretically' because the Arts Council questioned the legal status of the minimal board and its right to receive money from the council, just as Stewart had predicted.

Indeed, on 24 November the Arts Council said it was 'holding in abeyance' part of the Lyric's grant until it had a board of five trustees. The overdraft loomed ever larger. So Pearse set about reconstituting the board. Dr Colm Kelly, a colleague of Pearse's, a radiologist, was persuaded to join, as was the businessman Charles Carvill. Mary, who seems by this stage to have had enough of life on the sidelines and was also incensed by recent events, was suddenly remotivated and became a trustee again.

On 15 December 1969 a virtually new board set about clearing up the financial mess. Creditors were becoming menacing – fearing that, such was the perceived state of the theatre, they might not be paid. The *Belfast Telegraph* refused to take any more Lyric advertisements until the account was settled; and the Belfast Corporation sent a £1250 rates bill. Much more alarming was the fact that friendly McAlpine's had now turned unfriendly – sending out a summons demanding rapid payment of the outstanding balance of £14,000. Mary now took over the day-to-day management of the theatre and began battling on all fronts with her usual tenacity. This became possible because Denis Smyth, after doing strong productions in the autumn, departed; he had been given leave to take up a Leverhulme Trust fellowship at the Royal Shakespeare theatre, so artistic control devolved back to Mary. She wrote to Roger McHugh in November 1969, saying that 'with "businessmen" lurking around every corner I sometimes feel apprehensive'. McHugh remained resolute in his support for her and Pearse.

The 1970 season had begun with O'Casey's *Juno and the Paycock*, directed by Pat Brannigan, and continued with *The Field* (John B. Keane). This received high praise from an anonymous critic in *The Irish Times* for its relevance to the current unrest, the way it portrayed 'the terrible driving hunger for land, both actual and symbolic, the brutality and the fear – these are all only too clear'. A powerful performance by Michael Duffy in the lead role was praised as was Denis Smyth's direction. Two reasonably popular choices, Ben Jonson's *The Alchemist* and *Luther* by John Osborne, were followed by a classical French drama, Racine's *Phaedre*, translated in rhyming couplets by Robert Lowell. This was a step too far for Belfast theatregoers and despite a determined-to-like-it review from Betty Lowry and the presence of a French actress, Nicolette Bernard, in the title role, audiences plummeted to such an extent that the Arts Council had to step in to guarantee the loss.

Mary says in the autobiography that her return was 'reluctant.' She grumbles that she had 'handed over a thriving organisation in 1968 – and a year later it was minus Irish Handcrafts, the New Gallery and, if some people could have their way, without its traditions as well.' This is a little disingenuous. Part of the theatre's financial problems stemmed from debt carried over from the generally loss-making ancillaries – the products of her hectic expansionist era. Also her early appointments and her absence in the vital first year of the new Lyric's life had probably played their part in creating the 'chaos' which she found when she came back.

In her effort to run a better-organized ship, she was able to affect what happened on the stage more quickly than the stumbling finances. The latter was to be long and painful job. First, a schedule of payment by instalment was agreed with McAlpine's. Mary made the first payment in 1970 with difficulty, some of it 'handed over in a canvas bag', thus avoiding the distinct possibility that her theatre might have been put into the hands of the creditors. Another payment was made in April and quarterly from then on. McAlpine's withdrew their summons. Mary and Pearse took the rates issue to court: long delays ensued, and it took until 1972 for the legal system to decide that they were not liable for rates. The most immediate threats had been lifted and the Art Council's interim grant for the *Phaedre* losses had arrived. There was now a financial breathing space, but fundamental administrative problems remained at the theatre.

'It seemed to me incredible,' Mary says, 'the amount of chaos created during my year's absence from the theatre. When I took it over, I simply could not sort it out and subsequent appointees [presumably artistic directors who followed her] were similarly unsuccessful. I merely tackled some of the immediate and major problems and looked after the productions.' This suggests that a smooth-running operation was impossible to achieve at the Lyric. Running a subsidised 300-seater theatre profitably is a task which has been achieved successfully by many professional theatre managers. The job should not have been beyond Mary. However, when civil unrest unsettles the cultural climate and putting on particular plays and running a theatre in a certain way becomes politically suspect, when financial support is, for a time, insufficient, when the trade unions are militant, when the fabric of the theatre and its operation are threatened almost daily by unpredictable events on the streets (there was a bomb to come), when audiences fall below 50 per cent for several years running, and to 35 per cent for part of 1971, then damage limitation and survival become the primary goals. Mary, with a great deal of help from Pearse, was about to achieve both those goals and a whole lot more than that in a city which was fundamentally theatre-sceptical.

15

Troubles

MARY'S RETURN TO the front line is the beginning of a new chapter in her life and career. She could not return to the free-wheeling expansionism of the Derryvolgie days; she would no longer direct half a dozen plays a year; no more would she enjoy the satisfactions of having a familiar, talented team of theatre-practitioners available to do her bidding. Instead, she would have to manage a hard-up professional theatre staggering through a murderous political and social upheaval. The widescale and calculated violence affected her deeply. From 1970 the Troubles took a new, vicious turn. The Provos were now ready to take on the British army, which soon outlived the warm welcome it had received the year before and became a target for snipers. It was not long before the melancholy headline: 'Last night another British soldier ...' was becoming commonplace. And the Loyalist paramilitaries were clearly not going to stand for this attrition much longer. She also became increasingly anxious about her own personal safety and that of her family: a high-profile husband who drove into the heart of the city every day and sons who were constantly crossing the border as they shuttled from Belfast to Dublin and back.

This was the context in which Mary set about deficit reduction. The play programmes from 1970 onwards cite a figure for the money still owing and month by month there is a gratifying reduction in the sum. At Christmas 1969 the capital development debt is quoted as £23,000, followed by an appeal: 'DONATIONS ARE URGENTLY NEEDED TO CLEAR THE BALANCE'. By 31 March 1970 the debt was down to £21,000 but then progress was slow – it was still £17,000 in July 1971, just before internment came in and delivered another blow to turnout. Mary's plan was to keep Lyric audiences constantly aware of the fact that the theatre was in debt but also that something was being done about it. The financial situation had, of course, been helped by the disappearance of the New Gallery and Irish Handcrafts. But at this stage Mary could not be certain that the support of a disaffected Arts Council would continue.

In 1970 audiences began to improve after the *Phaedre* debacle. By Christmas Mary's choice of programme began to justify itself. *She Stoops to Conquer*, directed by the talented Bernard Torney, was a big hit. It played to capacity houses for four weeks over Christmas. Mary loved seeing 'cheerful, happy audiences' every evening and rejoiced in the 'busy click of the bar-room till'.

Stella McCusker, who played Kate Hardcastle, was to become a regular in Lyric casts during the 1970s. She had begun in the Studio, where she had been the victim of one of director Mary's less tactful remarks: 'I think we'll have to cover your arms; you know they're not your best feature.' Stella says that she has 'had a thing about my arms ever since'. Despite this faux pas, they got on well. 'Mary was wonderful about knowing when something was wrong with a scene but couldn't always tell you how to put it right.' Stella admired Mary's abilities as a hostess: 'She was always feeding people, always being kind to people.' Stella knew Helen Lewis and was saddened that Mary and she were never so close again after the rupture: 'It was an absolute shame, but I couldn't tell you why [it happened].' Stella regarded Pearse as 'a wonderful husband and a terrific strength to Mary'. She says that Mary 'definitely wasn't the kind of feminist we know today'.

Mary was by now back in multitasking mode, not only introducing cheese-paring management but, later in the season, directing *The Plough and the Stars*. In the programme she hid behind the pseudonym of 'Mary McCarthy'. Props for the *Plough* proved tricky. Guns were hired from England and duly arrived at Aldergrove airport. But despite the 'evident harmlessness' of the weapons, the authorities refused to release them. Appeals were in vain until the very, very last moment. 'We made a final effort during the first act of the play; we rang Lisburn barracks once more ... After further parley, they agreed to release the guns if we could send someone out. One of the soldiers from the fourth act, in full costume, made the journey at speed and returned [with the guns] in time to save the day.' The mind boggles a little at the vision of an actor dressed in the 1916 uniform of a British soldier and perhaps in full make-up, knocking on the door of Lisburn army barracks and asking, urgently, for 'the guns'. Mary's efforts were rewarded; box office takings for the O'Casey were good. After *The Magistrate*, directed by Louis Lentin from Dublin, came the Yeats: *The Dreaming of the Bones*, *Purgatory*, *Calvary* and *The Resurrection*, all relevant to the Easter season. Mary, re-energized, directed and Colin Middleton designed.

Ray Rosenfield of the *News Letter* wondered if 'it might be time for a reassessment of the place of Yeats in the theatre – to judge from the astonishingly large house for the first night ... a house, moreover, where young people were well in the majority'. Rosenfield, who had seen many of Mary's Yeats productions before (rarely attended by an audience of this size), was enthralled by the way 'the occasion gave force to the concept of the theatre as a temple, audience and performers being brought together as in the exploration of a mystery.' This, she said, 'was most successfully achieved in *Calvary* and *Resurrection* – not because of their obvious relevance to this season, but more because of the torment of incomprehension, despair and ecstasy conveyed by the performers'. She singled out Peter Adair for the depth of his performance as Judas and Liam O'Callaghan's 'mystic nobility'. The O'Malley magic was still in working order, even if now presented pseudonymously. But the management seems to have calculated, probably accurately, that Yeats could not draw in audiences over several weeks. This production ran for just five days.

Something very different followed – Sam Thompson's shipyard drama *Over the Bridge*. Ten years before, its depiction of rampant sectarianism had caused a furore. Now, with the sectarian dragon breathing deadly fire all over the province, its revelations were common knowledge. Gerald Rafferty in the *Belfast Telegraph* mined some encouragement in audience reaction: 'One hopes that it was something of a healthy sign to hear the audience laugh during the delivery of rather dramatic exchanges between Prods and Taigs ... at the shipyard, although I'm sure Thompson never meant any part of his work to be taken so lightly.' Rafferty sees in the play 'a monument to the fearless man who wrote it – a man who detested bigotry and hypocrisy in all shapes and forms. It is well worth going back to see this fresh production.'

The season was going well: 'The siege of the theatre has been partly lifted,' Mary wrote to Roger McHugh. By the time *Much Ado ...* was in rehearsal, Mary felt confident enough to give herself a break by taking a fortnight off in America. She and Pearse had been invited to attend a seminar on Ireland at the University of Southern Illinois at Carbondale. The 'Northern Irish question' was being discussed worldwide.

The seminar was predictably inconclusive and coincided with tragic events at another midwestern university, Kent State, where a protest against the US invasion of Cambodia led to the shooting of four students. The event resonated for some days afterwards. When Mary and Pearse went to see what turned out to be a lively production of the musical *Hair*, at the curtain call the audience was asked to stand in solidarity with the dead students. 'A solemn moment, we stood with the greater part of the audience, whilst some left noisily, indicating a different point of view.'

Mary and Pearse returned to Belfast refreshed but empty-handed: a fundraising visit to the Mellon Foundation had fallen flat. When they got back, they found that all had gone well with *Much Ado* and audiences had been good. John D. Stewart was delighted with the production and so was most of the audience on the night he went. '"It's just like a modern play," a lady explained, giving it the highest accolade she could find.' Stewart reports that the audience 'chuckled, laughed and finally roared' and he enjoyed the way there was a 'tell-tale hubbub of appreciation' during the interval. This was followed by a Brian Friel: *Lovers*, directed by George Mooney.

Attendance had been reasonable for the season, but the theatre's finances were still parlous, and efforts were made to get a further overdraft facility because the Arts Council subsidy had not been paid for more than six months. The reasons for this are not entirely clear, but it's likely that the reduction of the board to three at the time of the 'helpful' fundraisers' crisis, plus a lack of audited accounts and, possibly, Pearse's resolute gesture of independence in refusing offers of potential business-generated gold, were contributory factors. But at last, in June, the Council expressed its positive belief in the future of the theatre and £2000 was offered 'without prejudice to any further negotiations'; and in August the Lyric received a grant of £18,000 to cover the period up to March 1971.

Mary gives herself some credit for this turn of events. Back in 1969 she had written to James Callaghan, some time before he had made his calming, Home Secretary visit to Ulster. She says she had put the case for the Lyric Theatre and 'the right to life of the two traditions'. This appeal had taken a long time to bear fruit, but just before the Labour government gave way to Edward Heath's Conservatives, Mary had received a letter from Callaghan in May 1970 saying, 'I take it you are reasonably happy with the Arts Council grant, though, no doubt, you would have welcomed an even larger sum.' Mary thought it likely that Westminster was at this stage encouraging the Arts Council to support an independent theatre, whatever the 'constitutional position' of its founders was.

With some money in the bag it was now possible for Mary to plan the 1970–71 season. In the previous one, nine out of fourteen plays had either been set in Ireland or written by Irishmen and three had been Ulster plays. She and the trustees sought to achieve a similar balance in the upcoming season. Mary's thought processes may have gone like this. Why not an O'Casey to start with, the third great Dublin tragicomedy, *The Shadow of a Gunman*? Then give the Belfast audience a chance to see whether Tom Stoppard's *Rosencrantz and Guildenstern Are Dead* was as clever as audiences in England had found it to be; then the necessary Irish play, *The Becauseway*, an absurdist drama submitted by Wesley Burrowes, a writer from Bangor, Co. Down (this play was another winner of the Irish Life competition). Mary dug into her repertoire for the next play, the huge-cast *Peer Gynt*, to be followed by Miller's *Death of a Salesman*, directed by the returning Denis Smyth. For the Christmas holidays, Sheridan's cheerful comedy, *The Rivals*. This autumn season was the good old Studio mix of serious contemporary plays and classic pieces from world drama, but it was still a little light on home-produced fare. This lack was now likely to be made good, however, by the appointment of John Boyd, a former BBC producer, as literary manager at a salary of £500 a year. He was soon to start filling the local gap: first by writing Ulster dramas himself, often dealing with the impact of the Troubles.

Meanwhile *Threshold* was in the bookshops. The 'Northern Crisis' Summer 1970 edition had a startling cover. In Colin Middleton's arresting piece of graphic design, a black angular figure, club upraised, races towards orange flames as black, jagged debris flies around. This was a striking, simple summary of the shocking images which by then were appearing nightly on television screens in the largely law-abiding UK and farther afield. John Montague's Foreword states that 'the religio-political tension' in Northern Ireland has

> produced very little literature. We have a Brian, but not a William Faulkner. Talking to Ulster writers, one encounters either the impotence of rage, or a certain weariness: they wish that the local problem would go away and leave them to more central concerns. And yet it is something that we are stuck with, and only through absorbing its bitterness, it seems to me, can Ulster writers hope to grow.

He feels that now 'our woes have become a world-wide concern, it seemed important to give a more intimate picture of the crisis'. This aim was achieved, and 'Northern Crisis' was perhaps the finest *Threshold* Mary produced as managing editor.

———

In the autumn of 1970, proud of the splash her magazine had made (even if it gave some hostages to the anti-Lyric brigade), and with her play programme in place, Mary carried on with debt reduction. The uncertain security situation continued to bite into audiences but *The Shadow of a Gunman* did well enough in a city now living under the shadows of many gunmen.

Next came *Rosencrantz and Guildenstern Are Dead*, directed by Sam McCready. Gerald Rafferty in the *Telegraph* suggested that not only knowledge of *Hamlet* but also *Waiting for Godot* would help audience comprehension. The word games played by the two Hamlet sidekicks trapped in Beckettian stasis were, he said, sometimes 'stagnant, but this was amply compensated by flashes of brilliant dialogue and faultless acting'. He concludes a little enigmatically: 'This play is something quite new to Belfast. Whether we are really ready for it remains to be seen.'

The Becauseway, by Wesley Burrowes came next. This absurdist drama presented a challenge to the *Telegraph*'s Betty Lowry. 'If you go to see *the Becauseway* at the Lyric Theatre you'll be amused, you'll be stimulated and you'll be puzzled,' she says. Much of the action takes place in 'a crazy law-court' and she divines that the play is about 'the pursuit of love and the illusions in which despairing people take refuge'. Ian Hill was relatively benign: 'Mr Burrowes' humour is gentle stuff (he missed out on the Theatre of Cruelty), but very funny.' It also had a satirical edge: the dialogue carried coded anti-sectarian messages.

For *Peer Gynt*, Colin Middleton designed an impressively chilly snow-bound mountain environment using large sheets of fine steel. The costumes were experimental: the trolls were to be dressed in heavy-duty polythene. Mary suggested that this covering could be worn over bare skin. 'Too revealing,' said most of the men, demanding underpants. A female member of the cast bravely demonstrated that on a lit stage the costumes revealed shape but no detail. Nevertheless, some of the bashful males wore underpants on the first night.

The critical reception for Mary's second *Peer* was mixed. The *News Letter* said that it suffered from 'slowness in the first half, drab dressing and confusing choreography. The second half made ample amends: it was brisk, bright and brilliantly inventive.' Ian Hill satirizes the first half with glee in a way that, understandably, was to eventually get under the trustees' skin:

The elements of the play, till the interval, are those which tempt the Lyric most; they are also, I fear, those at which they are worst. Symbolic sets that don't give the actors room to stride about symbolically, lumpy tweed costumes, little interludes for dancing the interpretative dance, the poetic tones and much, not very athletic prancing. The house style, if you like, at its worst. It was a grim start to the evening and

then, suddenly, when the trolls were dispensed with the director, Mary
McCracken found her feet …

In the end he thought that Ibsen's magic worked, but the earlier barbs must
have hurt.

Betty Lowry found the play long and raises an interesting question
about one of the scenes: 'The audience laughter during the impressive and
horrific madhouse scene puzzled me.' It also puzzled Peer or rather the actor
playing him, Patrick Brannigan. In an interview given not long before he
died in 2014, he remembers Mary's handling of the madhouse scene and it
getting out of hand – there was superb mute acting by the inmates but they
distracted from the serious, central point of the scene. 'Very undisciplined,'
he called it. (Brannigan was one of Mary's stalwarts who, much later, refused
to work at the Lyric again when he felt that she had been unjustly treated by
the trustees.) Although he admired her visual sense and the way she held out
for the theatre's independence in those troubled days, he was disturbed by
the toll running a playhouse under almost impossible pressure took on her.

Putting on *Peer Gynt* did not please the Arts Council. Small-cast
plays were cheaper; there were forty parts in *Peer*. Mary defends the choice
of large-cast plays: 'A large cast made use of all of one's inventiveness. It
provided for total theatre, involving music, dance and all the other skills.
There was also the chance to try out a number of people in minor roles.'
She stood by the value of the project, but admits that, second time round,
this *Peer Gynt* lacked the excitement of that first production in the Studio
in 1957.

Mary was finding that directing plays and theatre administration did
not mix. Denis Smyth returned from London and directed what was, by all
critical accounts, a magnificent production of *Death of a Salesman*, starring
the Dublin actor George Alexander. Smyth had gained useful experience
during his year's absence on a Leverhulme scholarship and Mary and Pearse
had high hopes that he could be signed up as productions director. He could
act and was an excellent director, he had local roots and, as someone who
had played and directed at the Studio, he was well aware of Lyric traditions.
But when a contract was offered Smyth would not sign. Talking to him

almost fifty years later he explained that, on his return, he had found the Lyric 'chaotic'. It may be that he saw the indebted theatre as being so far from the relatively ordered processes of the Royal Shakespeare Company, where he had recently been, that the prospect of driving this leaky ship forward seemed too daunting.

He may well have been alarmed also by the contract he was asked to sign. It offered a salary of £2000 a year, specified office hours (including a one-and-a-half-hour lunch break), and promised four weeks holiday a year. The 'Responsibilities' section, however, was onerous. He would have had to ensure 'efficient operation of all theatre activities at Ridgeway Street, Cromwell Road and any property owned or held on lease by the theatre'. He had to oversee 'the clerical system and any proper keeping of records and preparation of reports etc. as directed by the Trustees'. He was also contracted to oversee the Academy of Music and Dramatic Art; *Threshold*; the bar, and coffee sales. Additionally, he was to be in charge of the scenic workshop, the storage of costumes and props and 'the maintenance of all theatre buildings and property'. He was also to be responsible for the 'discipline of all theatre personnel and the front-of-house organization' as well as preparing 'all publicity material in collaboration, of course with the Artistic Advisor' (Mary). The contract made quite clear that he was 'responsible to the Board of Trustees, via the Secretary' (Pearse).

What must have been the key sentence for Smyth, read: 'Expenditure, planning and direction of all theatre presentations [must be done] in collaboration with the Artistic Advisor, subject to the approval of the board of Trustees.' The contract loads him with administrative responsibilities while providing very little artistic freedom from the diktat of Mary and the trustees. Smyth, by the accounts of friends and acquaintances, was innately cautious, so his refusal to sign up for a more than Herculean task is understandable. He was big loss to the Lyric, particularly as he was passionate about promoting local writing, telling the press in an earlier interview that he hoped in future to produce a play by Stewart Parker and looking forward to the day when the theatre might have a writer-in-residence. Smyth's decision to leave the Lyric was a blow to Mary and Pearse, but she had no option other than to carry on as artistic advisor and general factotum.

Over the Christmas period Mary wanted to spread some Christmas cheer in a cheerless Belfast. *The Rivals* did well and was followed by the ever-popular *The Heart's a Wonder*. (Pearse remained sceptical of musicals; he saw a danger of the Lyric becoming too 'commercial'.) Mary directed it herself, for the fourth time. Even Ian Hill enjoyed the production ('It makes a pleasing enough evening') but rather spoilt the effect by describing the dancing as 'leppin'. Elsewhere the 'sprightly' production' and Stella McCusker's performance as Pegeen were praised. The piece kept the box office busy and provided a favourite Lyric anecdote: the mouse story. One night, during the final act, to the audience's delight, a mouse appeared on the stage. Unphased by the lights, it explored the set, including the huge fireplace, which was its centrepiece, even sniffing the soda bread being baked on a griddle. The actors ignored the intrusion with amateur/professional aplomb, but the audience revelled in it. A local newspaper report says that the mouse continued to play 'his small but entertaining part until just before the final curtain when he made a quiet exit'. Mary responded with a droll statement that the mouse was an Equity member and 'on the pay list for a quarter of a pound of cheese per week'.

She had a brief respite after this with John Boyd's *The Flats*, a play about a real block of high-rise flats with the ironic name of Unity Flats, largely populated by Catholics but close – too close – to the Protestant Shankill. From the earliest moments of the Troubles there had been incidents at the flats: an Orange parade had been pelted with bottles thrown from the block; Protestant mobs had replied by smashing most of the windows and at one point Ian Paisley had felt that his and his supporters' presence outside the flats was necessary and pitched battles had taken place. The play was bound to be controversial, Mary thought; trouble was anticipated at the theatre. The army was consulted about how to deal with incendiary bombs: the answer – put them down the lavatory. In the event the play's reception was peaceful and mostly approving.

The Flats was an important event in the new Lyric's history; a Troubles play by a local writer. Boyd, as literary manager, was determined to find relevant local contemporary plays: when they were slow to appear, he had written this one. *The Flats* had benefited from a procedure which the theatre had long needed – a rehearsed reading of the play had taken place earlier in the year. It didn't iron out all its weaknesses, but it must have helped. Ian Hill liked the documentary element in Boyd's play, but says it required 'a tougher, less sentimental production'. By contrast John Midgley liked the direction (by George Mooney). What many critics did *not* like – the neo-McCooey dialogue – may have appealed strongly to a portion of the Belfast audience. (The McCooey family were the working-class heroes of a long-running radio soap which, at its peak, had as fervent a fan base in Belfast as *EastEnders* has in London.) Boyd's first venture at the Lyric had not been a complete success, but it was a brave, and closely scrutinized, step into painful Belfast realities. The play drew good audiences, large enough for a revival towards the end of the season, and it had the advantage of an in-house designer: Mary had done the job herself.

She was hyperactive in the spring of 1971, mounting her second production of *The Silver Tassie* and preparing some more Yeats for the end of the season. Colin Middleton designed the abstract set for the *Tassie* and 'Mary McCracken' appeared in the programme as director once again. Betty Lowry didn't think this version of *The Silver Tassie* worked: 'Yeats rejected the play in 1928. After seeing it at the Lyric, I'm inclined to agree with Yeats.'

Mary had a brief pause before mounting the third Yeats evening in the new theatre: the late play *Words upon the Window Pane* and her old favourite, *The King's Threshold*. She designed as well as directed both pieces. Reviewing the plays, John Midgley in the *News Letter* raised the familiar point, that 'poetry, however well-wrought is not synonymous with drama'. He says that *Words upon the Window Pane* 'is simply embarrassing in its total lack of concession to the demands of the theatre'. But for him *The King's Threshold* 'came near to greatness'.

On 20 March 1971 the ineffective premier Chichester-Clark resigned, and the ambitious and capable Brian Faulkner took over. His job was going to be difficult. In the early summer of 1971, when the Yeats plays went on, the situation on the streets was beginning to deteriorate into a guerrilla war. Faulkner was already struggling and agreed to a rash course of action, the internment of over 300 republicans and civil rights advocates. This desperate measure failed. Republican reaction was intensified by the fact that hardly any Protestants were imprisoned. Internment was a disaster from the start: for the whole month of August Belfast and towns all over Ulster were rocked by explosions, rifle fire and mass evacuations of denominational groups who feared for their lives in certain urban districts. Belfast was in a state of shock. Some British soldiers had begun to even the sniping tally by shooting alleged terrorists in the streets.

Only eight people turned up at the Lyric for Yeats on the first, violent, post-internment evening. The cast numbered twenty-two – or should have, but one member could not get to the theatre and John Boyd read in for him. It was a low point in Lyric attendances. Between April and September 1971, the audience size was averaging 35 per cent. The American writer Mary Manning, in an undated newspaper comment, praises the theatre's defiance: 'My admiration for the administration and for the actors at the Lyric is unbounded. What with bomb scares and the natural reluctance of people to go out anywhere at night, they have managed to keep going and maintain a high standard of performance.' In fact, by now the Lyric was the only live theatre left in Belfast; the Troubles had closed all the others.

In *The New York Times* Colin Middleton, one of Mary's favourite artists and Lyric designers, confessed to an interviewer that he doesn't go to the city centre any more:

> 'We're all interned here,' he said bitterly. 'You're locked in physically and psychologically. You don't talk to people beyond a certain point. You can't get a perspective of what's going to come out of all this. There's no intelligence, just lawlessness. You have a feeling of being a refugee in your own city. It leaves you so sick and helpless that it drains energy from your work. But it's never occurred to me to leave – this is my home, my own home.'

It would be hard to find a more eloquent description of how it felt to live in Belfast in the early 1970s.

16

Survival

INTERNMENT HAD resonances for the O'Malley family – an uncle of Pearse's, James McKee, had been interned on a prison ship in Belfast harbour in 1922 – so when the internees' treatment in prison was referred to the European Court of Justice and the Dublin government asked Pearse to give expert medical and psychological evidence of their behalf, he was very willing to do so. It took a long time for a verdict to be reached, but eventually the prisoners were found to have suffered 'inhuman and degrading' treatment. The deliberate cruelty involved in the handling of the prisoners – being thrown out of helicopters hovering a few feet above the ground, for example – seems quite close to torture, a word not used in the judgment.

Internment stoked up the conflict, rather than dousing it. Huge numbers of people were now displaced from their homes, moving out of mixed areas to safer neighbourhoods. Jonathan Bardon says 60 per cent of the movements were made by Catholics and 40 per cent by Protestants. Residents often destroyed their homes before they left. Bombings, sectarian murders and sniping at soldiers continued unabated. Despite this chaos the plays went on, doggedly, at the Lyric. The new season began with Shaw's *John Bull's Other Island*, then *Lysistrata*, with Doreen Hepburn in the title role. Mary directed Eugene McCabe's *King of the Castle* with Tomás Mac Anna. She did a ten-day stint at the beginning and then he came up from Dublin to finish the show. The Christmas production was *The Importance of Being*

Earnest, beautifully dressed in costumes on loan from the Gate Theatre (courtesy of Messrs MacLiammóir and Edwards) in Dublin. *The Lads*, a new Irish play by Joe O'Donnell, started 1972. It was about five Dublin lads' consumption of alcohol and pursuit of girls, yet O'Donnell had chosen the Lyric rather than the Abbey for his play's first outing. Alan Simpson came up from Dublin to direct.

Meanwhile the fallout from internment continued into 1972. The Provos, who should have been in jail but weren't, provoked the army and, arguably, gained recruits by doing so. The new year provided the worst moment in the Troubles so far when on 30 January a huge civil rights demonstration was confronted by the Parachute Regiment in Derry. No one knows who fired the first shot, but after 108 rounds had been discharged by the Paras, thirteen local citizens were dead, seven of them under nineteen. The coroner described it later as 'sheer, unadulterated murder'. 'Bloody Sunday made its mark on the calendar,' is how Mary puts it. The next day she got a call from the theatre, '… should we play? I felt we should, and despite the personal feeling of many of the cast, the show went on … it seemed right to keep going, if only as an act of self-preservation.'

The task of keeping the theatre running consumed Mary and provided a distraction from the horrible events on the streets of Ulster. She and Pearse talked about the situation a great deal. Pearse was certainly a little unusual among Northern nationalists in that he had respect for England: 'He had worked in Bristol and London during the war years, and knew it,' says Conor. Pearse and Mary bought into the civil rights agenda: they wanted a level playing field for Catholics in Northern Ireland. To them this was not an option but a necessity. However, they remained constitutional nationalists, always keen for the factions to move along the tortuous, talking road to power-sharing, always hoping that one of the IRA's intermittent ceasefires would become permanent. Neither had any time for the use of violence for political ends. And both knew that their profile was high enough for them to be added to the lengthening list of prominent people who had been murdered. Pearse, when he drove to the Mater Hospital, was careful to always vary his route. A colleague who had not done so was shot at and his passenger – his son on his way to school – killed. One of Pearse's patients, who came for regular appointments, was assassinated after his route and routine were observed by gunmen, and he was struck down as he walked away from the hospital.

At this point Pearse, in his psychiatric consultations, sometimes found himself hearing the confessions of murderers. To give an idea of the levels of fear and intimidation, Kieran tells the story (presumably confided to him by his father as a fellow psychiatrist) of the murder of Máire Drumm, a high-profile nationalist in the Mater hospital:

> One of his patients was in the bed beside Máire Drumm. She had a photographic memory of the fella who did the execution. And Dad had to say: 'You saw nothing.' So, she remembered nothing because, if she had, she would have been killed. There were things you could say and things that you couldn't.

As a known nationalist, and one with relatives who had served the cause, Pearse was seen in certain quarters as someone who might be able to play a part in this new struggle. Conor O'Malley says his father received a visit from 'them' at Deramore Park. When Pearse told him about the visitors he was not precise about who 'they' were, but the story suggests that they were likely to have been the 'hard men' of the Provos rather than representatives of the newly formed SDLP – the party which would have been congruent with Pearse's political stance. 'They' asked Pearse if he 'would be disposed to be part of the struggle. Or in some way might support it.' Conor says, 'Dad told me he listened to them with courtesy and said no ... that whatever the troubles of the North were – and they were very difficult – they did not warrant any acts of violence.'

Mary's autobiography shows how deeply the human pain and the political frustration of the Troubles affected her. She remembers specially the bombing of the Abercorn Restaurant in Belfast (almost certainly the work of the IRA):

> We were in Dublin for the weekend. A face flashed on the television screen and before a name was mentioned, I recognised a young girl as

a past member of the drama school. Her father, an anaesthetist at the Royal Victoria Hospital, was tending the many injured that day, as his only daughter was brought in. The deaths and injuries from this event were horrific. The centre of Belfast started to look like No Man's Land.

———

The season continued, with the English actor Robert French playing Hjalmar in *The Wild Duck*. He was a fine performer who stayed for several years to play major roles. Mary went back into directing mode with *Red Roses for Me*, continuing her exploration of the later O'Casey works, which were largely ignored by the Abbey and considered to be too simplistically tub-thumping to be of general interest. Mary ('McCracken' again), ever faithful to her old company, cast Lucy Jamieson as Mrs Breydon and Louis Rolston as Brennan. Gerald Rafferty in the *Belfast Telegraph* records 'a tumultuous first night reception – the company, all 25 of them, rose to the occasion in a fine production, ably directed by Mary McCracken'. He was greatly enthused by the play which, he says, 'hovers far above *Juno* and the *Plough* for sheer poetic beauty'. He praises a relative newcomer, Linda Wray, as 'one of our best actresses'.

The production was bedevilled by more of what the trustees' minutes referred to quaintly as 'disorders on the streets'. The security situation now had become so serious that the Westminster government decided to shut down Stormont and sent over William Whitelaw as secretary of state to institute direct rule from London. Faulkner resigned as prime minister and there was uproar as 10,000 gathered outside Stormont to say an emotional au revoir to the white monolith on the hill (Stormont was prorogued for only a year in theory, but direct rule was to continue for a further twenty). Industrial action now became a new political weapon in the Troubles. The Protestant power workers showed their dislike of direct rule by striking. This led to frequent power cuts, which left the Lyric with a cold, unlit theatre. The staff met the challenge with Calor Kosangas heaters to warm the few patrons who were turning up and used

Tilley lamps to light the stage. Mary recalls one evening when, among an audience of forty-five, were two well-equipped 'elderly ladies who turned up with rugs and flash-lamps'.

Somehow Mary got through to the end of the season. The Yeats had been done earlier – three plays this time, *The Dreaming of the Bones*, *The King of the Great Clock Tower* and *The Countess Cathleen*. Mary herself directed the first but had quite suddenly run out of energy and had delegated the other two to Frank McQuoid and Patrick Brannigan. Mary's implosion can be explained by the fact that her theatre did much more than put on eight or ten plays a year. There were one-night events and performances of various kinds, just as used to happen in the Studio. Recitals by Davy Hammond, a ballad singer with a relaxed and amiable style, were regular events; he had been entertaining Lyric audiences since the 1950s. There was no reason for him to stop now. There were Gilbert and Sullivan evenings; harp recitals by Grainne Yeats; and John Molloy's one-man show *From Inniskeen to Baggot Street*. Mary took every opportunity to lift the pervasive gloom. She even persuaded the Abbey Theatre to send players across the border to perform a play in Irish at the Lyric. They were apprehensive about coming, even more so when bombs went off nearby at Queen's University, and even in Ridgeway Street itself. 'Against this background the Abbey Players performed splendidly and did the Irish language proud. I think, however, that they were glad to get back to Dublin the next day.'

At home Mary was facing the dispersal of her nuclear family. Kieran passed his finals in medicine, took a holiday and came back on the morning of the graduation ceremony, bearded and scruffy. Mary was not impressed, so he was transformed into an acceptable-looking doctor just in time for the conferring, which was followed by an O'Malley party, 'the only one in my life,' says Mary, 'which I couldn't enjoy because my first-born was on his way to Canada'. Kieran had found a post at St Anne's Hospital in Montreal as a first-year resident psychiatrist.

He went the next day and Mary found the parting traumatic. But at least Donal wasn't too far away – he was still training in England; Conor was finishing at Clongowes and about to start an arts degree at UCD. At least he would be on the same island. Domestically things were probably a little easier for Mary now – fewer mouths to feed at home and fewer visitors from the South because of the troubled times. The stalwart servants still came on alternate days, city riots permitting. The Catholic Mrs Hughes lived in the Ardoyne, the Protestant Mrs McDermott in the Donegall Road, neither area exactly peaceful. Mrs McDermott was the better cook; she baked apple cakes and would often leave Sunday lunch prepared in the oven. She was 'reserved and undemonstrative' and when, a few years later, she died, relatively young, of a brain tumour, Pearse and Mary were shocked and missed her very much. But the extrovert Mrs Hughes continued to battle her way across from the Ardoyne, hardly ever missing a day.

The Lyric was still underfunded, but gradually the grant was levered up until it was adequate. It went up from £25,000 in 1972 to £40,000 for the year ending March 1974. A guarantee was also given, should audiences fall below 55 per cent, which they did in several years. More property was acquired: a small house in Ridgeway Street to accommodate the costume collection, then a larger one to provide a green room for the company and an office for *Threshold*. This may seem extravagant, but Mary's justification was sound: 'The houses were bought at the time for very modest sums indeed and were of inestimable value to the organization.'

Although the administrative and financial side of the theatre were now better regulated Mary still had to choose the plays, find directors and designers, help throughout the year with casting and provide – after discussion with Equity – the necessary backstage staff. She started off the 1972–73 season with a controversial play, *Within Two Shadows* by Wilson John Haire, a Belfast man with a Protestant father and a Catholic mother. *Within Two Shadows* had already been put on at the Royal Court Theatre in London in early 1972. Mary now took the opportunity to present a play showing a family 'caught between the shadows of Orange and Green fanaticism'. Directed by Patrick Brannigan, it is a vivid, sad, hopeless protest against prejudice and Conor O'Malley believes it reveals 'in a way no other plays did the innermost motivations of the Northern Protestant'. Ray Rosenfield regrets that the author did not integrate the external conflicts on the streets with the ferocious conflicts within the family but praises Haire's ability to 'give in the heady, sometimes brilliant and often wastefully metaphoric dialogue, the details of unlovely family warfare that is fatally destructive of personality and mutual regard'.

The season that followed was nicely varied. After the gloomy Haire play came two more works by Irish authors: *Lady Windermere's Fan* (directed by Donald Bodley); then Brian Friel's *The Gentle Island*, directed by Barry Cassin, probably the first Irish play to depict a homosexual couple. Next, more Shakespeare – *The Merchant of Venice*, with Robert French as Shylock and Jeananne Crowley, from Dublin, as Portia. The Christmas production needed to lift spirits and find an audience. Mary had seen a production in London of *Man of La Mancha* by Dale Wassermann. It had taken a while to secure the right to perform this musical version of the Don Quixote story. She put energy into the project because she knew she had the right actor to play Don Quixote: Louis Rolston. Bill Skinner directed. Audiences took a while to grow but eventually they did, and Mary says, 'Some returned time and time again.' And she saw 'people weeping on occasion'. Betty Lowry in the *Belfast Telegraph* was positive: 'Charm and humour, pathos and philosophy, all presented with verve to the accompaniment of familiar tunes – that is what you will get in the Christmas show at the Lyric …' She has special praise for the choreographer, Sheila Wartski, who has the company 'folk-dancing, belly-dancing and fighting with style and realism'. She notes that the cast act better than they sing but reserves particular praise for the 'touching and comic' performance of Peter Templar as the faithful retainer Sancho Panza.

The Quixote story is about reality and illusion. Belfast, as 1972 turned into 1973, was suffering from too much reality. The Troubles were putting off investors in Northern Ireland; the shipyards were struggling; Westminster money was being poured in because there was a need to make direct rule work. Meanwhile, the Provos were doing their best to get the British out of the North. They wanted to make Northern Ireland ungovernable and began to take mayhem to the mainland. Nine soldiers and a mother and her two children were killed when a bus transporting an army family from Manchester to Catterick was blown up. Pubs in Birmingham were bombed with terrible loss of life. Talking about constitutional solutions seemed almost pointless at this stage. Mary and Pearse shuddered as atrocity piled on atrocity.

Later Mary did the fifth Irish play in the season: *Purple Dust*, by Seán O'Casey. She was continuing her thorough exploration of the maestro's later work, much of which had never been seen in Ireland. That was the case with this play, which had surfaced first in the Liverpool Playhouse in 1945, then run for fourteen months off Broadway in the 1950s, then had productions in London, Paris and Berlin. Its merits, however, were clearly not obvious to the Abbey Theatre (the rift with gone-to-England O'Casey was still deep), so Mary's was the first Irish production. It deals in slapstick and stereotype and would have been something of a shock for audiences familiar only with the great Dublin tragicomedies. Pitt Wilkinson, another newcomer from across the water, played the emblematic Englishman Poges with gusto and he, like another import, Robert French, became popular with Lyric audiences. Gerald Rafferty in the *Belfast Telegraph* was enthusiastic; he shared in 'the uncontrolled laughter of a packed house' on the first night. He enjoyed the broad-brush humour as Messrs Stoke and Poges come from England to live in a crumbling Tudor mansion in Clune na Geera and have 'the Irish experience', accompanied by two lassies they are 'looking after'. For Rafferty, the play was an undiscovered gem.

It had been an adventurous season, which included a test of stamina for the company: a one-night performance of *Within Two Shadows* at the Listowel Writers' Week in Co. Kerry. After the curtain-down on Saturday night the players set out on the 200-mile journey, which involved the tricky operation of crossing the border. They put on Haire's gloomy play in front of 600 people on Sunday and left in the early hours of Monday morning to be in time for the dress rehearsal of the next play, *Pantagleize*, on the Monday afternoon. Mary says that the audience in Listowel was somewhat shocked by the 'the language, the bitterness and the complete lack of hope' in *Within Two Shadows*.

Mary's autobiography takes on a lighter tone at this juncture. In the summer of 1973, her theatre was functioning reasonably well. She had been able to announce earlier in the year that the capital debt had been completely cleared. There were still some difficulties: with, for example, technical staff – finding a satisfactory permanent stage manager, a designer and a wardrobe mistress, proved almost impossible. Staff came and went, 'like birds at a feeding station'. Mary had more luck with finding workshop space. An old cinema on the Lisburn Road became available, rent free, and there the joiner and his assistant worked. As a painful sign of the times, it also doubled as a store for the furniture and belongings of those who had lived nearby but had either been burned out of their homes, or felt so fearful of their neighbours that they had felt they must leave. Another sign of the times was the need to employ a security guard for the Lyric building. The post was heavily subsidized but hopes that it might be just a temporary one were not fulfilled; there was still a long road to travel to peace.

Mary and Pearse now led a much quieter existence than in the busy days of the 1950s and '60s. Mary notes that 'there was little social life now … and when we got home (after their nightly but often short visits to the theatre) we usually closed up and watched in comfort the day's happenings on television'. Mary's unease about the political and security situation – and her anxiety about her personal safety – were not improved by the fact that at this point the O'Malleys found themselves under surveillance. They had a rather odd visit from an army officer, accompanied by a young private. Mary describes their interrogation. First, the usual identification questions, then, 'how many cars – colour and licence numbers? When we went out and when we came back? Our family's whereabouts and visitors? It was a minor inquisition – without the rough stuff.' There were queries about 'seeing anything unusual around?' Yes, Mary had seen 'something': a man who each morning came up Deramore Park and returned late evening. Mary explains that the strange man had dyed hair and 'might have passed, to the undiscerning eye, as a beggar'. After the interview Mary found out that, as far as she could ascertain, 'we were the only household visited in Deramore'. But she also discovered that another family in the next road 'had been subjected to the same questions and they too had noted the strange man. Like us they had the prefix "O" to their name'. Was 'the strange man' a member of the security forces or a potential paramilitary assassin staking out the territory? Mary never knew – fear and suspicion were endemic in early 1970s Northern Ireland. This visit from the army was disquieting; so was the fact that whenever she and Pearse returned from a visit to Dublin the phone would ring, obviously checking on something. 'I would always answer: "Yes, we're home."' Their frequent visits to Dublin, and perhaps Pearse's republican pedigree, must have made them persons of interest to the security forces.

17

Bomb

THE LYRIC WAS now beginning to hit its stride as a professional theatre, although audience size varied with the perceived level of safety in the unpredictable streets. Mary and the trustees had now acquired a dramatist-in-residence, courtesy of the Leverhulme Trust. He was a Cork man, Patrick Galvin, a poet as well as a playwright. His play *Nightfall to Belfast*, directed by Mary, started off the 1973–74 season in which the tide of the Troubles was to wash right up to the doors of the theatre. The Galvin piece was the only locally generated play in a programme which was, nevertheless, not lacking in Irish work. There was to be more O'Casey (*Within the Gates*, in its first Irish professional production, directed by Jim Sheridan, later a successful film-maker) and two Yeats plays, directed by Mary. There was more Shaw (*Saint Joan*), *Macbeth*, Molière's *School for Wives*, *The Cherry Orchard* and Brecht's *Schweyk in the Second World War*, which was an Irish premiere. Two modern pieces were also on the menu: Peter Barnes's wild, satirical English hit, *The Ruling Class* and, daringly in view of Ulster's religiosity, *Jesus Christ Superstar*.

Nightfall to Belfast opened in July and ran through August. Mary's cast was strong: Doreen Hepburn, Louis Rolston and Maurice O'Callaghan, an actor who had previously done popular work in the Group and the Arts theatres, supplemented by Pitt Wilkinson and Peter Templar. The subject was grim: life in one of the Catholic ghettos of Belfast. The play did not reflect well on the British army: a boy is arrested and kicked on the ground. At the Q&A afterwards (chaired by Mary), a couple visiting from England objected to the scene ('No British soldier would do that'). Mary had to explain that the fictional incident had been based on a piece of newsreel footage.

Conor O'Malley calls the piece 'a frontal assault on the political system itself'. The play should have drawn the crowds, but in Ulster in July and August there are many distractions, including sectarian parades, so audiences were thin. Kane Archer in *Hibernia* magazine is critical of Galvin's dramaturgy, noting

> vivid and penetrating exchanges between the characters, but these exchanges hardly ever add up to scenes … and such half-formed scenes do not coalesce into a viable dramatic framework. The play holds its audience for other reasons. It is through performances, and the mood created by them, running from laughter to near-tears, that we garner our rewards.

He singles out Doreen Hepburn, Michael Duffy and Louis Rolston for their vivid portrayals. (Conor O'Malley, who was stage-managing, also singles out the nuanced performance of J.J. Murphy, later to become a 1970s Lyric stalwart.) Whether it was the whole Lyric project or, more specifically the production of *Nightfall to Belfast*, which provoked paramilitary action, we will never know. Whatever the reason, by the time the next play went on, the building in Ridgeway Street had become a target for demolition.

The Ruling Class was the second play of the season. It had first appeared in the Nottingham Playhouse, then gone to London. Harold Hobson of *The Sunday Times* had found it interestingly packed with 'wit, pathos, exciting melodrama, brilliant satire, double-edged philosophy, horror, cynicism and sentiment'. Mary had seen a film version of the play and embarked on a long search for a leading man. Finally, she was able, with considerable help from *Spotlight*, to cast the English actor Paul Hastings in the lead role of the Earl of Gurney. In his first job at the Lyric he was to find himself in an alarming real-life crowd scene in the theatre's biggest offstage drama.

Nightfall to Belfast closed on Saturday night. The dress rehearsal of *The Ruling Class* was scheduled for Monday, with the play opening the next day. The late evening of that Monday, 4 September 1973, was mild and still in Ridgeway Street. A vehicle drove up the sloping street and stopped close to the Lyric Players Theatre. It was followed by a police car. Men got out of both vehicles. Inside the playhouse Mary was sitting with Pearse in the stalls, closely watching the proceedings on stage. Suddenly there was an outburst of shouting backstage. Mary says: 'The Security man dashed in and told us to evacuate immediately, there was a bomb. The cast and stage staff were already on their way out backstage when we joined the queue – so quickly that I left my glasses and handbag on the floor.' (Mary shared with her bête noire, the Queen of England, a strong attachment to her handbag. Black, shiny and sizeable, it is her default accessory in many group pictures.) She and Pearse rushed out through the stage door into a lane behind the houses. There they found actors in full costume mingling with British soldiers who were asking people to leave their homes. The residents were not pleased: it was 11 pm and they were ready for bed, if not there already.

As the little band of players stood, waiting, under the streetlights, with the shape of the theatre outlined against the night sky, Pearse began to worry about the family car. Because bomb attacks had become frequent, he had parked it defensively to block off the Lyric's side entrance. Now the suspicious car, which had been followed by the police, was parked beside it. There was intense activity. Men had been arrested and the area was being cleared. There was nothing Pearse could do, so they waited …

Mary's description of what happened next is strangely ambiguous. 'A controlled explosion, after what seemed like hours, finally took place. Smoke and flames enveloped the theatre and there was palpable anguish all round. My feelings were mixed. Escape at last, an end to fatigue and worry; sadness of course.' This strange fatalism is followed by quiet pleasure that Pearse's choice of parking spot had helped to save the fabric of the building. 'The vehicle with the bomb had backed against our car which was destroyed by the impact of the explosion with the chassis ending up on the green in front of the theatre. Our car had served its purpose and prevented more serious damage.'

As they moved back towards the theatre it was clear that, astonishingly, not one pane of glass had been broken and 'in true thespian spirit we marched back into the theatre and finished the rehearsal in the early hours'. The show opened the next night and its crazy, violent satire was popular with Belfast audiences. Only the set suffered from 'the bombers' visit. The delay it had caused prevented all the buttons on the padded cushions being in place before the first-night curtain went up.

The next day the press reports were low-key. 'Only blast damage to the Lyric and houses in Ridgeway Street when the car bomb went off a few minutes before midnight.' In the *Belfast Telegraph* this incident in the city is just one in a round-up of other potential tragedies all over the province. In the Falls Road in Belfast 'a masked man burst into a house … occupied by three pensioners and opened fire at soldiers across the street'. In Derry a man opened up with a Thompson machine gun on an army patrol, putting at risk the lives of children playing in the area. In Lisburn youths who had been stoning taxis were arrested. Such was life in Northern Ireland when the Lyric was almost obliterated.

The bomb turned out to have been a 200-pounder; the bombers motivation was unclear, although they were almost certainly Loyalists. Why a window-cleaner, an unemployed salesman and a joiner wished to destroy almost the only centre of live entertainment remaining in Belfast was not explained when they eventually appeared in court. The playwright, Peter Barnes, horrified by the turn of events, sent from England a warm thank-you letter to the cast, director and crew. One of the actors involved, Linda Wray, adds two first-hand details to the story. 'There was a sort of alleyway up to the stage door and the car was parked there – we didn't know it was the car with the explosives in it and we all just ran past it and up into Ridgeway Street.' After the controlled explosion she remembers going back into the theatre and finishing the dress rehearsal despite the 'unbelievable smell of cordite'. But the show had to go on – and did.

The theatre was still standing in October 1973 with *Saint Joan* onstage when its fifth anniversary in Ridgeway Street came around. Mary ensured that the celebrations would be low-key. She and the playhouse needed to keep as low a profile as possible. It was also difficult to feel much optimism about the next five years in a province where more than a thousand people had already died in what seemed at times like an unstoppable sectarian conflict. The very day of the modest, celebratory lunch, which they had arranged, Pearse and Mary were to feel the impact of the mindless destruction on their own family. Conor read out to them a newspaper account of a bombing incident in Newtownhamilton in Co. Armagh. A fire had followed the bombing and in trying to extinguish it a fireman had been killed. It soon became evident that the house which had been destroyed was Pearse's family home. His mother, his eldest unmarried sister and the housekeeper were now homeless. Fortunately, the house and business premises beneath were being renovated at the time, so the occupants were staying elsewhere. The almost-completed rebuilding work was destroyed, many personal possessions lost and the effect on Pearse's mother's life was devastating. 'It left his mother travelling around and staying in the houses of her sons and daughters for an indefinite period.' This 'lively and purposive' woman who had reared ten children and run a successful business became 'melancholy and bewildered'. She lived on for some years, dying in her eighties, never recovering from the disruption.

Mary's state of mind cannot have been improved by these events. As a response she decided to take a sabbatical year off from May 1974 and set about finding a replacement. This she did – Michael Poynor became director of productions in November 1973, with a view to taking on Mary's job when she departed six months later. Poynor had been born in Argentina, trained at LAMDA, worked in theatres in the Home Counties and was a director of talent who specialized in lighting, stage combat and musicals. He had already given technical help on *Macbeth* and *School for Wives* and now began work on *Jesus Christ Superstar*. He was going to direct, design and light the show. The number of early enquiries threatened to overwhelm the box office; and evangelical drums began to beat in the Free Presbyterian heartlands as the opening approached.

The show was 'blasphemous' they said. On the first night the Rev. Alan Cairns of Ballymoney Free Presbyterian Church arrived with a busload of supporters – not to see the play (thereby avoiding the danger of moral pollution), but to march up and down outside the theatre, singing hymns. The Rev. Cairns handed in a letter and he was presented with a countervailing document quoting Billy Graham, who approved of the play. According to Mary, 'The reverend gentleman countered by saying, "Billy Graham is not God," only to get the prompt reply from the resourceful front-of-house manager Winifred Bell: "And neither are you."' The Free Presbyterians offered 'unreserved condemnation' of the musical and their letter stated that: 'The province has had a harrowing experience for the last four or five years. Spare it the final indignity of having the foulest obscenity and blasphemy produced in our capital city.' This newsworthy opposition probably helped with publicity; the piece was to draw capacity houses for eight weeks.

Oddly enough the next play, O'Casey's expressionist *Within the Gates*, had also already aroused clerical ire, having been banned by the Boston clergy when it toured America in 1934. It's easy to see why Mary chose it. She quotes O'Casey: 'I am out to get back to the poetic significance of drama ... All fresh and imaginatively-minded dramatists are out to release drama from the pillory of naturalism and send her dancing through the streets.' Ulster audiences were hard to wean away from naturalism and the play did not 'dance' for the critics. Audiences, inevitably, were down on *Superstar*.

When Mary went off for a family holiday in Guernsey, Michael Poynor was busy rehearsing Brecht's *Schweyk in the Second World War*. She and Pearse were reasonably happy that the theatre was in good hands and beginning to be financially viable. The state of Ulster was not so hopeful. For a while there had been some optimism, when the Sunningdale power-sharing agreement came into force earlier in that year of 1974. At last some sort of constitutional solution had been proposed and enacted. But the Unionists still objected to any agreement which involved the Irish government. That disagreement took active political form in a Unionist workers' strike declared on 15 May. The O'Malleys watched from afar as the strike was first tolerated by the security forces, then opposed as the workers took control of the power stations and commandeered petrol supplies. Sunningdale was dead. To make matters worse, the Protestant Ulster Defence Association then went on the offensive on the other side of the border. Bombs were planted in Monaghan and Dublin, where twenty-six died. Mary and Pearse spent frantic minutes on the phone trying to establish if Conor and other members of the family in Dublin were all right. This was a bad moment, politically and personally, for Mary: 'With the dissolution of Sunningdale, all prospects of peace disappeared. It seemed too late now for any resolution in my lifetime. In my bones, and for the first time, I felt a certain despair.'

Conor confirms the importance of this moment. He remembers his parents' shock and disillusion when they came back from their holiday in Guernsey and heard on the four o'clock news that the executive had collapsed. 'They felt this was a solution that could have worked, given time. They always had to believe that there was hope around the corner.' But now, with the agreement in tatters, there was very little.

Before she left Mary had made her usual Yeats contribution and the plays had reached their final four performances. But now there was no electricity and no stage lights. This had happened before and been overcome by using Tilley lamps. The cast had transport problems but those had been remedied in the past. There were only eight in the audience the night before the last four performances were cancelled. Mary was not pleased. Had she been there, she says, 'I certainly wouldn't have closed.' She made enquiries: only two trustees had been available at the time. John Hewitt felt strongly that they should close and so did John Boyd, by now labelled an honorary director, who was in the theatre at the time. Joan Evans, the manager, had a difficult decision to make but she chose closure – for the only time during the Troubles.

Mary was still on sabbatical during the rest of the summer. She spent July in Dublin. Her least theatrically minded son, Donal, was about to return from England and take up a post as an optician. He had become engaged to a Cork girl, Eileen Kelleher, and they planned to marry in the following spring. Then Kieran sprang a surprise. He rang up from Canada to say that he was going to work in Nigeria – after a spell of training in London – and that he would like to marry his Chinese fiancée, Elizabeth Chong, in Dublin at the end of December. The Hibernian Hotel was duly booked, but then the Nigerian plan fell through and Kieran, to his mother's great relief, decided to stay in London to do a course in community medicine.

Mary was free of day-to-day burdens at the theatre, but still had to choose the plays for the new season. There were to be two Irish pieces before Christmas. The first was a raw work by Patrick Galvin, *The Last Burning*. Galvin was by now well embedded as writer-in-residence and working with Mary on another play for the end of the season. *The Last Burning* was directed by Patrick Brannigan and had a set by the gifted Eddie Johnston – one of many he did for the Lyric in the 1970s. The play is based loosely on events in Co. Tipperary in 1895, which culminated in the death of a young woman whose husband believed her to be a witch. The play panders to the then current obsession with witchcraft (1973, the year of *The Exorcist*); it is melodramatic but because of Galvin's stagecraft, worked well in the theatre. Linda Wray and John Hewitt (the actor) played the young couple and Betty Lowry said they gave 'unfaltering performances in difficult roles'. The second pre-Christmas 'Irish' piece was more entertaining: *Pygmalion*.

After Christmas came *Rosmersholm*, directed by a Norwegian, Anne Gullestad, who had worked at the Bergen National Theatre where Ibsen himself had been resident playwright and director. There is pride in Mary's account of this production: 'The Lyric cast, with one exception, was drawn from our own company; the visiting director expressed herself well satisfied.' Anne Gullestad impressed Mary with her ability as a director and her appearance – 'extremely handsome, tall and graceful, with an abundance of beautiful auburn hair'. Gullestad wrote Mary an appreciative letter when she got home. She asked for a copy of the 'exciting' play now in the process of gestation, Patrick Galvin's *We Do It for Love*. This was to end the season, but the Yeats had to be fitted in first. Mary stepped out and gave the task of doing three plays to three different directors. One of the pieces was *Deirdre* – with the name part played by Linda Wray who gave, in Mary's words, 'an excellent performance'. Mary did not dole out praise for Yeats interpretation lightly. Linda had been rising through the ranks ever since Mary had asked her if she would do 'a wee part' in 1970. She had not been one of Mary's dedicated amateurs in the Studio, so Linda worked with Mary only in the professional Ridgeway Street theatre.

They seemed to hit it off from the start. Mary spotted Linda in a Sam McCready, Lyric Youth Theatre production of *The Caucasian Chalk*

Circle. She rang her the next morning. 'Would you ever consider becoming a professional actress?' she asked. She was twenty-five, had always been interested in acting and at that point worked for the Lyric's paymasters, the Arts Council. Her friends told her she was mad but she had no hesitation about handing in her notice. She got her Equity card when she appeared as Hero in *Much Ado* in May 1970. She was paid the minimum rate at first but was rarely out of work for the whole of the 1970s. The roles were varied: she played Rebecca West in *Rosmersholm*, Mary Magdalene in *Jesus Christ Superstar* and Varya in *The Cherry Orchard*.

Linda played in classics, new Irish drama and Yeats. She and her fellow actors were sometimes irreverent about the Yeats productions, referring to the annual event as the Yeating Season. Nevertheless, she like the discipline involved in working on Yeats and loved the eloquent words. She related a vivid story of performing *The Dreaming of the Bones* one Sunday afternoon in a churchyard in Co. Kerry as part of the Listowel Writers' Week. 'We did it in long, black costumes with full headdresses and masks, in broad daylight in the middle of the graveyard. The Americans loved it.' She remembered the day with rueful amusement: '*The Bones* only lasts maybe twenty-five minutes and we drove all the way from Belfast, and did it, and then drove all the way back on the same day' (in effect a 500-mile round trip):

> I always remember I was off-stage at one point – it wasn't a brilliant stage and you just hid behind a tombstone until you needed to go on again – and there I was crouched behind the tombstone and all these Americans standing around and there was this old boy, a farmer, leaning on his gate, almost shaking his head and with a look that said 'What the hell is this?'

Linda was sympathetic to Mary's anxieties about the Troubles – 'a very good friend of hers, a judge was shot dead coming out of mass'. She conjured up vividly the miseries of 1970s Belfast:

> Six o'clock at night everything stopped – people just barricaded themselves in, there was nothing happening, bars just didn't open. But

the Lyric was the one constant thing that stayed open and it was just like a beacon of hope, this little unassuming building at the bottom of Ridgeway Street – it just stayed open.

Mary directed Linda in Yeats and O'Casey plays. Linda remembers being intimidated by her at first. 'She was quite formidable-looking, severe black hair, dark eyes … but then I got to know her and there was a softness to her; she had a sense of humour and a good heart and kindness.' In directing, Linda found Mary had 'an awful habit of chewing on the inside of her mouth and when she started to do that you knew you weren't doing what she wanted. You'd look up and she'd be chewing away and you'd stop and say: "Mary this isn't right." And she'd say; "No, it isn't."' Linda would then ask for help, they would talk and Mary would say, '"Try it again," and when she stopped chewing, you knew you were getting it right.' Linda says she will always be grateful to Mary for introducing her to the plays of Yeats 'and therefore to Irish mythology, which I knew nothing about – after all I had a Protestant education.'

Michael Poynor had managed the theatre effectively in Mary's absence but was now 'restless' and was granted leave to direct for Gemini Productions. David Wylde filled in for him, but it was not clear that he would continue after Mary's return. Meanwhile, nothing could interfere with Mary's next project, Patrick Galvin's *We Do It for Love*.

18

Triumph

BACK IN THE mid-1960s Mary had asked Brian Friel to write a satire about Northern Ireland. He declined – he said he was too angry to have the necessary impartiality. We don't know if Mary put the same proposal to Patrick Galvin, her writer-in-residence. She says, she had discussed with Galvin 'a play about Belfast at this time, which would encapsulate the whole situation in the North – a wide canvas and preferably with music'. Mary suggested that Galvin should go into the working-class Protestant and Catholic enclaves and 'imbibe the atmosphere and collect the ballads. He did this so successfully that by the time he sat down to write there was a huge quantity of material.'

Mary seems to have supplied the central pivot for the play – the 'Merry-go-round-man'. She had seen a documentary about Mickey Marley, who had travelled the roads of Belfast with a horse-driven merry-go-round. This had been vandalized early in the Troubles, so the children of the mean streets had been deprived of their occasional treat. In the play Mickey Marley became 'Moses Docker' and his merry-go-round was centre stage. Mary knew that Galvin's first draft needed cutting and some rewriting. It was easier to fix than the second, which 'had difficulties which were eventually resolved'. The latest version was passed on to the chosen actors somewhat gingerly. Mary knew the content was, to put it mildly, contentious, so the scripts were not circulated until the night before rehearsals began. Only one actor showed reluctance to play, but in the end decided to take the risk.

Louis Rolston, the skilled, still centre of so many Lyric productions was to be Moses Docker. Mary was proud that her cast included 'Catholic, Protestant and Dissenter' and three Englishmen, Pitt Wilkinson, Peter Templar and Paul Ridley. The child cast came mainly from the drama school; two children were to alternate nightly in the main juvenile part. A small band had to play a variety of popular tunes, under the baton of John Anderson, a teacher from Methodist College who was making his professional stage debut. The set was by Clive Wilson and was composed of found objects from the riot fields of the Falls and the Shankhill. When the roundabout was part of a scene, it turned its 'good' side to the audience, which could see animal and human heads on the 'horses'. During rehearsals (which went on for three weeks), according to Conor O'Malley, there were considerable contributions from actors, director and musicians. The script which finally emerged was more daring, closer to the knuckle than anything the Lyric had yet put on during the Troubles. The dress rehearsal was a tense moment: 'Had we been mistaken; was there indeed any humour in this grotesque pastiche?' Mary asked herself.

The first-night audience in the spring of 1975 was quiet and puzzled in the first half. The tunes were familiar but the words that Galvin had put to traditional ballads, rebel songs, pop songs and children's play ditties 'would make you hair stand on end'. The anxious director and author were relieved when the second half went better. 'It began with a ballad, "The Men behind the Wire", which somehow got the audience on track …' From then the house responded appropriately to the shifting scene. At the end the reception was unmistakable.' *We Do It for Love* was to be an unlikely, huge, long-running hit: it found a suitable satirical form to express social and political truths. Galvin described the piece himself: 'An amalgam of prose and verse, ballad and dance. No continuous story; instead a kaleidoscopic series of scenes, all of them illuminating the caricature of existence in this part of Ireland … It is, in intention, an elegy and a celebration of a courageous people in the middle of a dark wood.'

The play had eighteen scenes and twenty-three characters who were played by eighteen actors. Early on the audience is told, 'If you hate the bleeding Troubles / Clap your hands (clap clap),' and then, hair-raisingly, 'If you hate the IRA / Then clap your hands (clap clap).' More knife-edge songs followed. A child steps forward to sing the heartrending and savage:

> Hop-scotch – hop-scotch – hop-scotch
> Me Daddy went to Belfast
> Me Mammy said 'Oh, no!
> For if you go to Belfast
> We'll not see you no more.'
> But Daddy went to Belfast
> And Mammy got a note
> We don't know if they've tortured him
> Or merely cut his throat.

In the second scene Moses Docker, the proprietor of the roundabout, talks to a British soldier. Then a sergeant comes in and gives some advice to the squaddie who, it transpires, is called Evans. He gives him a short lecture:

SERGEANT You can't trust these Paddies. Loyalist or Prod. Catholic or Republican – when it gets down to the nitty-gritty they're all alike.
EVANS Pity they're not black, Sarge.
SERGEANT What does that mean?
EVANS I mean if they were black we'd know what to look out for. As it is they look like us.
SERGEANT Evans – no Irishman ever looked like an Englishman. There's a vacant look about them. Look at the eyes. The eyes are the windows of the soul. And an Irishman's soul is like a glacier mint. You can see right through it. When you've been here as long as I have, you'll realise that.

In the darkest scene in the play, we move away from the merry-go-round and watch two very inefficient bomb-makers, Mr Rooney and Mr Gormley, at work. They are using their instruction manual, mixing the chemicals and chatting. The humour is, to put it mildly, black:

GORMLEY As I've said before, Mr Rooney – it's an art. People don't appreciate that.

ROONEY (*starts to make up the bomb*) Ignorance, Mr Gormley. People don't appreciate nothing.

GORMLEY I mean where would this country be without the art of the bomb-maker?

ROONEY Nowhere. Sure it's us that gets all the publicity.

More horribly funny exchanges take place between the pair. They grumble about having to pay for the materials – 'and the phone calls. Every time we make a warning telephone call it costs us two-pence.' They argue about whether the detonator is in the right place, and then Gormley has a riff about the strain of living in Northern Ireland: '... do they realise the strain we've been living under for the past six years? It's not easy making a bomb. It's not easy planting a bomb. You need nerves of steel, a dedicated outlook, and love.'

The second half begins with a remarkable *coup de theatre*. In a darkened auditorium, the spectators are raked by searchlights based on the stage. Soldiers come in and drag members of the audience onto the stage. Then the whole cast sings a song about internment – 'Now every man must stand behind / The men behind the wire.' (The moment when, Mary thought, the first-night audience began to accept and enjoy the piece.) Mrs Castle, a new character, comes in. Her husband, Billy, a Loyalist paramilitary, has been arrested that morning. This is his third stay in Long Kesh, his wife says. She tells Moses that her Billy has been arrested by the eccentric Sergeant Blanche. He interrogates Billy in the next scene.

BLANCHE ... Still in the UVF?

BILLY Never heard of it.

BLANCHE You're not going to be difficult, Billy? I'm not a well man.

BILLY I'm sorry to hear that, sergeant.

BLANCHE Nobody's sorry. I go through agonies every day. I've got pains in my back. Pains in my legs. I'm not well, Billy.

BILLY Have you tried vitamins?

BLANCHE I've tried everything, Billy. But it's co-operation I want. You and me are on the same side

BILLY What side is that, sergeant?

The hypochondriac Blanche, 'the face that launched a thousand quips', is a brilliant creation. In Scene 13 we are in a massage parlour and Blanche, in dark glasses and little else, is being given a massage by Miss Fairchild. 'Press harder, Miss Fairchild. I've had a hard day at the barracks' is how the scene begins. She asks him if he has been to other massage parlours. He says he has but 'I wasn't happy. I didn't get the release I required. Are you getting it now?' she asks. 'I'll tell you later,' he replies.

In the end Moses Docker burns down his beloved merry-go-round. The way it circles repetitively has come to symbolize the unending, vicious circle of violence. As the flames rise up Moses removes his hat and sings an affecting little verse:

> Tears, falling like rain
> Keep out the rain, ease out the pain
> Troubles away, Troubles away
> Troubles away from me.

Then the cast wanders onto the stage and the policemen add batons and handcuffs to the blaze. The soldiers lay down their guns and 'the people cast flags, slogan cards etc. on to the fire'. Then they sing with Moses the rest of the 'Troubles Away' song, ending with:

> Free, let us be free
> To walk in the rain, to dance in the sun
> Troubles away, troubles away
> Troubles away, away from me.

But this almost mystical incantation is then undercut when the bombers Gormley and Rooney reappear and reprise their outrageous song and dance number. The whole cast joins in the finale:

You must admit that we care, Mama
We're taking Ireland to the fair, Mama
We're shooting rockets in the air, Mama
We Do It for Love
We Do It for Love
WE DO IT FOR LOVE

The critics saw *We Do It for Love* as a triumph: 'This is the most important and undoubtedly the best play to have come out of the present Troubles'; 'It was one of the most exciting and moving evenings I have spent in any theatre for a long time'; 'Patrick Galvin's play shows the agony of Belfast'; 'The play is brilliantly directed'; 'The packed opening-night audience applauded the author and cast until the stage was dark and empty. It knew I was in the presence of something special.' The theatre was full for the whole of the run. Mary was delighted that

> people came to see this play who had never been in the theatre before; people whose prejudices might have kept them out. They sat and laughed at jokes against the other side, and the other side laughed in turn. But they did it together and under one roof, and that was hopeful.

Some nights she would sit at the back of the theatre and 'feel proud that here at last we had achieved something which had touched the minds and hearts of the people of Belfast'.

Mary had a timid hope that somehow the warmth and communal enjoyment the play engendered in its diverse audiences might 'influence someone, something'. Sadly, the torrent of violence flowed on regardless. A policeman was shot in Derry the day the play opened; a member of the audience found the undertaker's scene too much and had to leave (she had been bereaved by the Troubles that very evening); one of the children who sang the saddest of songs, 'My Daddy Went to Belfast ...', had actually lost her father in a sectarian murder. In the previous year Mary's good friend Judge Rory Conaghan, a mild and kindly man who had helped her when she was a councillor, had been shot by the IRA on his doorstep in front of his family. She may have imagined a similar fate for herself or Pearse.

Despite these horrors, Mary must have felt great satisfaction that, after a quarter of a century of aspiration, she had made the good popular and delivered sharp, imaginative, exciting theatre relevant to the state of Ulster. When it comes to remedies and solutions the play is inevitably simplistic, having little more to offer than a blind faith that if individuals can heal differences then society can as well. In form the piece is close to a revue, but it is a touching expression of a hopeful longing for peace, a return to the basic humanity eroded by the sectarian conflict. She and Galvin had brought to vibrant life the pain and desperation of the mid-1970s in Belfast. Her reward was to be, first, a visit to Cork and then, at the end of the forthcoming season a chance of touring the piece in Scotland, Wales and England.

The play had caught the moment. How effective it would be on stage today is open to question. The skill of Galvin the poet, the courage to say the unsayable, the exciting stagecraft – these sustained the play in the mid-1970s. In the twenty-first century its rawness may be a problem in a different political atmosphere. But its abundant dramatic life surely makes it ripe for revival.

19

Finale

POST-HIT EUPHORIA did not last long at the theatre. In late May Joan Evans, who had been managing the playhouse effectively for a year, resigned. She was replaced by Winifred Bell, the front-of-house manager who was a rare creature, someone who had joined the administrative staff in 1969 ... and stayed. She became a close friend of Mary's and was to play an important role in the theatre over the next five years. Then came further health worries for Mary. She discovered a lump on her breast; diagnosis took a while and her imagination began to take morbid turns. In the end, the lump turned out to be non-cancerous, but the waiting period had given her plenty of time to consider her own mortality. So many friends had been taken before their time, leaving tasks undone. Mary knew she still had plenty to do: in the immediate future, the transfer of *We Do It for Love* to Cork and the new all-Irish season 'From Farquhar to Friel' to be arranged and organized. Mary was still the unpaid 'trustee with artistic responsibility'.

Patrick Galvin was about to leave the theatre as his Leverhulme award came to an end. Mary tried hard to keep him because he had provided exactly the creative energy and the writing skill which Mary needed. But it proved difficult. So the next writer-in-residence needed to be chosen. Stewart Parker? Wilson John Haire? 'Mr Parker was not interested,' says Mary and beneath the slightly odd use of 'Mr' may lie some ambiguous feelings about Parker – a fierce critic of her theatre but also, clearly, a skilled playwright who would have liked her to stage some of his very original work. There is evidence of some effort by the Lyric to put on a Parker piece. The trustee minutes for 13 October 1975 had instructed the director of productions to 'investigate the availability of *Spokesong* by Stewart Parker for possible production later'. According to Marilynn Richtarik, Parker's American biographer, there seems to have been something of a Lyric charm offensive directed at the dramatist and his play. Mary tried to buy an option on *Spokesong* and Parker was offered the writer-in-residence position. Both offers were turned down.

Parker versus the Lyric is an important theme in Richtarik's deeply researched book on the playwright (2012). Her biography is a sometimes touching account of Parker's development as a writer and the continuous difficulty he had in getting his works performed. In dealing with Mary, Richtarik outlines her earlier activities at Derryvolgie Avenue accurately but then suggests that, to the aspiring young writer, who had studied at Queen's University in the early 1960s, the idea of 'insinuating himself into a private house off the Malone Road for the purpose of attending a coterie production of plays by Yeats, if it occurred to him, would have held little appeal.' There was, of course, much else besides Yeats on show in the Studio – and, anyway, as an aspiring playwright, he would surely have benefited from the relatively rare experience of seeing, rather than just reading, a Yeats play. He was also missing out on a wider theatrical education. (Michael Longley says he has never forgotten the production of *Oedipus* he saw at the Lyric as a schoolboy.)

Parker and his university friends, who included Ian Hill in their number, seem to have had little sympathy for Mary's project. And the young writer had fallen out comprehensively with her and the Lyric when he was sent by the BBC to review for radio three Yeats plays Mary directed in 1967. In his critique he said he was 'dismayed' by the fact that Mary had put on the three plays 'in the reverse order of their composition'. He savages the sets and the acting ('*Deirdre* needs acting in the grand style and it doesn't get it'). His radio script contains a devastating final paragraph, which seems not to have been broadcast – possibly excised by John Boyd, then still a producer at the BBC: 'I have to say that these productions are not what they could be. There's not enough evidence in them that Yeats's intentions and theories have been considered. There's not enough of an attempt to involve an appropriate ensemble style of acting. Attention to detail is lacking.'

A few days after this Parker was unwise enough to submit a new play to the Lyric. Its title was *The Sensational Real-life Drama of Deirdre Porter*. It is not entirely surprising that he heard nothing for two years. However, there is an interesting coda to the story. Denis Smyth, who was keen to stage local writing, spoke to Parker about the play. It may even have had a tentative place in his and Mary's plans for the 1969–70 season. But various complexities connected with the production of *Over the Bridge*, which was supposed to start the season but was postponed, led to Parker's play being dropped. *The Sensational Real-life Drama of Deirdre Porter* went into limbo.

Richtarik's view of the Lyric's record in the 1970s and Mary's role in it is a little simplistic:

> Although she was not on the Lyric's payroll and had no formal theatrical training or professional experience, she would act, in essence, as artistic director until 1976. Her unwillingness, or inability, to let go had an immense impact on the cultural landscape of Belfast, especially after 1971 when she held an effective monopoly on theatre production in the city.

Richtarik then charges Mary with amateurism, citing Connolly's Lyric study. Parker seems to have felt much the same.

When Parker began theatre reviewing for *The Honest Ulsterman* in the 1970s he lamented the lack of local plays on the Lyric stage. He says, 'The occasional production of a Brian Friel play being about as far as Mary O'Malley was prepared to go as a concession to local taste.' (This is not quite accurate; in fact, the Lyric had already done five Friels by the end of the 1975 season.) Parker goes on to claim that in the seven seasons from 1968 to 1975 'the Lyric premiered only three new Northern Irish plays – all of them by John Boyd'. This charge is also wide of the mark. Parker forgets *The Becauseway* (Wesley Burrowes, 1970), *Within Two Shadows* (Wilson John Haire, 1972), *Nightfall to Belfast* (Patrick Galvin, 1973) and *We Do It for Love* (Patrick Galvin, 1975).

That Parker was totally out of sympathy with Mary O'Malley's Lyric is made plain by his description of a 'local' play, John Boyd's *The Flats*, as 'atrocious' – although it was popular enough to be revived at the end of the season; and by his view of *We Do It for Love* as 'a stale, third-hand, vulgar, and soft-centred farrago of cheap stunts'. He dismisses Mary's theatre like this: 'Nothing has ever really come out of the Lyric, in terms of acting or writing, that has been permanently important or that has made any kind of impact.' On the question of acting the answers are easy to find – the list is long and strong, running from Liam O'Callaghan to Sam McCready, from Louis Rolston to Stella McCusker, from Liam Neeson to Ciarán Hinds. On the writing charge, as we've seen, it's more difficult: Mary encouraged Friel early on, but he eventually drifted away to Field Day Theatre Company; however, Patrick Galvin wrote his best Belfast plays when he was at the Lyric; Martin Lynch's *Dockers* premiered at the theatre in 1980 and survived well enough to be the choice for the opening of the new Lyric in 2011. Nevertheless, it is in the area of play selection appropriate to a Belfast community theatre and the encouragement of young local writers, that Mary's record is most fragile.

Parker's own plays took a long time to reach the Lyric stage, but eventually *Kingdom Come* was put on in 1982 and *Northern Star*, perhaps his finest play, in 1984. It is quite hard to discern why Parker was so deeply antipathetic to the O'Malley style and the O'Malley project. His attitude, his flailing antagonism, gives some credence to Mary's constant, but often unspecified, claims that she was disliked, that she faced relentless opposition, that she was seen as 'the enemy of the people' – claims that can seem paranoid, but may have had some basis in fact.

If Mr Parker could not accept the post of writer-in-residence, Wilson John Haire could – but on conditions. Haire wanted to be the Lyric's 'writer', but not 'in-residence'. He was living in London and wanted to stay there, which Mary, surprisingly accepted. 'He did send two plays which were not suitable,' she says. The Lyric's slush pile has not delivered up the plays, so we are in the dark about what she found unsuitable in them. Her view was that 'the association would have been more fruitful if he had come over and stayed with us for some time. It was a missed opportunity from all points of view.'

In the autumn of 1975 the *We Do It for Love* bandwagon, led by Mary, rolled on to Cork. A play written by a Cork man and directed by a Cork woman was always likely to prosper in the city, but its reception surprised Mary. It ran for two weeks in front of 'large and appreciative audiences' and drew more good notices: Fred Williams put it memorably, saying on the radio that the play had 'given us a sharp, sad, honest, funny, frightening, infuriating, warm, unsentimental and, finally humorous insight into the Troubles of present-day Belfast'. He noted that the play didn't offer solutions but that 'right down at the level of the ordinary people who are living and dying in Belfast and the rest of Northern Ireland – there is hope. What you might call "a hope in hell".'

Mary came to Cork twice during the run and with Galvin and basked in Corkonian admiration. The size of the audiences made her hopeful that a UK tour, planned for 1976, would prosper. The rest of the time she was in Belfast helping David Wylde to organize the new season. This was to begin with Farquhar (*The Beaux' Stratagem*) and end with Friel (*The Loves of Cass McGuire*). Wylde did *Waiting for Godot* and then his contract came to an end. Mindful of money, the trustees decided to do without a productions director for a while. Mary, who worked for nothing, could fill in very well. She wanted to direct O'Casey's *Cock-a-Doodle Dandy*, but held off, and Tomás Mac Anna came up from Dublin to take it on. Eileen O'Casey, Seán's widow, was worried that its criticism of Lourdes might cause outrage. Her fears were without foundation, perhaps because Ulster Catholics had more pressing concerns on their minds. Then came Goldsmith's *The Good-Natur'd Man*, directed by George Roman, a Hungarian who was on the point of becoming artistic director of Theatr Clwyd at Mold in North Wales. When he went back to Wales, friendly, reciprocal relations were established with his theatre and the following year *We Do It for Love* spent a week there on tour.

This entire Lyric season consisted of plays by Irish writers. The Christmas musical was *Innish*, based on a Lennox Robinson comedy reworked by Fergus Linehan and Jim Doherty. It had a huge cast, twenty-five musical numbers and money was so tight that the finale went on unrehearsed because when the dress rehearsal overran Mary couldn't afford the cost of the necessary band overtime. The lack of rehearsal did not show on the first night and, with Michael Poynor, the specialist in musicals, at the helm, the show was a success. The next Irish play was *The Risen People* (the Lyric's third production of it featured Liam Neeson, then rising quickly up the ranks). Brian Friel's *The Loves of Cass McGuire* had Ulster's premier dramatic actress, Doreen Hepburn, in the leading role. It was directed by Eddie Golden of the Abbey Theatre who had, for Mary, artistic director potential. (He was to be appointed for the 1976–77 season). Gerald Rafferty in the *Telegraph* goes on at length about the unsuitability of Doreen Hepburn's costume in the role of Cass, the ex-Skid Row skivvy who returns to Ireland from America and finds herself so at odds with her family that they pack her off to an old people's home. Costume flaws apart, and given that Doreen Hepburn is 'too good-looking' for the role, he praises the piece as 'a magnificent drama, full of vision, warmth and sadness'.

Liam Neeson played the role of Dom in the production and during the run he and two other young actors were interviewed in the *Belfast Telegraph* by Billy Simpson. There is a delightful picture of the six-foot-four, 23-year-old – gangly, longish-haired and serious-looking. The interviewer describes him as having 'a Lincolnesque face and a slow, deliberate Co. Antrim voice'. He had got his Equity card two months previously and explains: 'I didn't pick acting through an elimination process. It was the one thing that I could do well and that I enjoyed doing. It feeds the soul.' He had performed with the Slemish Players in Ballymena but the acting bug 'really bit' when he was at teacher-training college in Newcastle upon Tyne. Surprisingly he failed his exams there ('I'm not an examination person') but came back to Northern Ireland determined to make acting his career. Mary, always shrewd at casting, helped him to pass his early exams on the professional stage. He has stood up very well to examination pressure ever since.

By now the Arts Council had stumped up £58,000 to build an extension of the stage and dressing room area at the Lyric and with help promised from the Gulbenkian Foundation, work could start. This meant closing the theatre for two months in the early summer. Into this convenient gap

Mary fitted the tour of *We Do It for Love*. The initial invitation had come from Giles Havergal, director of the Citizens Theatre in Glasgow, who had seen the play at the Lyric 'and felt it could travel'. Clwyd in North Wales, Manchester, London and finally Dublin were added to the itinerary. Not all the original cast and musicians could make the tour; adjustments had to be made in major and minor roles. But at least the newcomers had a short run at the Lyric before they set off.

The first night of the revival in the Lyric in August 1976 was notable for happened on stage and then, more importantly, afterwards. 'Someone got the idea that we should make the evening a sort of celebration of the twenty-fifth season,' Mary says a little ungraciously. She was asked to be there at the end of the show when, in front of a packed theatre, she was feted and presented with a 'fine Wedgwood china dinner service and the obligatory flowers'. This public thank you filled Mary with anxiety: 'As I looked around the auditorium, I thought how foolish to have such a high profile at such a time!' 'Mary McCracken' and 'Mary McCarthy' were just aliases; her cover had been decisively blown and she was fearful – with reason, as it transpired.

The ensuing party ended at 1 am. Pearse drove Mary and Conor and the dinner service home. Deramore Park was a dead end and as they approached their house Mary saw two cars parked on either side of the road, close to their gate. Most of the houses had driveways and garages, so it was unusual for cars to be parked in the road. As Pearse began to turn in towards their closed front gate, ready to open it, Mary says they saw a cord, 'criss-crossed to block entry. Pearse immediately thought of a bomb.' Then both stationary cars began to move forward, 'presumably to press us on either side. Pearse reversed at great speed and I could only think of my precious china hopping up and down on the back seat. The impact of the situation hadn't registered with me, it had all happened so suddenly.' Pearse managed to evade the two predatory vehicles and drove through a gate further down the road and they hid in the shrubbery of a large garden. 'The cars waited around and eventually moved away. After some time, we cautiously emerged and rang the police from a neighbour's house, where we stayed until they arrived.'

The string tied to the gate proved to be harmless, and the police found nothing suspicious in the O'Malleys' house and garden. They went home and what was left of the night proved 'most uneasy'. The incident made Mary deeply anxious. An assassination attempt seems more likely than a bomb; or had it just been an attempt to frighten them? 'It certainly did frighten us. We had no desire to become another statistic.' She and Pearse wondered if had been related to *We Do It for Love* and the prospective tour.

Whatever the reasons for the incident, Mary and Pearse felt they had been 'earmarked'. They were already taking precautions: they no longer had papers delivered and window cleaners had been dispensed with. Their reaction to the incident was to get in a contractor to make the bedroom windows bulletproof. Mary was pleased to be out of Belfast at this point but was concerned about Pearse being in the house on his own. He assured her that 'he could look after himself'. This incident, perhaps as much as anything else that happened, made it likely that Mary's tour would be a swansong.

Mary set off without Patrick Galvin. The previous June the trustees had agreed that when his Leverhulme award came to an end he would start a short contract at £1500 a year as assistant director to Mary. He wrote her a lively letter after he saw the first night of the revival of his play. He is critical of several of the performers, recast from the original production, and says that the present production 'lacks cohesion and purpose'. He confesses that he spoke to a number of people who had seen the first production 'and they thought that this one was better. So, where are you?' He ends quite formally: 'In spite of any differences we may have had you must know of my sincere admiration for you and my respect for all you have achieved. Regards to Pearse and love to you, Pat.' Then he adds a PS: 'I'd say "love to Pearse" too, but I dread to think what could be read into that.'

20

Departure

THE COMPANY SET off on 26 April 1976, with the builders moving into the Lyric the next day. First stop, Glasgow. There, once the raked stage had been mastered (the moveable scenery on castors had to be prevented from rolling downstage), they opened successfully in front of a band of civic dignitaries. At a reception Mary 'got the feeling that they were shocked at this play which seemed to make fun of murder, death and all manner of tragedies. They sipped a medium-dry sherry and possibly went home and thanked God they didn't live in Belfast.' The audiences over the two weeks liked the show but, as Mary says, 'we could have done with more of them'. The daytimes were spent exploring Loch Lomond and the Trossachs, sometimes, whenever Pearse came over, making outings with him and the child actors. She had a strong sense of almost parental responsibility for her young performers.

Next stop, Mold in North Wales. Theatr Clwyd was so new it had not yet been officially opened. Queen Elizabeth was to do that a week later. The complex must have seemed like a sort of paradise to Mary: it contained a 500-seat theatre and a smaller studio; another flexible studio space; a big function room and even a cinema – all a little different to the Lyric, struggling to expand on its tiny site. The disadvantage of visiting Mold at this point was that the new theatre hadn't had time to build an audience. The turnout was 'adequate' but George Roman, the director, clearly rated the cast because he employed some of them later in his own productions.

On to Manchester and the Library Theatre: a big, underground, circular space. Audiences were better here – a large Irish community saw to that. Old friends of Mary's Studio theatre turned up, regular attenders with a pile of programmes to prove it. And then an actor from those early days appeared, Denis Tuohy, who had acted in *Volpone* and *Hippolytus*. He was now a television reporter for the *BBC Tonight* team. The director of the programme's short report chose to film the undertaker scene from the play, which had been the touchstone for controversy in Belfast. Manchester audiences were at capacity.

In a letter to Mary, George Hawkins, general manager of the theatre, called the increase from normal attendance levels 'astronomical' and 'a fitting tribute to the power of the show'. He expressed pleasure at working with the Lyric Players and suggested that they should bring over more productions. Mary adds a surprising comment: Hawkins was 'not to know that I was unlikely to be back. This tour was in the nature of a "last hurrah".' She had made up her mind: departure was imminent.

The next stop was London. Mary had already made a day trip from Manchester to check out the Young Vic Theatre, but despite this preparation the run began badly. 'Vital sound and lighting cues went awry,' Mary complains. Evidently local and visiting stage staff found it hard to communicate. Mary was so disappointed she avoided meeting the many guests: 'Those who appreciated our work must have wondered what had gone wrong, but perhaps it wasn't quite so obvious to the uninitiated.' As the play settled down, there was a leaflet assault by 'The Workers' Association for the Democratic Settlement of the Northern Irish Question', attacking the play in uncompromising terms: 'It utterly misrepresents the nature of the Provisional IRA and it insults the army and the police who daily risk life and limb to combat terrorism. Furthermore … it views the war as a merry-go-round to which there is no solution …' The production survived this verbal assault.

In London Mary indulged in more tourism, kept the child actors out of mischief and saw Kieran and his wife, Elizabeth. Nevertheless, she was glad to move on to Dublin to prepare for the next week at the shrine of modern Irish theatre, the Abbey. Pearse came down from Belfast with Winifred Bell, the Lyric's administrator who was by now a close friend of the O'Malleys. It was a poignant moment for both Mary and Pearse. 'A warm-hearted audience responded with such generosity to the spirit of the evening that we felt at last fulfilled.' The theatre was sold out for the week: the President, Cearbhall Ó Dálaigh, asked Mary, Pearse and selected members of the company (chosen by Mary) and the two children to lunch at Áras an Uachtaráin.

At the end of June 1976 Mary submitted her financial report on the tour and resigned as a trustee and artistic advisor. It's clear that the process of reaching the decision to depart had been going on over a long time. Several factors contributed. The robust health and astonishing stamina of her thirties and forties had deserted her – she now had Meniere's disease, which leads to a disturbing loss of balance. Another factor was the state of her adopted homeland. Since the collapse of Sunningdale, the British government had almost abandoned any hope of getting the Unionists to make any concessions. And meanwhile the IRA remained firm in its belief that it could end British rule in Ireland by a relentless campaign of assassination and destructive bombing. Dublin, which had happy memories for her, and which she had always loved, must have seemed a much more attractive option than a tormented Belfast.

Mary records that in the first two months of 1976 there had been 129 explosions. 'I can remember during a dress rehearsal ... counting about twenty explosions in one night alone.' The targeted killing by both sides shocked Mary; three of the Miami Showband had been murdered the year before; then there were the pitiless bombings in England. Sectarian murder reached new depths: five Catholics killed in South Armagh one day, and on the next, the tit-for-tat slaughter of a busload of Protestant workmen in Rostrevor. The horrors spread, briefly, to Dublin: the British ambassador and his secretary were murdered. And the appalling treatment by both sides of anyone thought to be a traitor to the cause was an added horror. This was very close to a civil war.

There had been another hopeful moment – arising out of another tragedy. The army was in hot pursuit of a suspicious car which ran out of control and killed three children of the Maguire family who were out for a walk. This pitiable tragedy somehow made people in Ulster draw breath.

It was the beginning of the peace movement, led by Mairead Corrigan and Betty Williams. For a while there was optimism, even euphoria, but the country was not going to draw back from more killing. New atrocities happened, and Mary knew bulletproof windows and Pearse pulling the wardrobe across the bedroom door every night, might not – would not – be enough to prevent the life of another combative, high-profile person being added to the statistics.

That was the personal and political background to Mary's decision to leave her home and her theatre and move to Dublin: 'On tour I had time to think. I was now thirty years in the North, our sons had gone; whereas Pearse's family was firmly in South Armagh, I had no relatives north of the border and since my mother's death I had felt a little isolated.' She goes on: 'I had really lost the sense of purpose which had informed my actions in the past. I think I was war weary. In the prevailing political climate, I might even be an impediment to the theatre's progress.'

The birth of their first grandchild, Donal's daughter Klara, opened up a new role for them. Desultory house hunting began in Dublin where they spent most weekends. In Belfast Mary was disengaging from the theatre, going to the plays but not attending meetings. Eddie Golden was in charge and the autumn season mixed Greek tragedy (*Oedipus* and *Oedipus at Colonus*, both directed by Sam McCready) with world drama (Eugene O'Neill's *Ah, Wilderness!* and Brian Friel's *Philadelphia, Here I Come!*).

By now one of Mary's casting hunches, Liam Neeson, was revelling in leading roles. What critics thought of his skills is indicated by the *Philadelphia, Here I Come!* reviews. Gerald Rafferty in the *Belfast Telegraph*: 'Liam Neeson is certainly proving his worth with the Lyric Company ... He has all the attributes of his craft going for him, he's tall, he has a fine voice he is fast moving on stage and his timing is faultless.' In the role of Private Gar,

> Neeson is so good as the 'conscience' of Gareth O'Donnell that, as far as I was concerned, he just wasn't there at all. Yet phantom-like as he was, he carried the whole story along with effervescence, now making us laugh hilariously, now bringing tears to our eyes.

In *The Irish Times* on 25 October, Ray Rosenfield wrote of

> the brilliant startling effect of the first sight of Liam Neeson as the door
> swings back and he cues into the restless mood of the young Gar … from
> then onwards he darts, leaps, coils, his every movement an inescapable
> gloss on every probe into the conscience, every bitter resentment, every
> witty or cynical comment on the uncommunicative father …

The Lyric was unlikely to be able to keeps an asset such as this. Much later
Neeson expressed his gratitude to Mary: 'She gave me a professional start at
the Lyric and believed in whatever raw talent I had. Her love and pride in
the Lyric Theatre was infectious and she became a sort of mother to us all
in Ridgeway Street.'

The Christmas musical was *A Little Night Music*, which did not draw
the crowds, and got into trouble with Equity. So did *Mother Courage and
Her* Children later in the season, the first professional production directed
by 22-year-old Conor O'Malley. His mother cast all the roles including that
of the heroine (her usual practice), which she gave to the star of Ulster
variety theatre, Leila Webster. Conor reports difficulties with getting her
to learn Brecht's lines (in the end they shortened and simplified them),
and with another actor who wanted to walk out but was persuaded not to.
The Equity problems were part of a lengthy conflict between the theatre
and the union, which was certainly another factor in Mary's professional
disillusionment.

She details the *casus belli* in the Brecht production. The old issue of
the cast handling props and scenery arose again. Mary justifies the practice,
in this case: on an apron stage 'the production moved from scene to scene
without interruption … it was patently absurd to bring on stage staff to
set up the big gun when the soldiers in the cast were available …' Conor
also suggests that actors moving scenery helped to fulfil Brecht's desire for
'alienation'. She was outraged on her own and Conor's behalf when Equity
blacked the production. She had seen the play done in England with the
Equity cast moving props and scenery. She checked with director friends
in England and they thought Equity's objections were 'unreasonable'. The

union threatened a strike, with Equity representative Louis Rolston painfully placed in the middle of the dispute, but the Lyric held firm and the play went on. Mary adds that there was a cast of twenty-two, plus some children; 'to finance such a production in the times was no mean achievement'. She did not wish to compromise; she wanted to do 'big' plays. There had been relatively good years between 1973 and 1975, but now the Lyric was in deficit again, despite an average audience of 63 per cent in 1975–76, presumably helped by the huge turnout for *We Do It for Love*. So the budget for a big production like *Mother Courage* had to be scrutinized. Paying for what she thought of as unnecessary backstage staff was something that Mary wanted to avoid.

The Equity conflict, which had gone on since the new Lyric had opened, left her with a residue of anger and incomprehension, which she expresses in the closing pages of the autobiography. She had known from the start that once the Lyric became a subsidized professional theatre, the union would have to become involved. She was a paid-up Equity member herself and recognized its role in preventing the exploitation of its members. 'But I was not strictly the Employer, I was simply a custodian of the public purse, accountable to the Board, and there was very little [of the subsidy] to go around.' Attempts had been made in 1972 to create a special local agreement aimed at dealing with 'the problems facing a theatre with an obligation to present plays of cultural and educational value'. But it came to naught.

As for actors, Mary resented the way the union restricted the entry of newcomers to the theatre by allowing only two cards per year. She liked to hold open auditions as a way of finding local talent. In 1973 Equity objected to these and Mary, incensed, had responded in the *Belfast Telegraph*, stressing that maximum local involvement was the key to the theatre's survival: 'It is … of the highest importance that as many local actors as possible be employed, and it seems absurd that a theatre subsidized by this community cannot employ people from within the community.' She observed the pool of young local actors getting smaller and according to Conor O'Malley, it became harder to maintain consistent acting standards. The Lyric made attempts to increase the flow of younger actors by setting up a training scheme, which would fulfil Equity requirements, but these were also unsuccessful.

Mary had made protests to Equity's head office in London in 1973. The distinguished president of the union, actor André Morell, replied from 8 Harley Street. He was not prepared to concede anything on Equity rates, but suggested that if 'the agreement' (full Equity rates) is affecting the work of the theatre, then Equity and the Lyric Board should make an attempt to jointly persuade the Arts Council to increase its subsidy. But inevitably, Mary would want to use 'amateurs' – hadn't she trained them, and were they not highly competent performers? The gulf was unbridgeable. Mary finishes her indictment of Equity by quoting what she said in a press statement: 'We had hoped, in vain, for some flexibility in the Equity approach during these difficult years.' Some explanation is required.

The 1970s were a period of union militancy and intransigence. Equity in Northern Ireland (actually a branch of Scottish Equity) was naturally keen to provide maximum employment, on the best terms, for actors and stage staff. The union seems to have been determined to make the Lyric follow the rules for their members to the letter. By now the Lyric was the only professional all-the-year-round theatre still operating in Northern Ireland. Therefore, with their opportunities so limited, professional actors in Belfast must sometimes have reasonably objected to losing a role at the Lyric to one of Mary's 'amateurs' – no matter how talented.

In 1976 Mary and Pearse's Dublin house hunting eventually located a bungalow some twelve miles south of Dublin, at Delgany. It was further out of the city than they had wanted, but its setting – with a view of the sea at the front and of the Wicklow Mountains at the back – was attractive. Their old house was put on the market and they searched for temporary accommodation for Pearse, who would have to remain in Belfast because he was only fifty-eight and needed to work a few more years until he could retire. They rented a house called Piney Hills, where he would be looked after by the ever-reliable Mrs Hughes and commute to Delgany at weekends. And he could continue in the role of secretary to the trustees of the Lyric Players Theatre, which he did very comfortably for a time.

Mary began the slow process of disengagement from home, friends and Belfast. They still held their famous New Year's Eve parties, but she thought they had lost some of 'their fun and zest'. At the last one she remembers some of the guests gathering round the television to watch the news; she felt that apprehension rather than optimism predominated. The Troubles had taken their toll of everybody. And a new element had crept into their social life, a dose of 'whatever you say, say nothing'. It had become dangerous to make positive statements:

> I remember being invited to a friendly neighbourhood house one evening for drinks … I was set upon, not physically but verbally, by one of the ladies who disapproved of my lack of capacity to conform. I might have replied but I didn't wish to embarrass my hosts. There was always that slight sense of unease on social occasions.

She confesses that she had lost friends, 'didn't entirely lose them, they just moved to the side a little'.

Nevertheless, Mary knew, as she went around the house dismantling the past, that whatever the present difficulties, here in Belfast she had enjoyed good times. In the garage she sorted through the old costumes and props, which included weapons, ancient and modern. They went off to the Ridgeway Street store. The boys' rooms were harder: 'sports trophies and personal souvenirs; now that they had their own home, would they reclaim them? Where had the years gone?' Mary had an office at the theatre, but at home there was an immense pile of Lyric papers: these she had thrown into cardboard boxes (thereby laying the archival foundations for this book). Mrs Hughes was helping with the clear-out, hurrying Mary along if she lingered over old souvenirs or letters. Eventually all that was left was a huge pile in the wash house. Mrs Hughes attacked this 'with recklessness'. Mary had to keep an eye on her 'lest a precious part of my world disappear into the bin'.

Moving day came. Mary had slept at Piney Hills; she and Conor had arranged to go to Dublin ahead of the removers in order to be in Delgany before they arrived. This decisive moment is the cue for her summary of the Belfast years: 'I was naive, but I truly hoped to influence change. The welfare state had come but it seemed only to sharpen the differences between the privileged and the under-privileged working class in the North. I had much to learn.' She had felt that through the medium of theatre she could make an impact, 'plant a discreet message now and then'. To her,

> the theatre was a great joy. If I worked myself nearly into an early grave, as Ernest Blythe once described it, I still enjoyed the plays, above all directing and living in the world of imagination. There was never-ending change and constant challenge and great artistic satisfaction. And because I believed so strongly, I think, people came with me. At times, I'm sure, they thought I was slightly crazed, but they were behind me. And were it not for the assistance … of all these people the theatre couldn't have prospered. The list is endless – designers, artists, musicians, poets, writers of every description, wardrobe people, backstage staff, audience and backers, friend and foe, to stimulate action when I flagged. I was completely engaged in the process of being in the North. After all, out of unlikely material we had created a poets' theatre together. I loved it but I would have to leave it.

The night before they left, she and Pearse reminisced. They remembered the Christmas cribs at Derryvolgie Avenue. Each year she had been able to persuade a different, and usually distinguished, Ulster artist to design the crib and it would be unveiled on Christmas Eve, carols sung and readings delivered. The theatre would be open every afternoon from then until 6 January so that families could come and enjoy the stable-within-a-stable. Sometimes a choir from a local church would come in; at others Davy Hammond would bring along his guitar. Those had been the quiet years with Northern Ireland, uneasily, at peace.

They seemed very far away in 1976. When the removal van came to Deramore Park it had an evangelical tract on the windscreen. This seemed to offer a safe and sober journey to distant Dublin. At Delgany the move was accomplished easily – no stairs to contend with. The removal men looked 'somewhat askance' at a large drum, inscribed by the Tandragee Pipe Band. It had cost Mary £5 in the 1950s. It had played its part in the Yeats plays and travelled all over Ireland with the Lyric Players. Mary told the removers a little of its history, but 'they really weren't interested'. There were three of them – an older man, a middle-aged one and a 'young fellow'. Conversation was in short supply and they refused all Mary's hospitable offers of food and drink. They departed, still uncommunicative, and Mary finishes her autobiography with a gloomy question: 'I had truly left the North now after thirty years, and had I related so little to my fellow citizens that these three would not break bread in my new house?' For Mary the removal and arrival were life-changing and emotional moments. For the men this was just another day's work; they probably wanted to get back to Belfast as soon as they could. She saw intent when, perhaps, there was none.

Some months after arriving in Dublin, Mary gave an interview to *The Irish Press* which adds a little extra explanation for the move. Questioned about the Troubles she says, 'It is remarkable how we [the theatre] survived. In sense I myself did not survive – where I was concerned a slow despair set in. It was a lonely road for the Lyric.' She also mentions the difficulties with Equity. 'These problems wear you out,' she says, 'and you should only be worn out by artistic problems.' The interviewer must have caught Mary on a bad day: she was rarely that gloomy.

21

Disengagement?

WHEN MARY ABANDONED Belfast ('fled' or 'escaped' might be alternative verbs), she was almost sixty. Her life's work was nearly complete; she would never again operate at the intensity which running a theatre and its offshoots had required. Her daily existence became easier; she became less fearful. She had some minor health problems, but she still had energy to live a full family and social life, a different life in a more peaceful city. She enjoyed her retirement, but there were moments when events a hundred miles away made her existence anything but peaceful.

Mary had physically left Belfast, but almost inevitably she found it hard to disengage from the theatre, which had been her life for more than a quarter of a century. She would speak on the telephone with her close friend Winnie Bell, the theatre's stalwart administrator. Pearse, of course, was still spending time in the North, continuing to tend to his private patients and completing his service at the Mater Hospital, and so was in close contact with the theatre's activities in his role as secretary to the trustees. This arrangement continued relatively harmoniously until Pearse retired as secretary in 1980, although staying on as a trustee.

He and Mary needed a leader to succeed them, someone to secure the future of their theatre. Pearse saw the youngest trustee, Ciaran McKeown, a high-profile leader in the Peace People movement, as a potential successor in the role of secretary. Before considering him in that light, Pearse should perhaps have paid closer attention to an article McKeown had been commissioned to write in 1979 for a celebratory booklet, *A Needle's Eye*, published by the Lyric on the tenth anniversary of its arrival in Ridgeway Street.

In his piece McKeown asks provocatively: 'Can Belfast live with a poet's theatre? It was an outrageous ambition to create such a theatre in the first place, let alone in Belfast.' He praises the 'vision' and 'will' of the O'Malleys in creating the Lyric, but there is an edge to the piece. He sees their 'almost jealous nurturing' of the first ten public years as ensuring 'that a tradition has begun'. He raises doubts about the appropriateness of that tradition: 'a tradition of high standards in a Poets' theatre subsidised by the Arts Council, set in a community containing some who would even regard theatre of any kind as evil, and poetic drama as the most insidious canker of all'. (McKeown was exaggerating the amount of 'poetic' drama then being offered at the theatre. Belfast audiences had already had a Yeats-free year and, in the season when McKeown was writing, had to gasp for air in the rarefied atmosphere of poetic theatre for only three weeks – a small part of a long season.) McKeown had, nevertheless, pointed up an important issue: the choice of play was crucial if the Lyric was to become a theatre for the whole community.

McKeown goes on to examine what an O'Malley-less future *might* look like, now that Pearse and Mary have begun what he calls 'a controlled withdrawal'. He asks why the Lyric is not more popular. He adduces some interesting reasons: the image of a 'private' theatre persists; also, the Lyric is seen as 'Republican'. He believes both Republicanism and Belfast's anti-theatre puritanism are 'nihilistic'. He forecasts 'a wider company of midwives' will be needed if the Lyric's ten-year tradition is to be turned into 'a hundred-year, permanent tradition'.

McKeown was such a key figure in what followed in the 1980s at the Lyric that it seemed important to contact him. He had become so low-profile in Belfast that he was difficult to find, but contact was established, and he provided me with what he called 'a draft memoir on Lyric Theatre involvement'. It differs considerably, both in facts and emphasis, from Pearse's version of the painful events of the early 1980s that were to drag on into the 1990s and which involved a long-lasting split among the trustees and intense frustration for both Pearse and Mary.

The stepping stones towards an understanding of what happened are unsteady. Roy Connolly, in *The Evolution of the Lyric Players Theatre, Belfast*, asserts that the O'Malley influence on the theatre was still considerable in the late 1970s. Connolly comments on Mary's close relationship with the theatre's administrator, Winifred Bell, and notes that 'after 1977 Bell's powers were gradually increased, until she held authority over the front of house, the theatre correspondence, contracts and the theatre's finances'. So, although two directors of productions, Eddie Golden and Tony Dinner, followed each other in the new Lyric in the late 1970s, Connolly claims that 'the spirit of Derryvolgie Avenue continued to pervade the theatre'. This surely exaggerates the local power of Winnie Bell, and also the ability of even as potent a person as Mary to influence the playhouse from afar, although with Pearse still playing his part in the key role of secretary, O'Malley influence at the Lyric was unlikely to wane rapidly.

Connolly suggests that this situation lasted till 1980, when McKeown took over as secretary. As a trustee, Pearse and Mary had seen his potential; McKeown says:

> They were highly conscious of the fact that they were perceived as Republicans, not least because Mary had been a Republican councillor and Pearse was from South Armagh, whereas, not only was I neither Nationalist nor Republican ... but I was seen as an advocate of basic civil rights and active non-violence ...

The choice of McKeown as secretary indicates that the O'Malleys jointly wished to disengage from the theatre and it is likely that they believed that in the journalist and peace activist they had found someone with ideals at least similar to their own, and also someone with the force of personality to ensure the theatre's continued existence.

McKeown was the youngest trustee and had, at first, enjoyed himself greatly, going to the plays and becoming good friends with fellow trustees John Hewitt, Colm Kelly (the chairman) and with the literary manager,

John Boyd. But, according to his draft memoir, gradually McKeown became 'uneasy' – uneasy about the O'Malleys' attitude to Equity; and uneasy about Winnie Bell's frequent conversations with Mary in Delgany. So when Pearse retired from the post of secretary in 1980, and McKeown took on the job, he was able, as Connolly puts it, 'to pursue his work at the theatre with considerable vigour'. In his management of the Peace People McKeown had shown great confidence in his own judgment. As secretary, McKeown believed that change was necessary at the Lyric, and he was determined to implement it.

Tony Dinner's spell as productions director came to an end in the middle of 1980 and Sam McCready, with his wife, Joan, acting as his administrative assistant, was made artistic advisor. Ciaran says he tried to get Sam to become full-time artistic director but could not prise him away from his permanent job as a lecturer at Stranmillis University College.

Robert Hutchison, an English actor who was hired by McCready to play Lazarus in *Resurrection* (part of the Cuchulain cycle) and also had a part in *Bent* gives an interesting insight into how the board was functioning during the 1980–81 season. He came over from London in the summer of 1980 and did the Yeats play, for which the theatre was less than half full most nights. He was also supposed to help Winnie Bell with administration, so he went to trustee meetings. He felt he was not doing as much acting as he had expected and, as a trustee minute from 9 October 1980 shows, he was not backward about expressing his views about the theatre: 'He offered the opinion that the structure and style of the theatre's management showed weaknesses.' Talking to Hutchison nearly four decades later, he explained that the trustees relied heavily on Winnie Bell but did not treat her well. And Sam McCready did not have the respect from the board, which Hutchison felt was due. Hutchison afterwards went into arts administration, where, among other projects, he helped to found the Winchester Poetry Festival. What he saw at the Lyric cemented his ideas of how a theatre should be managed:

Basically, theatres should be run by an Artistic Director (who chooses the plays) with very strong support from a financial/managerial person and a good chair of the Board who has the overview and guides the process but doesn't generally interfere. As far as I could see this was not the model at the Lyric where a self-confident board thought it should run the theatre. I thought the Lyric Trustees had a completely misguided view of their role.

McKeown's first Lyric-changing move was to try to reduce Mary's role in casting. He was determined that the artistic advisor should have the last word on hiring or firing actors. He knew that, through Winnie Bell, Mary was still having some long-distance influence on this task. (It is quite possible that Mary's input was useful, in view of McCready's preoccupation with other projects.) A confrontation finally came about over the casting of Oscar Wilde's *An Ideal Husband*. Sam McCready was involved and explains:

> The difficulty … finally came to a head when we cast Ian McElhinney as Lord Goring in *An Ideal Husband*: Mary objected, suggesting we cast an actor, unknown to us, from Dublin. At this point, some of the Trustees took control. They sat in on an audition for Ian McElhinney and approved of our casting. It was a major challenge to Mary's authority …

At the time Mary happened to be up from Dublin for the unveiling of a portrait of John Hewitt in the theatre. McKeown's version of what happened is that he had felt Sam tugging his sleeve saying he wanted 'help with an audition'. McKeown says he told Sam that it was *his job* to cast actors but agreed to help. After the brief audition, McKeown had no doubts that McElhinney was the man for the role: he returned to the portrait party and told Mary that Sam was casting McElhinney. She disagreed with his choice, but let the matter go.

McCready and McKeown went on to challenge O'Malley influence in another area – play selection. McCready again: 'I was given the responsibility for choosing the season's programme, but decisions had already been made before Joan and I took over.' Sam succeeded in challenging some of these choices and in steering away from the idea of doing Eugene O'Neill's mammoth trilogy, *Mourning Becomes Electra*, 'which runs 5/6 hours and has a huge cast. I knew it was beyond our resources and substituted three plays by Synge, directed by Joan. Synge was on the school syllabus.' (The implication here is that the O'Neill play was Mary's choice; it may well have been, but it had also been approved by the trustees.) In principle, McKeown and McCready felt that remote control was never going to be as sensitive an instrument in choosing plays as on-site management, and was undesirable anyway.

So what sort of plays were appearing on the Lyric stage during the four years Pearse was secretary and Mary was in Dublin? The choices were less southern-oriented than in previous years, but locally generated plays were still rare. In one of the seasons, 1977–78, no Ulster play was scheduled at the Lyric. In the other three years there were two plays by Brian Friel and two by John Boyd. There was also a production of Sam Thompson's *The Evangelist*. So, ten years on from the birth of the new Lyric, no young Belfast playwright was represented on its stage for four seasons. To deal with this, the Lyric set up a playwriting competition in 1978 in the hope of finding local writers of talent and the first winner, *The Dark Rosaleen* by Vincent Mahon, was staged in the 1979–80 season. In the next season *Dockers* by Martin Lynch had a huge success, but by the time the plays of Graham Reid, Marie Jones and Christina Reid came on tap in the 1980s Mary and Pearse were no longer a force in the theatre.

According to McKeown the production of a play called *My Silver Bird* in 1981 'signalled the end of the O'Malleys' reign'. The production looked promising: the play had been written by the Lyric's most successful playwright, Patrick Galvin, and was to be directed – after a five-year absence from the Belfast stage – by the theatre's founder. The piece was to run for a month, starting on 6 May 1981. (This happened to coincide with a tragic moment in the Troubles: first Bobby Sands and then nine other hunger-strikers starved themselves to death for the Republican cause. Sands died the night before the play opened.) *My Silver Bird* used specially composed music by Peadar, son of Seán Ó Riada, and it focused on Grace O'Malley, the pirate queen of the West. Mary directed, assisted by Conor, with Mary still, confusingly, 'Mary McCarthy'. It was sad that, in directing a play about one of Pearse's ancestors, Mary still felt she could not use the O'Malley name.

Well before it opened, McKeown says he was beginning to have cold feet about the production. (In the trustee minutes before the production there is an apology from McCready and Boyd, the literary manager, that work had not been done on the first draft of Galvin's script. It would probably have benefited from their attention.) Pearse and Mary wished to sign an agreement with the Cork Opera House that the play would visit Cork after the Belfast run. The board had approved the tour, subject to a £10,000 guarantee against loss being secured from the Cork theatre. But in a sequence of events that is far from clear, McKeown decided that the tour should not go ahead, probably because he feared the play would make heavy losses. He was stubborn; he told the O'Malleys he needed board approval of the arrangement. He says, in his memorandum, he had reached 'a kind of tipping point'. He wasn't sure whether he should resign or continue. So he rang chairman Kelly who told him not to resign. They met and Kelly made it plain that McKeown's refusal to support the tour would have his backing and probably that of Denis Nichol (the Lyric's accountant and now a trustee) and John Hewitt as well. McKeown now had a majority of the trustees on his side, should the issue come to a vote at the board. McKeown's account of the story of *My Silver Bird*, or 'My Silver Albatross', as it was sometimes called in the theatre, stopped at that point, so the rest needs to be told by others.

In the programme Patrick Galvin describes the play as 'an entertainment rather than an historical drama because, although the incidents and characters are based entirely on fact, I have taken certain liberties with time, place and circumstance'. Patrick Brannigan, who played Grace's jealous husband, says, 'It had a large cast and wasn't a great play.' The quality of the production is also doubtful: the *Belfast Telegraph* carried an ambiguous review, with the headline 'Musical strikes a wrong note'. The review then begins: 'The regular and generous applause of the audience testified to the excellent entertainment provided by the large cast ...' The reviewer, Martin O'Brien, praises the acting and 'the lovely lyrics of Mr Galvin,' but criticizes the construction of the piece: '... there is no theme through this disjointed series of adventures,' adding that although the play does not purport to be an historical drama, 'it could and should have had an essential unity'.

My Silver Bird was costly to stage. Accountant Denis Nichol noted overspending. And the theatre had just given all its actors a 10 per cent pay rise. Money was tight. Mary, now sixty-three, found this one of the most difficult moments of her life. She and Pearse had hoped the play would go to Cork, but when McKeown dug his heels in and, with the support of the majority of the board, effectively cancelled the tour, it must have come as a fierce blow: the director, the author and Ó Riada, the composer, were all Cork people – this was to have been a triumphant homecoming.

How painful for Pearse and Mary these manoeuvrings were, is indicated by a note Pearse wrote to his fellow trustees in June 1981, after *My Silver Bird* had closed in Belfast. He was by now a full year into his retirement as secretary and his note took the form of a sharp memorandum. He feels 'it is necessary to express uneasiness about recent developments and the present situation'. Since his resignation there had been' a serious deterioration in artistic and financial management and control ...' Pearse objects to Sam McCready taking on a double workload and then adding to it: 'Regrettably Mr McCready continued to accept commitments outside the Lyric and Stranmillis College. These included adjudications, BBC work and other productions ...'

This is how Sam, in a 2018 email, responds to these criticisms:

> The date indicates that it [Pearse's memorandum] was written out of anger after the cancellation of *My Silver Bird*, but the accusations he makes ... reflect something much deeper. Put bluntly, during my tenure, Mary and he lost control of the Lyric. The year Joan and I spent as Artistic Advisors was a watershed year, a tumultuous year which saw major changes in the administration of the theatre, changes effected by the Trustees: Colm Kelly, Ciaran McKeown, and Denis Nichol, supported by John Hewitt.

Pearse's sharp memorandum continues with criticism of Ciaran McKeown. He has 'exceeded his power as Secretary and has taken on personal administrative functions. As a result, the Administrator [Winnie Bell] is now not even aware of much that is happening at an administrative level and yet is expected to accept responsibility for business and financial control.' He ends unequivocally: 'Two Trustees [himself and Roger McHugh] no longer have any confidence in his [McKeown's] ability to act responsibly on their behalf. It is quite clear his actions have been divisive – and it is felt that his conduct as Secretary is not in the best interests of the theatre.'

These are serious criticisms. McKeown had got under Pearse's skin like no one else. Marilynn Richtarik's biography of Stewart Parker provides another perspective on McKeown's actions and attitudes as secretary of the theatre. Richtarik interviewed McKeown for her book, and he gave her this account of his motivations:

> Despite his regard for what the O'Malleys had achieved in founding the Lyric, he [McKeown] soon came to believe that their continued dominance posed the greatest single obstacle to its growing into a truly professional and distinctively Northern Irish theatre. If the price of overseeing the Lyric, in what McKeown regarded as a responsible way, turned out to be the loss of their friendship, then he was willing to pay it. In successive showdowns through 1981 and 1982, McKeown led a board of Trustees, split four to three between reformers and O'Malley loyalists [who included McHugh and the Unitarian minister Frank McQuoid] in asserting his own pre-eminence as Secretary and establishing that senior staff members of the theatre should be empowered to wield authority in their respective fields.

In the memorandum McKeown sent me, he admits that in order to oppose the O'Malleys' regime, 'people, including myself, would have had to stretch the elastic of their own ethics in order to deliver an alternative way of working'. This is a significant admission. The next opposition step involved calling a meeting, held in a rush just before Christmas (two trustees were missing), in which a staff member, who was an O'Malley loyalist, was effectively dismissed. Pearse was so angry about this he took a legal action against the validity of the decision as the board meeting had not been convened according to the rules. Not only were two trustees absent but no observer from the Arts Council was present. The case was eventually lost in the High Court, the judgment prioritizing the primacy of a majority over procedural correctness. Pearse and Mary had been rebuffed; the McKeown faction, with its numerical advantage, was now strengthened.

The board's minute books for this period make dismal reading. Colm Kelly, the chairman, and long-time friend of Pearse's (he was a groomsman at his wedding) gives trenchant support to the majority. Pearse trusted Kelly, who had been his colleague at the Mater Hospital for many years, and the falling-out must have been personally poignant for Pearse. After Pearse's death Kelly expressed regret about what had happened. The board's records give some clues as to what transpired but the emotions which lay underneath are not expressed.

After 1981 the O'Malleys had almost no influence at the Lyric. Pearse came to fewer and fewer meetings and eventually just went to AGMs where he would vote against the adoption of the accounts. A sad incident, witnessed by Conor at Delgany, indicates the depth of the rift. During the *My Silver Bird* period Mary had been on the phone to Sam McCready in Belfast; Conor says, 'As I was leaving the house after a family visit, she came to the front door and blurted out that Sam had put down the phone. I suspect that my father had counselled her not to tell me what had happened. He appeared at the door and said unambiguously that it was not a matter in which I was to become involved.' The situation ultimately became so acrimonious that in Delgany in the 1980s what was going on in the Lyric, according to Conor, hung over the O'Malley ménage like 'a dark cloud and they didn't discuss it. They would have rows, so they parked it. It was not a solvable problem.'

In 1982 Leon Rubin, a graduate of the RSC, was appointed artistic director of the Lyric. McKeown was delighted with the relationship that developed between himself as secretary and the new director: 'I hardly had to tell him that he was responsible for the hiring and firing of actors and on the other hand he understood that I had a responsibility that each season must end with the financial ability to plan the following season.' Rubin began to mend fences with young Ulster writers and McKeown speaks with pride of the plays of Stewart Parker, Martin Lynch, Graham Reid and Christina Reid taking their place on the Lyric stage. David Grant, in *Stepping Stones:*

The Arts in Ulster, 1971–2001, says that the emergence of this rich vein of playwriting talent made the 1980s 'a golden age' at the Lyric. McKeown felt great satisfaction when a play as good as Parker's *Northern Star* went on at the theatre.

Mary's relationship with local writers – or the lack of it – has been noted from very early on in the Lyric. But it is simplistic to see the rush of strong Ulster plays in the 1980s as the bursting of a dam after Mary and Pearse's departure from the Lyric. In truth, apart from Stewart Parker, the playwrights who became big names in the 1980s did not offer their work while she was in post at the Lyric, and only to a limited extent during her twilight period of 'influence' in the late 1970s. This point is illustrated by an interesting exchange in the Dublin press in April 1982, when one of the new Ulster dramatists blames Mary (now six years on from her official role at the Lyric) for frustrating the 'Protestant writers'. In an interview in the *Irish Press* with Nell McCafferty, Graham Reid had complained that his plays are not produced in the North or at the Lyric. He says: 'Mary O'Malley, director of the Lyric [*sic*] says she won't produce plays which have been premiered in the South. On the other hand she won't premiere mine in the North. Catch 22. None of the Protestant playwrights has been produced by her, so we all come South.'

Mary's reply in the letters column of the *Irish Press* is spirited and sharp. She says unequivocally that Reid's statements are 'contrary to the facts and need to be corrected'. She begins with a body blow, explaining that plays come mainly to the Lyric's Literary Advisor, the 'Northern Protestant', John Boyd. She then lands a series of further punches: *Won't produce plays which have been premiered in the South?* 'Totally untrue. While I was artistic director, several plays by Brian Friel were presented at the Lyric, following their initial Dublin production.' *Won't premiere my play in the North?* 'Again untrue. As far as I am aware the Lyric did not at any stage receive a play for consideration from Mr Reid.' *None of the Protestant playwrights have been produced by her, so we all come South?* 'Totally untrue. Plays from the following "Protestant playwrights" were presented during my time at the Lyric – Sam Hanna Bell, John Boyd, Sam Thompson and Wilson John Hare.' This is skilful defensive footwork, but the query over Mary's ability to nurture Ulster writing remains.

In the late 1980s the Lyric's still-divided board had a new set of problems to deal with. The Arts Council had supported the theatre since 1968, cleared debts when audiences were reduced by trouble on the streets – or plays some way from popular taste – and paid for extensions of the theatre. But in the mid-1980s the Council took on more commitments and the Lyric's financial place in the sun was threatened. It had to compete with new theatre companies, which the Arts Council had decided to support – among them Field Day and Charabanc. And the Council had spent £3 million refurbishing the Grand Opera House. Not surprisingly the Lyric's grant fell by 20 per cent in real terms. This caused such problems that in one season the theatre went dark from mid-April until the following September – an unprecedented hiatus.

The question of the Yeats commitment continued to hang over the theatre. In the early 1980s the artistic director, Leon Rubin, had tackled the issue head on, writing to the trustees in uncompromising terms:

> I think we should reconsider the accepted practice of mounting a full-scale Yeats production every season. I am not anti-Yeats; on the contrary I would like to see him celebrated and brought to life. The ritual performance every year of a Yeats play to an empty auditorium by a demoralised cast is the worst possible way to keep this tradition alive … Why should we lose seven or eight thousand pounds on a Yeats play, just because that has always been the case?' Rubin suggests that there are other ways of honouring Yeats – through readings, poetry recitals, lectures, rehearsed readings of plays …

The relatively poor audiences for Yeats need some explanation. A guess might be that the plays are far from the realism, the comedy, the traditional naturalistic forms, which the bulk of Belfast audiences seemed to like. Yeats is demanding, the language mixes obscurity with beauty, there is minimal action – all a long way from 'entertainment'. Connolly quotes from an interview with a Belfast taxi driver about what was on at the Lyric in the

1970s: 'A load of bloody rubbish … heavy stuff. Morbid Irish stuff. With our Troubles we want a bit of musical comedy, not more bloody troubles.'

Doing the plays was a symbol of Mary's devotion to the Irish Literary Revival, to the Yeats canon and to an all-Ireland cultural vision. She was able to develop this vision at Derryvolgie Avenue and made it almost her trademark. She took it with her, as an accepted tradition, to Ridgeway Street and strove to keep it alive there, until her influence ceased. When she was not there to schedule and often direct Yeats productions, urgent answers were needed for the questions reasonably asked by Leon Rubin. Even when the plays were done with skill and devotion by Sam McCready, it was plain that their lack of popular appeal in Belfast was unlikely to change. So from the early 1980s the Lyric became almost a Yeats-free area. From 2007 the theatre's constitution no longer required an annual Yeats production. None of the above should minimize Mary's astonishing achievement in giving theatrical life and frequent exposure, over two decades, to twenty-six extraordinary plays, the best of which can provide deeply satisfying drama.

———————

The long administrative nightmare of the split trustees finally came to an end in the early 1990s. The trust was reconstituted and later became a company limited by guarantee in 2007. All shareholdings were abolished. The theatre had zigzagged forward into the present century, going through multiple crises and reassessments, employing numerous artistic directors, shedding pieces of the O'Malley legacy as it went (like the Lyric's harp logo, known as the Motif, and 'Players' from its title), and at one stage surviving a threat of being moved lock, stock and barrel to the Grand Opera House.

Conor O'Malley was close to his parents in Dublin: he had directed at the Lyric and shared his mother's beliefs about the practice and purpose of theatre. Although busy himself with work and family, in the 1980s he was able see the rationale behind his parents' behaviour and how the conflicts which arose affected them. When his mother first arrived in Dublin he says she was 'not really accepting mentally that she is fully finished with theatre life and perhaps gossiping with Winnie (Bell) as friends do, and offering views and advice, as those who are natural leaders will do to address problems'. But Conor believes that Pearse knew that Mary needed to be out of the picture at the Lyric, and that Pearse himself strongly wished to step away – leaving the theatre in safe hands. On McKeown, Conor sees his father as being horrified when he found out that the man from the Peace People was far from being the safe pair of O'Malley-friendly hands he had hoped for, but 'he had no one but himself to blame as *he* had brought him in'.

This account of the Fall of the House of O'Malley emphasizes Pearse and Mary's pain. It is reasonable to ask what gain there was from the McKeown revolution. The answer is that, despite a succession of life-threatening financial alarms, the theatre survived to become – to put it perhaps a little grandly – one of Northern Ireland's arts institutions. The new regime showed as much determination to keep the Lyric alive as the O'Malleys had done. And the departure of the founders gave the theatre a new neutrality; it no longer had a perceived political affiliation – the socialist, republican, national anthem *refusenik* was not in residence anymore. It could become a *Belfast* theatre – free to be shaped, and reshaped, in the image of the artistic directors, the playwrights and the cast and crew who came through the door, perhaps glancing briefly at the bronze head of the woman who had started it all, before setting down to work.

22

Retirement

BEFORE THE O'MALLEYS could wholeheartedly enjoy the sea air on the Wicklow coast they had to bear another disappointment. Not long after arriving in Dublin, encouraged by Conor, Mary put into action a plan that had been in her mind for some time: to create something like a second Lyric theatre, in Dublin. Before she left Belfast she had taken the trouble to get the board to agree to her proposal. Conor drove the idea forward and in 1978 they leased the sizeable Pavilion Theatre in Dún Laoghaire, five or six miles away from the city centre, and put on four productions: two vintage plays, Boucicault's *The Colleen Bawn* and Lennox Robinson's *The Far-off Hills* and two contemporary pieces, *We Do It for Love* and Tom Coffey's *Sink or Swim*. In the cavernous former cinema, which could seat a thousand, audiences began as low as forty but were moving slowly upwards, towards a hundred by the end of the season. Money was lost – so much so that before the final play the actors were paid off, with a view to cancellation, but then emergency funding arrived from the Arts Council and, although they could have taken the money and run, all the actors came back and played their parts in the final play, *The Colleen Bawn*.

Conor remembers the season ruefully: 'The concept was to create a double Lyric, north and south, but it was overreach, big-time. It was a financial disaster. Budgets were not exceeded, but audience projections just did not materialize. It was a real wake-up call for what's in your head and what can actually occur.' Despite the public's indifference, he thought Mary had not lost her touch as a director. 'The Lennox Robinson play, *The Far-off Hills* ... was beautifully done – lightness of touch, excellent casting, a splendid production. She was still well able to direct, once she was given the opportunity.' But he felt personally chastened. His production of *Sink or Swim* opened the season and his *The Colleen Bawn* had closed it. Still in his early twenties, he had felt he needed to do things in incremental steps, but that it has been sink or swim for him too with the Pavilion venture. 'It [the Pavilion season] was a lifelong lesson for me and it was also, effectively, the end of her career. But at least we had shown that the Pavilion stage had some potential as a home for professional theatre.'

———

Despite the distress this setback and the events in Belfast mentioned earlier must have caused, generally Mary and Pearse had the pleasant, thoroughly normal, retirement they had probably hoped for. Their bungalow, Derabeag, was further out from Dublin's city centre than they had intended but still within easy reach of two of their sons' homes. The garden was sizeable and the whole ensemble ideal for entertaining children, which the grandparents did with enthusiasm. Donal, an optician, and his wife Eileen, a teacher, had a family of four: Klara, Rory, Terry and Anna. Conor, a civil servant, and Sara, a teacher and town planner, had three: Evelyn, Eoghan and Clare. Kieran and Elizabeth, a theatre executive, lived in Canada in the 1980s and 1990s and also had three children; naturally the grandparents saw less of Daragh, Nora and Brendan. Kieran's career (as a psychiatrist and sometime theatre director) was much more peripatetic than that of his siblings. When he and his family were in Canada, Mary and Pearse came out to see him. Kieran's wife, Elizabeth, was Chinese and 'Mum struggled with the mixed-race marriage – Dad was better,' says Kieran. 'The different culture fazed her. Mum was very conservative about food. Dad was too ... but he would try ... Dad was, after all, in a service industry and you just had to connect with whoever came in the door.'

Because they had infinitely more time than they ever had for their own children – especially after Pearse retired fully and came back to Dublin – they were able to enjoy being active, hands-on grandparents. Kieran remembers how Pearse, especially, took to the role. The rather un-tactile father 'became metamorphosed – as a grandfather he was holding kids'. Kieran is convinced that both his parents felt immense relief to be out of the North.

Mary was as good at children's parties as she was at adult festivities; junior events were frequent and every Christmas she would organize a crib and a nativity play in which all participated. In 1986 the Christmas play was *The Mistletoe Bough*. The surviving script is contained in an exercise book into which the printed version has been cut and pasted along with professional-looking lists relating to sets, costumes, casting, etc. The grandchildren could not have failed to acquire some skills when performing quite a complex, forty-minute musical. The Christmas play was much loved, and this piece of theatrical nurture, as well as the thespian genes which came down from Mary, may have had something to do with the fact that three out of the ten grandchildren now have careers related to the stage.

In Dublin Mary and Pearse were able to entertain friends, for meals or visits, something which had become increasingly rare and difficult over the previous decade in Belfast. There are plenty of letters from their friends in the archive. John and Elizabeth Boyle had encouraged Mary to dive into politics and had also been involved with the Derryvolgie Avenue beginnings. After they moved to Canada in the 1960s, Mary had kept in touch by letter and they came to Delgany for a visit in 1990. Years before, the Boyles had given the O'Malleys a Colin Middleton painting before they left Belfast. Three decades later it had become extremely valuable and Pearse and Mary offered it back. The offer was refused, and Elizabeth's thank-you letter after the visit was warm: 'Again Mary thanks for all you have done for us, not just on our visit but in the past.' Ties were also re-established with another family, the Brookes. Presents had been sent by Mary; Arthur Brooke came over from Wales to stay in August 1991 (Florence had died in 1987). The rift had obviously been healed. Mary also had visits from theatre friends including Robert French and Louis Rolston. A painful bereavement came with the death of the long-time and loyal trustee of the Lyric, Roger McHugh, in 1987.

Maeve McGibbon and Wolsey Gracey as Rosie and Fluther in *The Plough and the Stars*. Studio 1966. NUIG

Sam McCready as Captain Boyle and Louis Rolston as Joxer in *Juno and the Paycock*, directed by Mary. Studio 1965. NUIG

Smock Alley, (or *The Fortunes of an 18th Century Theatre*), a historical musical entertainment devised by Mairin Charlton. From left Joan McCready, Sam McCready and Maureen Ashe. 1967. NUIG

Source abbreviations: **O'MFA** = O'Malley family archive   **NUIG** = National University of Ireland, Galway

Terence Nonweiler, powerful Lyric actor in the lead role as Seanchan, Yeats's *The King's Threshold*. 1961. NUIG

Erna Kennedy as the Dancer in Yeats's *The Death of Cuchulain*. Movement choreographed by Helen Lewis. 1965. Photograph by George Mooney. O'MFA

Frank McQuoid, another stalwart Lyric actor (later a trustee) as The Greek in *The Resurrection*. 1968. NUIG

Mary's heroic Yeats style in *The Resurrection*, last night Studio theatre. 1968. NUIG

Austin Clarke lays the foundation stone for the new theatre at Ridgeway Street, 12 June 1965. NUIG

The foundation stone is set in place during construction works at Ridgeway Street, spring 1968. On the stone the sculptor, Michael Biggs, had carved Yeats's words 'Look Up in the Sun's Eye'. NUIG

The last night at Derryvolgie Avenue in June 1968. Among the Lyric Players, their friends and associates is Mary in the middle of the balcony with Sam McCready on her right, and Alice Berger Hammerschlag and Helen Lewis on her left. The indomitable Mrs Hughes is in a sleeveless dress, in the front, far right. Behind Mrs Hughes is director Denis Smyth; to her right George Mooney, Lyric actor, director and chronicler. 1968. NUIG

The Lyric Board crisis in 1969/70: four trustees have resigned. Rowel Friers has them leaving what may be a sinking ship. O'MFA

The madhouse scene from *Peer Gynt*, directed by Mary with Louis Rolston, third from right, and Patrick Brannigan (Peer) extreme right, at new Lyric. 1971. O'MFA

Threshold No. 23 – Colin Middleton's cover for a special Northern Crisis issue. Issue edited by John Montague. 1970. NUIG

John Hewitt as paramilitary Billy Castle in the huge hit, Patrick Galvin's *We Do It for Love*. 1975. NUIG

Mrs Ellis, Mrs Ryan and Mrs Castle, played by (*left to right*) Sheila McGibbon, Trudy Kelly and Linda Wray in *We Do It for Love*. 1975. NUIG

Cast of *We Do It for Love* outside Abbey Theatre. 1976. Mary in front, with her characteristic handbag. Winne Bell, theatre manager and ally on her right, also with handbag. The children are Sharon Smyth and Michelle Neeson. Liam Neeson is fourth from right. NUIG

Leila Webster in the lead role in Brecht's *Mother Courage*. 1977. NUIG

Stella McCusker leads in John Boyd's *The Street*. 1977. NUIG

Liam Neeson as Mr Hardress with Margaret McCann as the Colleen Bawn in Dion Boucicault's *The Colleen Bawn*. 1977. NUIG

Mary and Pearse in the early 1980s with (then) eight grandchildren in their garden in Delgany, Co. Wicklow. *From left to right* – Terry, Evelyn, Klara, Nora (on Pearse's lap), Eoin (on Mary's lap), Anna, Darragh and Ruaídhri. Yet to be added are Clare and Brendan. o'mfa

Mary had kept in touch with the poet and diplomat Val Iremonger during her early years in Belfast. By the 1950s his letters had become more decorous (he had stopped calling her 'baby face'), but they were still amusing. He was working in London and noted 'Brendan Behan has taken London – and us – by storm. Dylan Thomas is only trotting after him.' In another letter he eloquently refused to write an article for *Threshold*. His time is limited, he says, to 'the office, necessary social engagements (how I hate them), and trying to teach the children a bit of Irish and Irish history... I concentrate entirely on poetry to the exclusion of everything else'. Diplomatic postings in Scandinavia, New Delhi and Luxembourg followed London. By the 1990s he was back in Dublin and, like Mary, not in good health. His wife, Sheila, writes saying he enjoyed reading her autobiography, 'but he just wasn't up to writing a letter'. He died, aged seventy-three, in May 1991.

Contact with old friends, holidays abroad and private entertaining took a fair share of Mary's retirement time. But public service still had its appeal. She was involved at the Abbey where she was a shareholder. At one stage she became particularly exercised by what she saw as the underuse of the resident Abbey company. She was persistent: at one point she demanded an explanation, 'in layman's language', of the proposed new Abbey constitution. She relished the theatre's sometimes turbulent politics, often making a formidable alliance with Ulick O'Connor. According to Kieran he and Mary became 'bosom-buddies'; he inscribed a book for her: to his friend 'who like myself has fought against the dying of the light'. Mischievous rebel as he was, O'Connor may have encouraged her to make a major change to her image. The dark, elegant, Celtic lady of the Lyric suddenly went blonde for a time. Her hair might change colour but her fidelity to the Lyric family did not waver; she proposed one Eugene Downes as a potential Abbey shareholder. He just happened to be the son of Neil Downes, the architect who had designed the first version of the new Lyric and with whom she now had friendly meetings in Dublin.

Mary also did some broadcasting. Back in 1988 she was asked to do three *Thought for the Day* talks on BBC radio. They were touching, elegiac and lyrical, one talk focusing on the early death of her niece, Anne.

She finished it like this: 'Today a sapling fell outside my window and I thought of Anne, and the little boots, and her will to life.' She also took on more traditionally feminine activities. She was a member of the International Women's Club, with whom she watched demonstrations of French cookery and visited the Abbey and an ESB power station. She also organized a huge fundraiser, the Golden Fête. This involved marshalling twenty-two helpers, finding large numbers of empty biscuit tins and entering into a bond for £100.

Mary and Pearse also combined for the O'Malley clan rallies, which Pearse and a sometimes-reluctant Mary had been attending since the 1950s. He had been elected chief of the clan at the fourth annual rally back in 1956. These O'Malley events were centred on Clare Island, off the coast of Co. Mayo in the West of Ireland. The island was the home of the legendary Grace O'Malley, whose story Patrick Galvin had told in *My Silver Bird*. Early expeditions of Clan O'Malley to Clare Island sometimes involved travel on a rickety boat in choppy seas to the rocky isle where mass would be said. However, by the 1980s it was easier to get to the island and a fully functioning clan association had been formed. Its aims were to foster friendship, hold an 'annual clan rally', investigate the history of the O'Malleys and try to preserve the buildings associated with the clan. Conor remembers: 'Every year all the grandchildren would go ... and Dad would make speeches. In June you would go off to this – all round the west of Ireland.'

Pearse was able to find time to do what *he* wanted to do. He compiled all his writings for medical journals in a single book. He wrote a memoir of his youth in Newtownhamilton. He kept up with his relatives, sometimes going North to play poker with them. He paid attention to northern politics and was delighted when Conor was sent as a civil servant to Armagh, just a few miles from Pearse's birthplace, to help the North/South Ministerial Council implement the Good Friday agreement.

In the early '90s Mary was honoured at the Lyric. Eddie Johnston, one of the theatre's best designers, had noted in a letter to the *News Letter* on 11 April 1988 that the Lyric had no portrait or image of her. He says the lack of a portrait is 'a glaring and sad omission'. He goes on: 'I know that Mary was not the easiest person to have dealings with ... but women of her calibre to my knowledge are strong-willed and consequently rather autocratic at times. Nevertheless, she made an inspiring effort to make her aspirations come true, and the Lyric, so far, has not acknowledged this wonderful effort …'

Nothing happened until, in December 1990, Deborah Brown, the distinguished Ulster artist who had designed many sets for Mary in the Studio, wrote to her in Dublin, noting the absence of a portrait and making a suggestion:

> I would like to see a bronze head of you in the foyer and feel that your friends should raise the money to commission it. Would you be willing to allow Philip Flanagan to do a portrait bust of you in bronze? He is a very good sculptor and has just finished a fine head of Seamus Heaney. Would you let me know what you feel about this?

Flanagan was the son of Sheelagh Flanagan (née Garvin), one of the original Ulsterville House actors. Mary was pleased to accept: 'I am greatly flattered by your kind thought and of course it would be splendid to have it done by Philip Flanagan, Pearse's godchild.' But then comes a telling sentence: 'I am not too sure about the Lyric, though – they may not welcome the idea. It might be as well to check.' (The administrative stand-off among the trustees was still going on.) The bust was duly commissioned, completed and unveiled on 27 March 1993. It has been on display in the theatre ever since. Mary was delighted, but her friends in the North must have been aware that at the unveiling she was only half-present. Dementia had been slowly encroaching since 1990.

Fortunately, she managed to write her autobiography before the illness took hold. Friends had been constantly encouraging her to write her life story. After all she had a huge archive of papers; in theory all she had to do was to put this lavish supply of raw material into some sort of order. She got down to it in the late 1980s and kept at it until *Never Shake Hands with the Devil* was published in 1990 by Elo Publications in Dublin. She wrote it at home and also worked on it at Annaghmakerrig, the writers' retreat located at Sir Tyrone Guthrie's old house in Co. Monaghan. The finished book stops in 1976, just before this chapter begins. Conor says that she came to a halt then because the rest of the Lyric story was too difficult for her to tell. The book is quite discreet: she does not name enemies (Ian Hill, for example, escapes without a mention) but she sometimes omits – the Helen Lewis conflict is an example.

Mary achieved a great deal in what was still, largely, a man's world, but the book avoids almost entirely any reference to feminism. She prefers to complain about the Unionists rather than grumble about male power and privilege or glass ceilings. She is a person, who happens to be a woman, who has an agenda to get through, which she mostly does. She is not daunted by male power; she combatively takes on males who oppose her although, in doing so, she may have felt that being female made it necessary for her to be tough and outspoken, if she was going to get what she wanted. Her book makes it plain that she had little doubt that she could 'have it all' – if she worked hard enough. So she took on without hesitation entertaining, directing, managing a theatre, mothering, running a household, editing a magazine, creating new organizations – here a gallery, there a shop or a drama school or a music academy. She just knew what she wanted to do and did it – with huge support, she acknowledges, from Pearse and her reliable domestic help.

Although Mary did not emphasize it in her memoir, a key factor in the viablilty of the Lyric as an emergent institution lay with female relationships that were sustained during the 1960s and 1970s. As well as the formidable ladies who kept Mary's home going, and made it possible for her to dedicate herself to her theatre, there were also close relationships with women who played major administrative and artistic roles in the Lyric. On the administrative side, there was Joan Evans who was secretary in Irish Handcrafts and for a period general manager in the Lyric in Ridgeway Street; another was the Lyric's charismatic caretaker, Marie Annett, later OBE, to whom Mary was intensely loyal. Perhaps the most substantial connection was with Winifred Bell who was at first house manager at Ridgeway Street and later on, general manager. Conor observed their interaction: 'It was a partnership based on mutual trust, robustness of dialogue, a strong commitment to the values of independence and fair play, and also a joint sense of mischievousness and fun – particularly when they were jointly facing common adversaries.' Mary's closest artistic relationships were generally with women. Much of the Yeats achievement, was aided by the close bond – sometimes fractured by rows, but close nevertheless – between Mary as director, Helen Lewis as choreographer and Alice Berger Hammerschlag as scenic designer.

The autobiography embodies the energy and the self-belief which Mary had in her prime. But she did not just love the theatre for herself and her own ends; she had the ability to transmit that love, creatively, to others – a considerable feat in the sometimes-chilly cultural climate of Belfast.

23

Endings

MARY WAS IN reasonable health until the slow onset of dementia from 1990. Then she began to decline physically. Her arteries had become severely blocked; she had a bypass operation, from which she never fully recovered. Her thyroid gave trouble; there were mini strokes and severe dementia set in. By now she and Pearse had left the fairly remote Delgany bungalow for a house in Booterstown. When Mary was still being cared for at home, Sam McCready visited her and Pearse. There had been a clash twenty years before, but he may have felt that accounts had to be settled with the person who had been such a huge and positive influence on his life and career:

> When I arrived, a nurse was with Mary and Pearse took me out to lunch. He was warm and cordial and appeared to be in wonderfully good health, so much so that I thought he must live for ever. Indeed, he appeared to have changed little from the time I first met him – some forty years before ... the same dark hair and ruddy cheeks, the same sardonic smile, but as we talked I sensed the strain he was under, coping with the pain of watching the woman he was devoted to, his closest companion for almost sixty years, gradually lose contact with this world and those around her.

Sam describes the touching scene when Pearse took him up to the bedroom to see Mary:

She sat on a chair, white-haired (I had only ever seen her with intensely dark hair), frail, paler than I had remembered her but beautiful, calm – almost beatific. It was as if she fought all her life and was now finding peace. 'She's happy,' insisted Pearse. 'As you can see, she's happy.'

I sat in a chair a few feet away from her. We spoke of her grandchildren and their love of the arts; we spoke of my work in America, but it was difficult to know how present she was, how much she understood the conversation since Pearse answered the questions, prompting her occasional remarks. Throughout, however, she focussed her dark eyes on me. They were not piercing and demanding, as I remembered them, but soft and loving. I almost wished we could sit there and be silent, for there is eloquence beyond words, but Pearse needed to talk. 'She understands!' he kept insisting, 'you see, she understands!'

Before Sam left, Mary opened his *Yeats Encyclopaedia*, which he had dedicated to her, looked out of the window at the fading afternoon light 'and recited word for word, without hesitation, the final lines from Yeats's play *The Countess Cathleen*:

The years like great black oxen tread the world,
And God the herdsman goads them on behind,
And I am broken by their passing feet.

Pearse visited his beloved wife every day – except for a single week of holiday each year, which he would spend in Surrey staying with his niece, Mary Pengelly, and her husband. He enjoyed walks in the country around Hindhead and going to the Yvonne Arnaud Theatre in Guildford. On one of his visits he confided something surprising to his niece. He said he 'probably wouldn't have married if he hadn't met Auntie Mary'.

Despite always looking the picture of health he died, quite suddenly and unexpectedly, in 2004. Two years later Mary went – on Pearse's birthday, 22 April 2006. Sam McCready was at the smaller family funeral. A larger public gathering had been arranged for the next day. At the church he met Neil Downes, the architect who drew up the original plans for Mary's new theatre. 'He was always a modest, courteous man and clearly, despite his disappointment over the design for the new Lyric, he has harboured no resentments. Since he was involved in the Derryvolgie years, I feel a special attachment to him.' Sam kept glancing at the coffin, 'a simple box, wreathed with flowers from the family. I try to convince myself that Mary is inside that box, but I can't. No box, I decide, can contain all that intensity and all that pride.' The priest, Sam observed, 'doesn't seem to know her well'. The cleric said some prayers and Sam spoke a few words. 'She brought culture to the north where it was in short supply; she built a theatre. I speak of her love of Yeats and the contribution she made to Yeats's drama.' There was a wake afterwards in a restaurant across the road from the church. But Sam and Joan had to leave because Joan was doing her one-woman show, *Coole Lady*, about Lady Gregory, in Rostrevor.

McCready's book ends with a touching portrait of Mary:

Mary O'Malley was demanding and uncompromising, but she never demanded more of others than she demanded of herself. She was ruthless in dealing with mediocrity, small-mindedness and limited effort. Some withered under her gaze but many blossomed. She had a devoted following of audience, actors and artists … but for each one of her admirers there was someone who resisted her, resented her presence in the North of Ireland and was at pains to undermine her. What her detractors didn't realise, however, was that their actions brought out the fight in her.

In his eulogy at his mother's funeral, Kieran stressed these fighting qualities. He said his mother had remained rebellious to the end: in her first nursing home she had gone to local garda station in slippers and dressing gown, protesting that she had been put in the home against her wishes; in the second she had refused to go in the wheelchair to the mandatory daily Mass; and in the third 'she floated as a butterfly on the water'. Kieran says he borrowed the last image from Carl Jung, the psychiatrist who had treated Lucia Joyce and told her father, James, that 'this was how she had slipped away'.

This biography has to some extent been a portrait of a family so it seems appropriate to end with part of a poem written by Kieran O'Malley – a psychiatrist like his father and a theatre director like his mother. His lines are entitled, 'For Mary and Pearse O'Malley on the occasion of the reopening of the Lyric Players Theatre, Belfast, 1 May 2011.' In the new building, the stuff of his parents' dreams, he sees Philip Flanagan's image of his mother, Mary's 'piercing bronzed visage':

> … Bringing a tale of united purpose,
> Creating something intangible and unknown.
> Now, sixty years later,
> A formidable Northern Playhouse
> Sits astride the Lagan waters.

24

Coda

BY THE TIME Mary died, the Belfast Agreement had created a structure that allowed the extremists of both sides in Northern Ireland to share power in a reasonably constructive way. At the start of the twenty-first century, the Lyric was thriving artistically, but the building was beginning to show signs of middle age. The theatre by the Lagan needed at the very least major refurbishment. Instead, rebuilding was the chosen option and after a huge fundraising effort, in 2011 a magnificent new playhouse rose up on the modest site in Ridgeway Street. It is delightful to imagine what Pearse and Mary would have made of the handsome, imaginative yet practical, new building.

At the opening there was a recognition of the role of the O'Malleys in creating the theatre, but at first her bronze head (by Philip Flanagan) was not given high visibility in the second 'new' Lyric. Instead it was a fine sculpture of Seamus Heaney (by the same artist) that greeted the public as it arrived. The great poet was a keen supporter of Mary and admired her theatre and her Yeats productions. His benign statuary presence lent lustre to the second new Lyric, but generous soul that he was, Heaney would probably have wanted to change places and allow the Belfast theatregoers, as they arrived, to gaze upon the likeness of the woman who had offered them such dramatic riches and managed to root a new theatre in the unpromising cultural soil of Belfast. Happily, that is now possible; the Heaney bust has gone to be celebrated elsewhere and Mary gazes on the customers as they come in – probably counting them. Mary's achievement will be long debated. But fortunately, there can be no debate about this one lasting contribution to cultural life in Belfast: her memorial is a visible, tangible, enduring mix of wood and concrete – as her son describes it, 'a formidable Northern playhouse' standing proudly beside the Lagan.

Remembering Mary and understanding the evolution of the Lyric has been easier since June 2001. That was when the theatre archive was formally lodged and launched at the Hardiman Library at NUI Galway. This rich store of cultural history was acquired for the university largely through the efforts of Lionel Pilkington, who teaches there. It is that archive which made it possible to write this book. So it is appropriate to give the last word to Pilkington, who knew the O'Malleys in Dublin in the 1980s and '90s and who has written authoritatively on Irish theatre and in particular about the politics of Irish theatre. He sums up the O'Malleys' contribution:

> Mary, supported by Pearse, founded their theatre as an attempt to establish a space of freedom in Belfast for Protestants and Roman Catholics that would be organised around a positive, non-sectarian and capacious Irish national identity. They were acutely aware of the sectarianism, gerrymandering and institutional injustices of the Northern Ireland state but they were determined in their idealistic way to oppose this narrowness with the liberating experience of theatre. I think that their achievement was magnificent, and that Northern Ireland owes them a huge debt for having established such a vibrant and ambitious theatre, and one that has left such a powerful legacy. Once the Lyric Players' Theatre became public, of course, they faced a barrage of hostile opposition. So, possibly, more could have been done to encourage local playwrights and they could have made a greater effort to plug themselves into the orthodoxies of Belfast in the 1950s and 1960s. But this would have been contrary to what they believed in, contrary to their ambition and generosity, and contrary to the possibilities that, for them, theatre offered.

This was a couple whose lives had been hurt by the long struggle in taking on the Unionist establishment in Northern Ireland, but whose determination to continue that struggle (or at least to have that struggle recognised for what it was) remained with them to the end.

Appendix A

An account of *Threshold* magazine, 1957–90

MARY WAS SOLE editor of *Threshold* for its first fifteen editions, from 1957 to 1961. In that year she became so overloaded with theatre, magazine and much else besides, that she decided to pass on her editorial role to a series of guest editors. In editing the early issues Mary had a great deal of help from Pearse and the short editorials sound more Pearse than Mary. From the beginning the tyro magazine team managed to attract good writers (usually paid pittance fees) and to express an all-Ireland vision. It was no accident that, although the magazine originated in Belfast, nearly half of the contributors to the first issue came from the Republic. This was policy. For Mary, Ireland was culturally one country, and the North needed to be kept informed about ballet in Cork, the Dublin Theatre Festival, the state of the Abbey and of the Irish language and similar topics.

The mix in these early editions remained fairly constant: short stories (by Friel and Patrick Boyle among others); historical profiles, for example a piece on the fabulously wealthy Belfast shipping magnate William James Pirrie; foreign reports (one on Israel by the distinguished commentator Uri Avnery); remarkably, a contribution from the then Taoiseach, Seán Lemass, about Ireland joining the European Free Trade Area; a doughty intervention by Roy McFadden in the *Over the Bridge* row; and some fine poetry, chosen by John Hewitt, and occasionally including some of his own. There were advertisements to defray the costs borne, once again, by the

O'Malley exchequer (regular support from the Arts Council did not come until Mary's tenure as editor was over).

Two short extracts from the earlier editions indicate *Threshold*'s quality. 'The first week in Lent' is a splendidly outspoken report in *T2* by the poet John Montague on the elderly de Valera making a speech in College Green in Dublin: 'He began in Irish. "What does he want to do that for," complained a girl, "sure half of us don't understand a word of it." Voices from the now crowded trees shouted: "We want Bill Haley." After this intervention Dev spoke in English.' Montague summarizes de Valera's message sharply: 'The language could be revived; partition could be solved; we could produce most of our needs in Ireland – the whole impossibly plausible old story.' Gloomily, he recognizes that de Valera is in effect hoping that Ireland '… might be able to resign from the twentieth century'.

Second, in *T14*, a tiny sliver from a long poem by John Hewitt. As poetry editor he was a little shy about publishing his own poetry until very near the end of his tenure, when he chose to include an eighteen-page delight, 'A Country Walk in May', which communicates the enjoyment of an uneventful but interesting country walk in good weather in the heart of England. Rhyming couplets give it a walking rhythm and are full of Hewitt's sharp wit. He describes the four hikers taking the walk – starting with himself:

> For thirty years my chosen part
> has been to play the middleman in art;
> not one of those sleek creatures, tall and bland,
> who lisp in jargon on the carpet stand,
> with long nose in the glossy catalogue
> to document the very latest vogue
> for rubber-jointed minor Mannerist
> or metal twister shinning up the list.

Threshold's circulation averaged about 800. These early issues were surprisingly diffident politically. As a party politician Mary had spoken out about the Unionists' misuse of power. But *Threshold* in the late 1950s and early

'60s did not say anything directly about discrimination or gerrymandering, or about sporadic and sometimes lethal IRA activity. Her nationalist stance was reflected only in *Threshold*'s inclusive subject matter; her approach was to try to create an Irish dimension for Northern Irish readers, to ignore the border and see Ireland as a single entity. When cultural or political issues came up, like the *Over the Bridge* row, she and her contributors were prepared to wade into the controversy. But on the broader picture, the social injustices suffered by many Catholics in their everyday lives, she and *Threshold* remained, like the rest of the local, national and international media, mostly silent – until the pressure cooker finally exploded almost ten years later.

It's possible that Mary took this line because, having achieved in her theatre a fully-functioning, non-sectarian amateur company – a relative rarity at that juncture in Belfast – she did not want the magazine to threaten the creative harmony of her players or put off any potential audience members by making political statements. She felt anger and frustration at the state of Northern Ireland, but did not want to demonstrate a too-obvious partisanship in her magazine. Perhaps she or Pearse sensed that the moment for effective, full-hearted protest, which eventually came in 1968–69, was not yet at hand.

Mary tried hard to delegate the task of editing *Threshold* after 1960 because her other activities were multiplying so fast. But this took a while to achieve, and she had to stay on as editor until the autumn/winter of 1961 when the 'new', sixteenth issue of *Threshold*, edited by the BBC producer John Boyd, appeared. It didn't look very different from its predecessors and Boyd's choices were very similar to what Mary's might have been. Boyd included two stories, Patrick Boyle's grim 'Death, Where Is Thy Sting-aling-aling?' and Brian Friel's 'The Potato Gatherers'. The second is a rite-of-passage piece, set in the potato fields of Co. Tyrone. Boys bunk off school to make some money, picking; the dialogue has all the dramatist's skill; the events are ambiguous and touching.

Threshold 17 is mysteriously undated, but probably came out in 1963. Its virtues were two excellent pieces of prose fiction. One, John McGahern's 'Waiting', is an extract from his first novel. It tells with poignant clarity of a woman's diagnosis with breast cancer and the fear and, briefly, panic she feels. The anxious woman, the kindly doctor and the moment of revelation are realized with a limpid simplicity of style. McGahern was about to 'arrive' as a writer. The second piece, by Michael MacIntyre, is a vivid Dublin story, 'The Fortune Teller', about a 32-year-old country girl, Maura, who is desperate for a partner and goes in search of a fortune teller. Her journey is described felicitously: 'as they waited, a blade of sunlight surprised the lane and hesitantly held its ground.' The ending is sad: 'Hearsed in a taxi they drove back to the city.'

There are some high-quality poems in this issue: contributions from Ezra Pound, Padraic Colum ('Lament'), Thomas Kinsella, and a lively offering by John Montague about coming home to Co. Tyrone:

> No Wordsworthian dream chain enchants me here
> With glint of glacial corry or totemic mountain,
> But merging dark hills and gravel streams,
> The oozy blackness of bog-banks, pale upland grass;
> Rough Field is the Gaelic and rightly named
> As a landscape for a mode of life that passes on.

In the autumn of 1965 *Threshold* made a new departure: its first themed edition (*T19*). Roger McHugh edited a centenary tribute to W.B Yeats and poses a penetrating question: 'Was he a dramatic poet who, both in range of theme and technique, raised drama to new heights; or was he simply a great lyrical poet who, using the theatre to extend his voice, never really faced up to the true nature of a very distinctive public art?' McHugh writes an informative piece, covering the whole canon of Yeats plays, and in the end, makes the judgment that Yeats was 'always a poet in the theatre rather than a poetic dramatist'. This Yeats edition is more directly related to the Lyric and to theatre history in general than any previous *Threshold*. (The idea of themed issues was to be taken up again very effectively in the following decade.)

Although by the mid-1960s the magazine was appearing less frequently than before, it had achieved enough presence to attract Brian Friel and Seamus Heaney as guest editors. Heaney had already submitted poems to *Threshold* – one of which he withdrew rather hurriedly. This particular edition was being edited by James Plunkett, but Heaney wrote directly to Mary: 'Could I withdraw 'Oh Brave New Bull' from *Threshold*? I do not suppose James Plunkett will consider it for publication anyhow, but in case he did, please restrain him?' Heaney explains that an earlier copy of *Threshold*, containing a fairly harmless story, 'The Metal Man' by Patrick Boyle, had been withdrawn from the reading room by the clerical management at St Mary's University College where he had just started work. He thinks that if the 'Brave New Bull' appears in *Threshold* with his name under it, 'such an eventuality would not be the ideal introduction to a new job'. He encloses a 'much less dangerous' substitute poem and adds, 'I need to say I find the situation as ridiculous as you must.' 'Oh Brave New Bull' does not appear in *Threshold* – Heaney may have been right to think that farmyard copulation might be offensive to the hyper-sensitive management of his Catholic training college. Fortunately, the poem has survived in the archives. Young Seamus has dragged 'a nervous Friesian on a tether' up a lane for it to be serviced by an unlicensed bull, presumably at a bargain price. He gives 'the clammy silver' to the bull's proprietor, Old Kelly. Perched on a gate, the poet watches proceedings. The potentially offensive lines are: 'His knobbled forelegs straddling her flank, / He slammed life home, impassive as a tank.'

Heaney had already fired a critical broadside at the magazine in *Hibernia* in April 1963, a few months before sending in 'Oh Brave New Bull'. He begins with some positives:

Irish politics, Irish art, Irish music – all have been treated with wisdom and urbanity. Yet *Threshold* has not taken over where other magazines left off. Why? Because it is not essentially a Northern magazine. It might as well be published in Dublin. It relies mainly on established reputations, rarely publishes new names and one generally feels that its contributors would be more at home on the banks of the Liffey than the Lagan. Mrs O'Malley will answer these charges by saying, very truly, that no significant writing is being produced in the North. If the writers are there, they should be writing. I agree. But no literary apprentice is going to produce a story or poem with the professional finish one has come to expect of *Threshold* ...

Heaney opines that *Threshold* failed because, 'it is more in the nature of a national literary review than a local magazine'. He is sure that 'a new magazine is necessary in the North in this period of literary revival and social and political thaw'.

Another literary magazine did eventually appear, four years later, in the shape of *The Honest Ulsterman*, edited first by James Simmons and then, for many years, by Frank Ormsby. It ran from 1968 to 2003, with the frequency of issues decreasing over the years. It outperformed *Threshold* in the end, achieving more than double the number of editions. It arrived at a propitious time, when new writing of extraordinary quality was bubbling up in Northern Ireland. *Threshold* also benefited from this rich flow and Heaney's strictures became irrelevant as successive editors of the magazine began publishing pieces by new Ulster writers and the Dublin bias, which Heaney had deplored, was moderated.

T20, which came out in the winter of 1966, is a slim volume. It was edited by a busy Brian Friel. He wrote to Mary on 17 May 1966 from his home at Marlborough Street in Derry, saying that he is prepared to waive his editorial fee, which 'would leave £100 intact for the contributors'. Mary has invited him to come and see *The Plough and the Stars* at the Lyric, but he declines. He explains he has been away so much recently that 'the children are beginning to see me as a casual handyman'. He signs off 'Ever, Brian' and then with charming modesty adds '(Friel)'.

Friel's busyness may have been a reason why his edition was somewhat slight. It contains a nicely characterized story with great narrative drive by John Boyd, 'The Air Gun', an extract from Eugene McCabe's new play, *Breakdown* and some 'work in progress' from Maurice Leitch. One of the best choices is a John Montague poem, 'The Road's End'.

But the thatch
Has slumped in, nettles proliferate
In the bedroom. Only the shed remains
In use, for calves, although fuchsia
Bleeds by the wall and someone
Has propped a yellow cartwheel
Against the door.

The next *Threshold*, Number 21, was 175 pages long: a large, confident cornucopia of Ulster writing, dated Summer 1967, and with a cover by Gerard Dillon. The editors of this rich compendium, Sam Hanna Bell and John Boyd, make little of the 'Ulster' label. Their selection includes writers who 'by birth or residence, have been associated with Northern Ireland'. Most of the issue is taken up with poems and short stories, but there was also an outstanding example of the Belfast memoir, 'A Spit of the Ould Da', Robert Harbinson's compelling and tragic account of his father – a jaunty, popular, heavy-drinking window cleaner – who one day fell off his ladder and was impaled on the railings below. The account of his final, bedridden months at home is almost too painful to read but is a remarkable piece of writing, which stands out in what was to become a familiar genre in *Threshold*.

To anthologize this sizeable anthology is difficult. The risk of the list is ever-present, but in both poetry and prose these are *some* lists. In the verse there is Louis MacNeice's 'Carrick Revisited' ('Memories I shelved peer at me from the shelf'); Seamus Heaney's 'The Follower', a marvellously visual piece about his father; John Hewitt's touching, carefully worked nature poems, 'The Swathe Uncut' and 'The First Corncrake'. Then there is W.R. Rodgers's boisterous 'Armagh':

There is a through-otherness about Armagh
Delightful to me,
Up on the hill are the graves of the garrulous kings
Who at last can agree.

Jack McQuoid, contributes one of his attractively rough-and-ready poems, 'The New Scythe Blade'; James Simmons is frank and touching in 'Ballad of a Marriage'; Michael Longley, not yet thirty, memorably remembers his father, a veteran of World War One:

> In my twentieth year your old wounds woke
> As cancer. Lodging under the same roof
> Death was a visitor who hung about,
> Strewing the house with pills and bandages,
> Till he chose to put your spirit out.

And Derek Mahon another, youthful pretender to the throne of MacNeice, muses by the grave of the older poet in Carrowdore churchyard: 'You lie / Past tension now, and spring is coming round / Igniting flowers on the peninsula.'

In prose fiction this *Threshold* puts on a parade of the older, established storytellers and the newer arrivals, like Maurice Leitch. There is great vigour and life in the writing but there is also a lot of death, or near-death in the stories. Michael J. Murphy contributes a terrible tale of tuberculosis, and the fear of it, in the Antrim glens; the fear of death appears again in John D. Stewart's brilliantly told story of a young boy bird-nesting and egg-hunting on seaside cliffs. Brian Moore is on top form with 'A Vocation', a savage parody of Catholic teaching as interpreted by two boys. They agree that the only way to avoid damnation, or at least a long spell in purgatory, is to become priests:

> 'If a fellow was wise, that's what he'd do. After all, it's the next world that counts.'
> 'That would be the best thing,' Joe said. 'To be a priest. An order priest. It would be the safest.'

Threshold was permitted to celebrate the opening of the new theatre in Number 22 (1969), edited by Seamus Heaney. Jack McQuoid makes a home-spun tribute to the achievement of his fellow players in the old converted stable:

The writer who wrote the play,
The actor who played the part,
The painter who painted the scene,
The poet who found the word,
And the musician the note.

This issue is strong on both prose and poetry. The stories come from Patrick Boyle, Mary Lavin, Redmond O'Hanlon and Hugh Bredin. Boyle's story 'Sally' packs a mild erotic charge, unusual in *Threshold*; it's a comeuppance tale of the confident male undone by a convent schoolgirl. Redmond O'Hanlon's story 'The Brothers' is about tribalism: is it OK to steal apples from Protestants? Yes, it is, but ... Mary Lavin's contribution 'Fond Mother' is pure gold – a marvellous monologue about motherhood. And there is another erotic charge (hardly surprising, it is, after all, the late '60s by now) in 'The White Flower', a story by Hugh Bredin, which includes a scene in a confessional where a young man, in response to the traditional priestly enquiries, happily confesses to having had sexual congress ten times in four days – with a woman who is not his wife.

With Heaney at the helm, the selected poetry is of the highest quality. He had noticed the talent of the young Paul Muldoon (just twenty-four at this point) and included two poems 'Still Born' and 'Snail'. The first, about the floating corpse of a sheep, is not cheerful:

Better dead than sheep:
The thin worm slurred in your gut
The rot in your feet
The red dog creeping at dawn.

'Snail' is a grim love poem. The possibly faithless lover is likened to a snail. The long-awaited letter is 'impatience clamped beneath a paperweight'. The poet hesitates to open it. When he does, the news is bad. He distracts himself by removing a snail from a bush: 'I turned it over through the grass / To watch your mucous lips withdraw.'

There are also fine poems by James Simmons, Michael Longley and Tom Kinsella and, from the less well-known Geoffrey Squires, 'The Farmer', a delightfully simple offering about mortality:

> He died
> Without really having reached any conclusions.
> He saw it coming
> Like a red bus on a country road
> A long way off.
> He saw it stop at the bridge
> To pick someone up.
> And as it approached, he could do nothing
> Except watch it
> Getting bigger and redder.

This issue naturally foregrounds the opening of the theatre and delivers strong new writing. But the magazine gives little sense that Northern Ireland's already septic politics are now threatening to become gangrenous. By the end of 1969 thirteen people had died as a result of communal violence. Full attention in the pages of *Threshold* to the escalating civil commotion had to wait till the following summer.

As we have seen, Mary chose John Montague to edit *T23*. The result was 'Northern Crisis' (1970), an edition full of sharp social analysis and, in its poetry, a strong feeling of the disorder in the streets. This was an exceptional issue, which included John Hewitt's 'Coasters'. Other poems caught the moment vividly. 'Barricades' by Francis Mulhern is dated 'Belfast August, 1969'. There is vivid understatement in the poet's description of street skirmishes:

> Timber, tyres, scaffolding;
> Whatever, whosoever, it all went on –
> To keep them out was the important thing.
>
> We heaved and slammed at paving slabs
> Till they came, leaving clinker and sharp rock.

Hard work it was, but it's a sturdy job.

Of course, it left the pavements treacherous.
Last night, my youngest took a fall –
The cut's a deep one, it'll leave a scar.

Brian Moore, the Irish-Canadian novelist who was then living in California, comes back and delivers a striking portrait of 'his' Belfast which, he says, 'still, foolishly, I sometimes call "home"'. There is an intense, despairing anger in the piece, which mixes vivid reporting of the current street scene with italicized memories of his early life and times in the Falls Road. Touring Belfast with his brother-in-law, strong memories of the city blitz in 1941 come to him; he wonders if perhaps Belfast has an 'incurable' sickness. But he immediately questions his right to pontificate: 'A Catholic who is no longer a Catholic, an Ulsterman who holds a Canadian passport, and lives in California, an Irishman who has lived longer out of Ireland than he lived in it. What can I know of Ulster's present troubles?'

Then comes a memory riff about the IRA, as he perceived it in the 1930s: 'We despised them. Because of them, Catholics were beaten up by special police. Because of them, the Old Etonians, our masters, could keep the silent Protestant majority in a state of dumb fealty to the British Crown and the Ulster Unionist party.' To Moore, the IRA 'was, and is, the perfect red herring'. As he continues to drive around, the car moves from a Catholic to a Protestant area. He finds the streets

are equally drear, the same shut little workingmen's dwellings, the same stale corner pubs, tawdry sweetie shops and gimcrack sludgy little grocery stores. Is this all that the right to vote, the pick of available jobs and housing, the welfare state, has brought the Queen's Irish Protestant liegemen and women? Yes, it is. They have so little they feel they cannot afford to share it.

So turn the Papish out.

Earlier in the article Moore makes a frightening prophecy, which we know now turned out to be true. He senses 'an exile's truth' – that if the 'news item', the coverage of the Troubles he has seen in California, dies, 'then nothing will change here'. He goes on: 'It must escalate. Blood must run in the streets. Ulster people must die like dogs. Unless they do, nothing will change.' These words were written in 1970 and at least 3000 more people had still to die.

There is high literary and journalistic quality and intense feeling in many of the contributions to 'Northern Crisis'. Seamus Heaney's offering is 'The Tollund Man'. The poem is about ritual murder, about the corpse found, fully preserved in a Danish bog. Heaney draws horrifying parallels with sectarian killings closer to home. The final stanza has a Yeatsian power and economy:

Out there in Jutland
In the old, man-killing parishes
I will feel lost,
Unhappy and at home.

There is space for only one more piece from John Montague's remarkable compilation. This is unfair to other notable contributions from Thomas Kinsella, Derek Mahon, John D. Stewart, Seamus Deane and Montague himself. However, the piece by Eoin Sweeney, a Dublin student who went on the People's Democracy march from Belfast to Derry in January 1969, one of the most significant early chapters in the Troubles, is a first-hand account of considerable value. There is room here for only the briefest summary, but perhaps the quotation will give some of the raw flavour of the original. Sweeney is frank about his motive for going on the march: he wanted to help to push the structure of Northern Ireland 'towards the point where its internal contradictions would cause a snapping and a breaking to begin'. He hitchhiked to Belfast, then set off on the Antrim Road with perhaps forty people. They overnighted near Antrim, wakened on this and other nights by the police with false bomb scares. Next day they headed for Randalstown and Sweeney has the sense that they are becoming a pilgrimage. Violence is avoided where possible through rerouting, but there are clear signs of fierce hostility. The marchers were heartened when they met supporters:

> The people we met on the roads and in the villages matured our purpose, gave the march a dimension of meaning that solidified the delicate structure of our hope and faith. I became conscious of the pressure of history, forcing people to express their anger, their need for dignity, in patterns of helpless conflict.

At Maghera they avoided confrontation and 'plodded up the mountain and over the Glenshane Pass, cold and bleak and beautiful'. They were now clear that they were 'a catalyst setting off a chain reaction'. They had a big welcome at Dungiven and then by sheer force of numbers managed to push the police aside. Next, they were ambushed at Burntollet, but despite casualties, continued to Derry. When they arrived at Guildhall Square, 'half of the group that had started out were either in hospital or bandaged'. But Sweeney felt that 'we had done what we promised to do – walked across the province without lifting a hand to any man'.

In choosing John Montague as editor, Mary knew what she was doing. At one time he had toured Ireland giving poetry readings in tandem with John Hewitt. They were advertised as 'The Planter and the Gael'. Inevitably the Gael in Montague was going to inform his choices for this *Threshold*. At this point in the Troubles, before any major changes had been made in the governance of Northern Ireland, and before the IRA had got into its murderous stride, it was difficult to make any sort of case for the Unionist majority. This *Threshold* did not try to do so, but it was unequivocal about sectarianism; it lay at the root of Ulster's troubles.

In the 1970s John Boyd played an increasingly important editorial role in the magazine: he became the dominant figure, editing or co-editing eleven issues in all despite also being the Lyric's chief play-reader and writing plays himself. Not surprisingly, from time to time he in turn devolved the task to others. He edited the twenty-fifth *Threshold* with Patrick Galvin in the summer of 1974 (there had been a long gap since 'Northern Crisis'). This

115-page edition, which had a striking grey and black cover by Clive Wilson, contains poetry that vividly conveys the atmosphere in troubled Belfast. Eleanor Murray in 'Fear' renders with perfect simplicity the poisonous, window-peeping anxiety, which street violence had brought to many ordinary citizens:

> The very walls
> Seemed to listen with me
> Until a lock clicked;
> And a strange car
> Glided softly back
> Into the darkness.

More than a year later the same editors did it again with *T26* (Autumn 1975). This was another large, 125-page edition, supported for the first time by An Chomhairle Ealaíon in Dublin as well as the Northern Irish Arts Council. It mixes anguished responses to the continued horrors of bombings and sectarian murder with pieces that relate more distantly to events in the streets. Padraic Fiacc despairs over Belfast with its chimney pots 'flowering smoke for tea-time',

> … Waiting for when or where the next blow
> Will fall. Against this black the white sea-gulls
> Glide in again, like lazy-eyed drunks, over dark.

Threshold 27, which came out in 1976, consisted exclusively of the text of Patrick Galvin's *We Do It for Love*. Otherwise these later *Thresholds* are not hugely different to their immediate predecessors, but there is a new element; more academic literary criticism, including a delightful piece on Beckett by Alec Reid. Editorials sometimes express explicit and incendiary political opinions, like this one from 1982: '… in the Catholic Republic contraception, divorce, abortion and the like remain acrid issues, precisely because their introduction would mark the end of Catholic hegemony and usher in the pluralist modernism the place so badly needs'. The writer then takes his bludgeon to Ulster Protestantism, which is dismissed as 'a negative religion, more accurately defined as being anti-Catholic than anything else'.

Some of the poetry in the last twelve *Thresholds* was of a high order. There was work from poets who had been there almost from the beginning: from Hewitt, Heaney, Montague and from newcomers like Tom Paulin and Matthew Sweeney. An example: Patrick Galvin is Lorca-esque in his use of mesmerizing repetition from this extract from his poem about murder in the snow at midnight in Antrim; here is just part of it:

> Death
> At midnight
> The eleventh stroke of midnight
> Death –
> In famine field and green beret
> In the clothes we wore
> At chapel, church and meeting
> Death melting in the snow
> Still falling lightly –
> My Antrim.

After they came to live in Dublin, Mary and Pearse's involvement in the afterlife of *Threshold* was minimal. They found it easier to let go of the magazine than the theatre. In *T30*, which Seamus Heaney edited, he published 'The Strand at Lough Beg', a poem he wrote in memory of his cousin Colum McCartney. It gives a terrifying account of how the victim may have been trapped:

> What blazed ahead of you? A faked road block
> A red lamp swung, the sudden brakes and stalling
> Engine, voices, heads hooded and the cold-nosed gun
> Or in your driving mirror, tailing headlights
> That pulled-out suddenly and flagged you down
> Where you weren't known and far from what you knew …

In the same issue John Hewitt is in good satirical voice, contributing 'Variations on a theme' in which he explains his own aesthetic very wittily. He is sorely tried by modern art:

> For cautious critics now define
> A work of art as something said
> To be just that; a coil of twine,
> A plank with nails, a broken bed,
> A tray of plastic gingerbread …

The last twelve *Thresholds* included three special editions: 'Forrest Reid' (*T28*, Spring 1977), an Irish-American special (*T34*, Winter 1983–84) and finally a tribute to John Hewitt (*T38*, Winter 1987–88).

The Forrest Reid edition contained a playful piece – which began life as a speech – on Reid by E.M. Forster:

> On his mother's side he was English, I am glad to think, but that side was never important to him. Every now and then he came to England, often to play croquet, and each time he came he found the English nicer than he expected, which showed what he had been thinking of them in the interval. I tried to persuade him that the English were always nice, but he wouldn't have that …

Forster visited Reid regularly in Belfast and enjoyed exploring the Lagan valley with him as well as the Down and Antrim coasts. There are diverting accounts of the attempts by the two bachelors, both incompetent in the kitchen, to cook for themselves. At the end of his speech Forster takes on the serious task of assessing Reid's work. He admits Reid's genius is not easily summed up: 'He was elusive and sensitive, yet at the same time he was tough and knew his own mind. He preached no dogma, and yet all his work is characterized by what he himself has beautifully called a sort of moral fragrance. Its final impact is ethical.' Other contributors were not prepared to celebrate the novelist so unreservedly.

The penultimate *Threshold* was dedicated to John Hewitt. He died, aged seventy-nine, in the summer of 1987. The next issue *T38* (Winter 1987–88) became a tribute to him, with a black-and-white picture of the poet in typical pipe-lighting mode. John Boyd, who was editor (with Desmond Maxwell), wrote a personal tribute, concisely assessing what the loss of the poet meant:

> John was a unique figure in Belfast, honoured by the city he himself honoured. He was born here, died here, loved the place, found it hard to hate when its follies demanded harsh words. But when harsh words were necessary, he spoke them fearlessly; he was never afraid of making enemies, and he certainly made a few in his time. Fortunately, they were very few compared to the great number of his friends and admirers.

Alan Warner, who chose the poems for a Blackstaff Press edition of Hewitt's work, notes that honesty is a prime quality in Hewitt's poetry and quotes approvingly Hewitt's own description of his style as 'a slow measured art / irrevocably plain'. Warner likes the scrupulousness and restraint of Hewitt's political poems, like 'Neither an Elegy nor a Manifesto':

> Bear in mind those dead:
> I can find no plainer words.
> I dare not risk using that loaded word, Remember …
> Bear in mind the skipping child hit
> by the anonymous ricochet;
> the man shot at his own fireside
> with his staring family around him.

The final *Threshold* gives no hint of dissolution. It is a healthy size – more than a hundred pages long – and has the plain cover, which was the norm from *T36*. The editors are John Boyd and Desmond Maxwell again. This is very much a late-*Threshold* mix, but it has a marginal feeling. There is little to force a browser to spend £2 on it.

In the end *Threshold* simply faded away. Once the O'Malleys had stepped back from the magazine it lacked consistent direction although it still delivered sharp, readable issues. In the 1980s there were intense uncertainties and urgent conflicts at the Lyric theatre, so running a literary magazine must have sometimes been a low priority for *Threshold*'s workhorse, John Boyd. He was approaching eighty when he edited the final issue. Perhaps he and his fellow workers had just had enough.

The O'Malleys had dreamt in the Derryvolgie Avenue days of making a 'contribution to creative writing and objective criticism' in the great tradition of Irish literary periodicals. This they did, paying to do it early on but later getting substantial support, right up to the final edition, from the Arts Council, who were always acknowledged on the first page. The magazine, which had been started with 'hope and a certain temerity', fulfilled its creators' aspirations: *Threshold*, now sadly little known, added a significant piece to the mosaic of Irish literary periodicals.

Appendix B

Lyric Players Theatre productions to 1981

Source: *A Poets' Theatre*, Conor O'Malley

1951–52

Lost Light, Robert Farren

At The Hawk's Well, W.B. Yeats

The Kiss, Austin Clarke

1952–53

Before Breakfast, Eugene O'Neill

Princely Fortune, Anon (China)

A Swan Song, Anton Chekhov

Wrap Up My Green Jacket, Valentine
   Iremonger

The Viscount of Blarney, Austin Clarke

The Dreaming of the Bones, W.B. Yeats

Icaro, Lauro De Bossis

Christmas Pot Pourri, The Company

1953–54

This Way to the Tomb, Ronald Duncan

Cathleen Ni Houlihan, W.B. Yeats

The Only Jealousy of Emer, W.B. Yeats

The Second Kiss, Austin Clarke

The First-Born, Christopher Fry

Blood Wedding, Federico García Lorca

1954–55

Seadna, Joy Rudd

Othello (Act 3, Scene III), William
   Shakespeare

The Falcons in the Snare, Elizabeth
   Boyle

Comus, John Milton

Calvary, W.B. Yeats

Hamlet (1603), William Shakespeare

The First-Born, Christopher Fry

1955–56

King Oedipus, Sophocles / W.B. Yeats

The Land of Heart's Desire, W.B. Yeats

The Family Reunion, T.S. Eliot

The Frogs, Aristophanes

King Lear, William Shakespeare

Hippolytus, Euripides

1956–57

Volpone, Ben Johnson

The King's Threshold, W.B. Yeats

La La Noo, Jack Yeats

The Dark Is Light Enough, Christopher
Fry

Antigone, Jean Anouilh

Macbeth, William Shakespeare

The House of Bernarda Alba, Federico
García Lorca

The Children of Lir, Joy Rudd

1957–58

The Seagull, Anton Chekhov

The Bloody Brae, John Hewitt

Purgatory, W.B. Yeats

Deirdre, W.B. Yeats

Under Milk Wood, Dylan Thomas

Peer Gynt, Henrik Ibsen

Medea, Euripedes / Robinson Jeffers

See the Gay Windows, Norman
Harrison

1958–59

The Three Sisters, Anton Chekhov

The Silver Tassie, Seán O'Casey

Julius Caesar, William Shakespeare

The Voice of Shem, James Joyce / Mary
Manning

The Land of Heart's Desire, W.B. Yeats

Purgatory, W.B. Yeats

The Wolf in the Wood ('A Christmas
Entertainment'), Dorothy Waters

1959–60

Oedipus at Colonus, Sophocles / W.B.
Yeats

Before Breakfast, Eugene O'Neill

The Emperor Jones, Eugene O'Neill

Wrap Up My Green Jacket, Valentine
Iremonger

Romeo and Juliet, William Shakespeare

Oedipus at Colonus, Sophocles / W.B.
Yeats

The Death of Cuchulain, W.B. Yeats

The Heart's a Wonder, Nuala and Mairin
O'Farrell

Red Roses for Me, Seán O'Casey

1960–61

Yerma, Federico García Lorca

At the Hawk's Well, W.B. Yeats

On Baile's Strand, W.B. Yeats

The Only Jealousy of Emer, W.B. Yeats

Riders to the Sea, J.M. Synge

King Lear, William Shakespeare

Lady Spider, Donagh MacDonagh

Mary Stuart, Friedrich Schiller

The Heart's a Wonder, Nuala and Mairin
O'Farrell

Purgatory, W.B. Yeats

The King's Threshold, W.B.Yeats

A Full Moon in March, W.B. Yeats

1961–62

The Kingdom of God, Martinez Sierra

Brand, Henrik Ibsen

Thompson in Tir-Na-Og, Gerard
Macnamara

Apollo in Mourne, Richard Rowley

The Rising of the Moon, Augusta Gregory

The Dreaming Dust, Denis Johnston

Doña Rosita, Federico García Lorca

Many Young Men of Twenty, John B. Keane

The Carmelites, Georges Bernanos

The Dreaming of the Bones, W.B. Yeats

The Hour Glass, W.B. Yeats

The Player Queen, W.B. Yeats

At the Hawk's Well, W.B. Yeats

1962–63

The Moment Next to Nothing, Austin Clarke

A Man for All Seasons, Robert Bolt

Romance of an Idiot, Christopher O'Flynn

Uncle Vanya, Anton Chekhov

Deirdre of the Sorrows, J.M. Synge

The Heart's a Wonder, Nuala and Mairin O'Farrell

Many Young Men of Twenty, John B. Keane

The Risen People, James Plunkett

Riders to the Sea, J.M. Synge

Grace (adaptation from *Dubliners*), James Joyce

The Rising of the Moon, Augusta Gregory

Calvary, W.B .Yeats

King Oedipus, Sophocles / W.B. Yeats

Oedipus at Colonus, Sophocles / W. B Yeats

Purgatory, W.B. Yeats

The King's Threshold, W.B. Yeats

On Baile's Strand, W.B. Yeats

1963–64

The Enemy Within, Brian Friel

The House of Bernarda Alba, Federico García Lorca

Endgame, Samuel Beckett

The Stepping Stone, G.P. Gallivan

Jacques, Eugene Ionesco

The Future Is in Eggs, Eugene Ionesco

Martine, Jean-Jacques Bernard

Richard III, William Shakespeare

Next Time I'll Sing to You, James Saunders

The Unicorn and the Stars, W.B. Yeats

The Cat and the Moon, W.B. Yeats

The Herne's Egg, W.B. Yeats

The Resurrection, W.B. Yeats

1964–65

The Possessed, Albert Camus

The Blind Mice, Brian Friel

The Rough and Ready Lot, Alun Owen

The Beggar's Opera, John Gay

The Cherry Orchard, Anton Chekhov

Long Day's Journey into Night, Eugene O'Neill

The Pot of Broth, W.B. Yeats

The Words upon the Window Pane, W.B. Yeats

The Green Helmet, W.B. Yeats

The Death of Cuchulain, W.B. Yeats

The Subject Was Roses, Frank D. Gilroy

The Only Jealousy of Emer, W.B. Yeats

The Death of Cuchulain, W.B. Yeats

The Dreaming of the Bones, W.B. Yeats

The King of the Great Clock Tower, W.B. Yeats

Purgatory, W.B Yeats

Calvary, W.B. Yeats

The Resurrection, W.B. Yeats

1965–66

The Heart's a Wonder, Nuala and Mairin
　　O'Farrell
Ghosts, Henrik Ibsen
Juno and the Paycock, Seán O'Casey
The Fantasticks, Harvey Schmidt and
　　Tom Jones
A Month in the Country, Ivan Turgenev
King of the Castle, Eugene McCabe
Caligula, Albert Camus
The Plough and the Stars, Seán O'Casey
The Duchess of Malfi, John Webster
The Shadowy Waters, W.B. Yeats
The Countess Cathleen, W.B. Yeats
The Dreaming of the Bones, W.B. Yeats

1966–67

The Field, John B. Keane
Heartbreak House, Bernard Shaw
Lower Depths, Maxim Gorky
Who's Afraid of Virginia Woolf?, Edward
　　Albee
The Shaughraun, Dion Boucicault
The Plough and the Stars, Seán O'Casey
Anna Kleiber, Alfonso Sastre
The Woman at Rathard, Sam Hanna
　　Bell
The Caucasian Chalk Circle, Bertolt
　　Brecht
The Green Desert, Patrick Hughes
Them, Thomas Coffey
Richard III, William Shakespeare
Deirdre, W.B. Yeats
A Full Moon in March, W.B. Yeats
The Words upon the Window Pane, W.B.
　　Yeats

1967–68

Smock Alley, Mairin Charlton
The Shadow of a Gunman, Seán
　　O'Casey
The Chair, Michael Judge
Breakdown, Eugene McCabe
All Souls' Night, Joseph Tomelty
Juno and the Paycock, Seán O'Casey
Nathan the Wise, Gotthold Ephraim
　　Lessing
The Wild Duck, Henrik Ibsen
The Plough and the Stars, Seán O'Casey
The Last Eleven, Jack White
The Promise, Alexei Arbuzov
Henry IV, Luigi Pirandello
Smock Alley, Mairin Charlton
The Dreaming of the Bones, W.B. Yeats
Oedipus at Colonus, Sophocles / W.B.
　　Yeats
The King of the Great Clock Tower, W.B.
　　Yeats
Purgatory, W.B. Yeats
Calvary, W.B. Yeats
The Resurrection, W.B. Yeats

In the New Ridgeway Street Theatre:

1968–69

At The Hawk's Well, W.B. Yeats
On Baile's Strand, W.B. Yeats
The Only Jealousy of Emer, W.B. Yeats
The Death of Cuchulain, W.B. Yeats
The Seagull, Anton Chekhov
Tarry Flynn, Patrick Kavanagh
　　(Adaptation: P.J. O'Connor)

A Penny for a Song, John Whiting

The Royal Hunt of the Sun, Peter Shaffer

The Quare Fellow, Brendan Behan

Smock Alley, Mairin O'Farrell

Pictures in the Hallway, Seán O'Casey (Adaptation: Patrick Funge, David Krause)

The School for Scandal, R.B. Sheridan

The Prime of Miss Jean Brodie, Muriel Spark (Adaptation: J.P. Allen)

Sive, John B. Keane

Black Comedy, Peter Shaffer

The Cudgelled Cuckold, Alejandro Casona

1969–70

Juno and the Paycock, Seán O'Casey

The Field, John B. Keane

The Alchemist, Ben Johnson

Luther, John Osborne

Phaedre, Jean Racine

Candida, George Bernard Shaw

She Stoops to Conquer, Oliver Goldsmith

The Plough and the Stars, Seán O'Casey

The Magistrate, Arthur W. Pinero

The Dreaming of the Bones, W.B. Yeats

Purgatory, W.B. Yeats

Calvary, W.B. Yeats

The Resurrection, W.B. Yeats

Over the Bridge, Sam Thompson

Much Ado about Nothing, William Shakespeare

Lovers, Brian Friel

The Passing Day, George Shiels

1970–71

The Shadow of a Gunman, Seán O'Casey

The Chair, Michael Judge

Rosencrantz and Guildenstern Are Dead, Tom Stoppard

The Becauseway, Wesley Burrowes

Peer Gynt, Henrik Ibsen

Death of a Salesman, Arthur Miller

The Rivals, R.B. Sheridan

The Heart's a Wonder, Nuala and Mairin O'Farrell

The Dance of Death, August Strindberg

The Flats, John Boyd

Richard III, William Shakespeare

The Silver Tassie, Seán O'Casey

The Flats, John Boyd

The Words upon the Window Pane, W.B. Yeats

The King's Threshold, W.B. Yeats

1971–72

John Bull's Other Island, George Bernard Shaw

Lysistrata, Aristophanes

King of the Castle, Eugene McCabe

Romeo and Juliet, William Shakespeare

The Importance of Being Earnest, Oscar Wilde

The Lads, Joe O'Donnell

The Wild Duck, Henrik Ibsen

Red Roses for Me, Seán O'Casey

Danton's Death, Georg Büchner

The Farm, John Boyd

The Resistible Rise of Arturo Ui, Bertolt Brecht

The Dreaming of the Bones, W.B. Yeats

The King of the Great Clock Tower, W.B. Yeats

The Countess Cathleen, W.B. Yeats

1972–73

Within Two Shadows, Wilson John Haire

Lady Windermere's Fan, Oscar Wilde

The Gentle Island, Brian Friel

The Merchant of Venice, William Shakespeare

Man of La Mancha, Dale Wasserman

Famine, Thomas Murphy

A Swan Song, Anton Chekhov

A Dream Play, August Strindberg

Purple Dust, Seán O'Casey

Arms and the Man, George Bernard Shaw

Pantagleize, Michel de Ghelderode

1973–74

Nightfall to Belfast, Patrick Galvin

The Ruling Class, Peter Barnes

Saint Joan, George Bernard Shaw

Macbeth, William Shakespeare

School for Wives, Molière

Jesus Christ Superstar, Tim Rice and Andrew Lloyd Webber

Within the Gates, Seán O'Casey

The Cherry Orchard, Anton Chekhov

The Hour Glass, W.B. Yeats

The Player Queen, W.B. Yeats

Schweyk in the Second World War, Bertolt Brecht

1974–75

The Last Burning, Patrick Galvin

Pygmalion, George Bernard Shaw

Guests, John Boyd

A Man for All Seasons, Robert Bolt

Indians, Arthur Kopit

Cabaret, John Kander, Fred Ebb and Joe Masteroff

Rosmersholm, Henrik Ibsen

It Would Be Funny…, Tom Coffey

Deirdre, W.B. Yeats

Purgatory, W.B. Yeats

A Full Moon in March, W.B. Yeats

We Do It for Love, Patrick Galvin

1975–76

The Beaux Stratagem, George Farquhar

The Playboy of the Western World, J.M. Synge

Waiting for Godot, Samuel Beckett

Cock-a-Doodle Dandy, Seán O'Casey

The Good-Natured Man, Oliver Goldsmith

Innish, Fergus Linehan, Jim Doherty and Lennox Robinson

The Risen People, James Plunkett

The Loves of Cass Maguire, Brian Friel

We Do It for Love, Patrick Galvin

1976–77

King Oedipus, Sophocles / W.B. Yeats

Oedipus at Colonus, Sophocles / W. B. Yeats

Ah! Wilderness, Eugene O'Neill

Philadelphia, Here I Come!, Brian Friel

Henry IV (Part i), William Shakespeare

A Little Night Music, Hugh Wheeler / Stephen Sondheim

The Gathering, Edna O'Brien

The Street, John Boyd

Mother Courage and Her Children, Bertolt Brecht

Black Man's Country, Desmond Forristal

The Rise and Fall of Barney Kerrigan, Frank Dunne

1977–78

The Whiteheaded Boy, Lennox Robinson

All My Sons, Arthur Miller

The Plough and the Stars, Seán O'Casey

The Colleen Bawn, Dion Boucicault

Uncle Vanya, Anton Chekhov

Europé, Dominic Behan

Filumena Marturano, Eduardo De Filippo

Talbot's Box, Thomas Kilroy

Equus, Peter Shaffer

1978–79

At the Hawk's Well, W.B. Yeats

On Baile's Strand, W.B. Yeats

The Only Jealousy of Emer, W.B. Yeats

The Death of Cuchulain, W.B. Yeats

The Evangelist, Sam Thompson

A Midsummer Night's Dream, William Shakespeare

Grease, Jim Jacobs and Warren Casey

The Mandrake, Niccolò Machiavelli

Facing North, John Boyd

The Second Life of Tattenberg Camp, Armand Gatti

Whose Life Is it Anyway?, Brian Clark

Once a Catholic, Mary O'Malley

1979–80

The Shadowy Waters, W.B. Yeats

The Herne's Egg, W.B. Yeats

The Tempest, William Shakespeare

Juno and the Paycock, Seán O'Casey

Jacques Brel Is Alive and Well and Living in Paris, Eric Blau and Mort Shuman

Spring Awakening, Frank Wedekind

Crystal and Fox, Brian Friel

Hobson's Choice, Harold Brighouse

The Drums of Father Ned, Seán O'Casey

Dark Rosaleen, Vincent Mahon

Not I, Samuel Beckett

The Death of Dracula, Warren Graves

1980–81

Marat/Sade (Drama School Production), Peter Weiss

Leila Webster's Summer Special, Leila Webster

The King of the Great Clock Tower, W.B. Yeats

Calvary, W.B. Yeats

Resurrection, W.B. Yeats

Purgatory, W.B. Yeats

Bent, Martin Sherman

In the Shadow of the Glen, J.M. Synge

The Tinker's Wedding, J.M. Synge

Riders to the Sea, J.M. Synge

Heritage, Eugene McCabe

The Threepenny Opera, Bertolt Brecht

Dockers, Martin Lynch

An Ideal Husband, Oscar Wilde

Victims, Eugene McCabe

Old Days, Frank Dunne

My Silver Bird, Patrick Galvin

Dockers, Martin Lynch

Appendix C
John Hewitt's 'Dedication'

Before he died John Hewitt revised his poetic tribute (printed at the front of this book) to the Lyric and its finder. The changes he made in this later version of his sonnet are minor but will be of interest to students of the great poet.

DEDICATION

I owe much thanks to players everywhere
who've placed such circumstance before my mind
that I've often shed my momentary care
in rapt occasions of the richest kind:
the mad king and his fool; the broken man
who sees flame make the saint; the peevish pair
who wait beside the tree; the harridan
urging her creaking wheels beyond despair.
With all to thank, I name in gratitude
and set among the best, with them aligned,
the little band upon their little stage,
tempered to shew, by that dark woman's mood,
O'Casey's humours, Lorca's sultry rage,
the Theban monarch's terror, fate-assigned.

– John Hewitt

Acknowledgments

BIOGRAPHERS NEED help from both people and institutions. People – no, a person first.

Mary O'Malley's youngest son, Conor, was the chief enabler of *Fierce Love*. After his mother died he provided information for an obituary I wrote in *The Independent*. And he didn't stop there. It is hard to imagine this biography being written at all without the help of someone who had a unique, front-stalls view of how – with a great deal of help from Pearse – Mary created and developed 'her' theatre. He has answered endless queries, commented on drafts, supplied precious family archives (including a tiny note Mary wrote to her beloved Pearse more than seventy years ago), sent me valuable sound recordings of Lyric events, worked hard to accelerate the writer's sedate pace and provided hospitality and continuous encouragement. He was even prepared to dive into the huge Galway archive on my behalf. We would sometimes agree to disagree on certain points, and I must stress that any errors in this volume are mine and mine alone.

The institution which helped most with *Fierce Love* is the National University of Ireland, Galway – more specifically the wonderful Hardiman Library and within that, the Special Collections unit. Sitting in the magnificent reading room, looking out over the green Galway campus as another box of O'Malley treasure arrives on a trolley, has been one of the great pleasures of the sometimes arduous task of finding a way through a complex life.

In Special Collections Kieran Hoare was consistently helpful and encouraging in providing access to the 72-box O'Malley Archive. So was Barry Houlihan, who has worked in the archive long enough and knew it well enough to find very useful material for me and to prepare copies of many of the pictures which I have used in the book. His expertise is now in the public domain; he has published two books with the self-explanatory title, *Navigating Ireland's Theatre Archive.*

All the staff in the reading room remained positive, helpful and encouraging during visits which stretched over at least half a decade.

Regular trips from London to Galway, although delightful, involved cost. The university's Moore Institute, run by Professor Dan Carey, and which grants fellowships for postgraduates engaged in projects like mine, provided me with vital financial support. Professor Carey was warmly welcoming, and it very enjoyable to participate in seminars and converse with the other Moore beneficiaries.

Lionel Pilkington, who has written insightfully about drama and politics in Ireland, and teaches in Galway, championed my project from the start and was kind enough to comment helpfully on an early draft. He also gave me licence to expound on the Lyric Theatre at a seminar (in which I failed to curb my enthusiasm and overran wildly).

Galway holds the main O'Malley archive, but the delightful Linen Hall Library in Belfast also has a sizeable collection of Lyric material including a fine assortment of play programmes. There I had great help from Mary Delargy who responded to my phone calls and email requests by turning up all sorts of valuable material.

I also had much assistance from the Belfast Central Library, a treasure trove of the Belfast and Dublin newspapers, which charted the often-controversial moments in the Lyric's history as well as delivering reviews of a great many productions. My thanks to all the staff who helped me.

There are many more individuals I would like to thank. Sam McCready, who has written with love about Mary, generously helped me find answers to questions about her stagecraft, her politics, her volatility and much else besides. Sam helpfully introduced me to Denis Nichol, an accountant who was involved in managing the theatre in the late 1970s and '80s. And I have drawn copiously on Sam's excellent memoir of Mary and the Lyric, *Baptism by Fire*. And he put time and effort into trying to tell it how it was after Mary had left. Ciaran McKeown proved hard to find, but when I did he provided a draft account of his years at the Lyric when, after he had left the Peace People, he became Secretary to the Lyric's board of trustees and, in opposition to Pearse O'Malley, created a different Lyric theatre. Sadly both Sam and Ciaran are no longer with us.

In Belfast I was delighted to share a noisy teatime at the new Lyric with the poet Michael Longley and Denis Smyth, a distinguished Lyric director, both reflecting perceptively on Mary and her theatre. In Dublin Andrew Parkes closely read the manuscript and saved me from countless errors. Robert Chesshyre in London did the same and delivered encouragement.

I would also like to thank the following for being prepared to go back in time to recall people and anecdotes relating to the Lyric's first forty years: Linda Wray, stalwart of many 1970s Lyric productions; Patrick Brannigan, to whom I spoke just months before he died, sadly far too young; Sheelagh Flanagan, wife of the painter Terence Flanagan and mother of the sculptor Philip Flanagan; Sir Kenneth Bloomfield, civil servant and survivor of the Troubles; Bernadette Keenan, who admired Mary's energy but did not share her enthusiasm for Yeats; and Stella McCusker, still a force on the Irish stage. I would also like to express my gratitude to Christopher Fitz-Simon. His frank interview is at the core of the book. Finally I would like to thank another interviewee, my friend Robert Hutchison, for his insights into the way the theatre was managed in those difficult days. Sadly, he has left us recently.

Conor and Kieran O'Malley both gave long and revealing interviews about their parents. Conor, whose PhD thesis was on the Lyric, was prepared to discuss at length the many facets of Mary and her theatre practice covered in this book. Kieran, less immersed in the theatre, but with his own insights into family dynamics and his mother's temperament, was also prepared to answer many questions. Donal O'Malley helped to fill in the picture of what life was like in the home that was also a theatre. And late in the day I was put in contact with one of the O'Malleys' Danish au pairs, Elsebeth Orntoft, who provided some very interesting domestic detail. And finally,

Mary Pengelly, Mary's niece, provided me with some hilarious anecdotes gleaned on her visits to Derryvolgie Avenue from Dublin.

Biographies need publishers. Part of this book began with Lagan Press. Pat Ramsey encouraged me to write a pamphlet about *Threshold* which could be published in time for the launch of the new Lyric in 2012. I did so but it grew and grew, and I got cold feet. I felt the pamphlet would not stand on its own – that it was a full biography or nothing. I abandoned the project – some of which survives in the *Threshold* appendix. Not surprisingly, communication with Patrick Ramsey and Lagan Press broke down.

Much later: enter Lilliput – in about 2017 Antony Farrell agreed to take the book but stipulated a length of around 100,000 words. When it arrived at nearly 150,000, he was dismayed and required cuts. This I did but it was not till Djinn von Noorden came on the scene that *Fierce Love* took on its present, relatively slim shape. Her amputations have been so skilful as to be painless, and she has been endlessly patient with my concept of 'improvement' – aka constant changes to the MS – and with the fact that I am an IT greenhorn. And finally Ruth Hallinan got the book over the line against what became a very tight deadline. She was calm and organized at a tense time – as was the proofreader, Niamh Dunphy, who patiently tolerated my last-minute re-thinks and put a printable MS together. Thank you Ruth, Niamh and Lilliput.

Authors usually have families. Mine has been tolerant of my absences, both physical and mental, as I followed the O'Malley trail. My wife, Mona, got used to conversations beginning, 'Must go to Galway ...' and would have been heartily relieved that the story of the Lyric Players Theatre is finally out in the bookshops rather than rattling round in my head. Mona, of course, was there right at the beginning: in the mid-1960s we used to go together to see how Mary had fitted another giant production into the tiny stage at the back of the solid Victorian residence in Derryvolgie Avenue. This book's origins lie in what we saw and heard there in those heady days of the O'Neill spring in Northern Ireland. Sadly, Mona died in 2019 before she could see *Fierce Love* in print.

Permissions

IN MY TEXT I have quoted from some authors multiple times. In the cause of brevity, I list only the first time an extract from their literary work or correspondence appears in the pages of my book. Because I found some authors, or their estates, uncontactable, I have weighed up whether the publication of often a very short extract from a letter will cause pain or embarrassment and gone ahead where I felt it would not.

The list is quite short because, using the conventions established on quotations from literary works, I have gone ahead when the prose extracts or lines of poetry were within the established norms for permissible quotation. So the extracts in question do not appear in this list

I am grateful to those who gave me permission to make use of the following extracts or complete works (listed in page order):

'Dedication', a sonnet, and other poems and letters – John Hewitt estate
Never Shake Hands with the Devil, Mary O'Malley's autobiography and
    other material – the O'Malley estate
Private notes exchanged between Mary and Pearse – Conor O'Malley
Letters to Mary from Val Iremonger – Iremonger family
Letter to Mary from Arthur Brooke – Brooke family
Extracts from *Baptism by Fire*, Sam McCready – Joan McCready
Letter to Mary from Helen Lewis – Lewis family

Letter from Nuala O'Faolain to Mary – O'Faolain estate

Letter from Brian Friel to Mary – Friel estate

Letter to Mary from Micheál MacLiammóir – Michael Travers

George Mooney Lyric speech – Mooney family

Letter to Lyric Trustees from Christopher Fitz-Simon – Christopher Fitz-Simon

Letter to Mary and poetry by John Montague – Montague estate

Extracts from *We Do It for Love* and a poem, 'Midnight' – Galvin family

A draft memoir on Lyric involvement – Ciaran McKeown

Letter from Leon Rubin to the Lyric Trustees – Leon Rubin

'For Mary and Pearse O'Malley', a poem by Kieran O'Malley – Kieran O'Malley

An assessment of the O'Malley contribution to theatre in Ulster, Lionel Pilkington – Lionel Pilkington

'Armagh' a poem by W.R. Rodgers – Gallery Press

'The Farmer', a poem by Geoffrey Squires – Geoffrey Squires

'Barricades' by Francis Mulhern – Francis Mulhern

In addition, the author and publishers are grateful to Faber and Faber Ltd and the Estate of Seamus Heaney for permission to quote the following:

Excerpts from review (on BBC) of Yeats play

Letter to Mary O'Malley

Excerpt from article in *Hibernia*, April 1963

'The Lyric Players'

'Oh Brave New Bull'

'The Tollund Man'

'The Strand at Lough Beg'

(All poetry from *Opened Ground: Poems 1966–1996*, Seamus Heaney (Faber and Faber, 1998) apart from two lines from 'Oh Brave New Bull' – unpublished.

All prose unpublished.)

Sources

AUTOBIOGRAPHY

Never Shake Hands with the Devil, Mary O'Malley, Elo Publications, Dublin, 1990

I have made frequent use of Mary's autobiography, particularly in the early chapters. Unfortunately, it ends in 1977 when she left Belfast, so there is no account from her standpoint of the painful conflicts within the Lyric's board of trustees in the 1980s.

OTHER SELECTED WRITTEN SOURCES

Jonathan Bardon, *A History of Ulster* (Belfast, 1992)

Sam Hanna Bell, *The Theatre in Ulster* (Dublin, 1972)

Kenneth Bloomfield, *A New Life* (Belfast, 2008)

John Boyle, *The First Five Years: The Lyric Players Theatre 1951–56* (Belfast, 1956)

Terence Brown, *A Social and Cultural History of Ireland* (London, 1975)

Mark Carruthers and Stephen Douds, *Stepping Stones: The Arts in Ulster, 1971–2001* (Belfast, 2001)

Fiona Coffey, *Political Acts: Women in Northern Irish Theatre, 1921–2012* (New York, 2016)

Roy Connolly, *The Evolution of the Lyric Players Theatre, Belfast* (Lampeter, 2000)

Lyric Players Theatre, *A Needle's Eye* (Belfast, 1979)

Barry Houlihan, *Navigating Ireland's Theatre Archive* (2019)

Helen Lewis, *A Time to Speak* (New York, 2010)

Sam McCready, *Baptism by Fire* (Belfast, 2007)

Conor O'Malley, *A Poets' Theatre* (Dublin, 1988)

Lionel Pilkington, *Theatre and the State in Twentieth-Century Ireland* (London, 2001)

Marilynn Richtarik, *Stewart Parker: A Life* (Oxford, 2012)

Clair Wills, *That Neutral Island* (London, 2007)

INTERVIEWS

Patrick Brannigan, actor and director

Christopher Fitz-Simon, first director of productions at Ridgeway Street

Robert Hutchison, actor and arts administrator

Bernadette Keenan, actress

Stella McCusker, actress

Kieran O'Malley, Mary's eldest son

Donal O'Malley, second son

Conor O'Malley, third son

Elsebeth Orntoft, au pair

Mary Pengelly, Mary's niece

Denis Smyth, actor and director

Linda Wray, actress

THE LYRIC THEATRE / O'MALLEY ARCHIVE

This huge collection of papers in the Hardiman Library, NUI Galway, was acquired through the good offices of Lionel Pilkington and Conor O'Malley in 2003. It was well catalogued by Sarah Poutch in 2011 but is so vast that I have not found it possible to read everything the archive contains. It covers, sometimes in dizzying detail, Mary's packed life: the evolution of her theatre, her time in politics and family events. It also includes some of Dr Pearse O'Malley's papers. Below is an outline of the archive, which gives some idea of the scope, interest and quantity of my main source. For ease of access, I have provided front and end archive references for each section. The list below is selective and represents what I found interesting in this unique collection.

Lyric productions T4/1–365

Play programmes, often accompanied by other material – photos, annotated scripts, design sketches and lists of props, 1950–99

Touring Productions T4/366–387

Proposed Lyric tour to USA, 1960; Yeats Summer School, Sligo, 1960–62; Dublin Theatre Festival, 1960–61 and 1967; Listowel Writers' Week, 1973; Limerick Festival, 1974; UK and Ireland tour of *We Do It for Love*, 1976; Lyric Players' season at the Pavilion in Dublin, 1978.

Production notebooks T4/387–404

Fascinating collection of miscellaneous notebooks relating to individual productions, starting with *The Falcon in the Snare*, 1954. These books of varied size contain attendance figures, notes on costume and design, auditions, casting, music, sound effects, costs and much more.

Unproduced scripts T4/405–460

A slush pile of more than sixty plays. Includes works by Dannie Abse, Eileen Atkins, Padraic Colum ('Moytura'), Henry de Montherlant, Brian Friel, John Hewitt, Eugene McCabe, Donagh MacDonagh, Brian O'Nolan, James Plunkett, Victor Price, William Saroyan, Gregorio Martínez Sierra and William Trevor.

Miscellaneous production material T4/469–485

Contains flyers, index boxes, address books, a provisional Lyric logo, an employee list (1969, includes salaries). Prime item: Mary's Macmillan edition of Yeats's plays: an intensely annotated volume containing production notes written on almost every page of the book.

Administrative papers T4/486–521

Annual Reports, 1960–78 and 1997; Minutes of Trustee Board Meetings, 1960–93 and 1997.

Legal documents T4/522–535

Includes relevant material from the establishment of the Lyric Players Theatre Trust (1960); correspondence about unpaid bills after the new theatre opened in 1968; papers relating to the High Court action taken by Pearse O'Malley against some other trustees (1981–85); Winifred Bell's proposed legal action against the Theatre, 1982.

Arts Council documents T4/536–542

> Correspondence relating to the laying of the foundation stone and the costs of building the Ridgeway Street theatre.

Financial Material T4/543–591

> Audited accounts, 1961–70 (Atkinson and Boyd, auditors); 1970–74 (Ashworth, Rowan, Craig, Gardner and Company); 1975–90 (Price Waterhouse); miscellaneous documents relating to fundraising, subscribers and development options.

Building of Ridgeway Street Theatre T4/592–624

> Neil Downes's original plans for a theatre on Ridgeway Street (1964); programme for the foundation stone-laying ceremony, performed by Austin Clarke; fundraising brochures; contract with the Wells Organisation, fundraisers; final architectural plans for the new theatre, drawn up by architects for McAlpine and Sons (replacing the original design by Neil Downes).

Administrative notebooks T4/625–637

> Notes in shorthand (almost certainly Mary's); handwritten minutes of trustee meetings; many to-do lists.

Press cuttings T4/625–56

> Nineteen files covering the period 1952–99. A monumental collection of press comment on the Lyric, mostly in the form of reviews.

Printed material T4/657–765

> A miscellaneous collection of books, magazines, memoranda and pamphlets. The welter includes: *An Appeal to Leaders of National Opinion in the North* by Ernest Blythe; Arts Council annual reports; copies of *The Dublin Magazine*, *Rann*, *Lagan*, *Fortnight* and *The Honest Ulsterman*; a brochure for the Ulster College of Music; a pamphlet, 'Women's Duties in Social and Political Life', Pope Pius XII.

Correspondence – individuals T4/806–867

> Letters to and from: Samuel Beckett, Alice Berger Hammerschlag, Ernest Blythe, John Boyd, John and Elizabeth Boyle, Arthur and Florence Brooke, Deborah Browne, Austin Clarke, Kenneth Darwin, Neil Downes, Gabriel Fallon, Christopher Fitz-Simon, Brian Friel, Patrick Galvin, Armand Gatti, Monk Gibbon, Harold Goldblatt,

Tyrone Guthrie, Wilson John Haire, Val Iremonger, Denis Johnston, John B. Keane, Tom Kinsella, Louis le Brocquy, Lord Longford, Donagh MacDonagh, Roger McHugh, Micheál MacLiammóir, Molly McNeill, Jack McQuoid, Mary Manning, Rutherford Mayne, John Montague, Eoin O'Mahoney, James Plunkett, W.R. Rodgers, Anne Yeats, George Yeats, Grainne Yeats, Jack B. Yeats and Michael Yeats.

General correspondence T4/868–958

Chronological collection which gives insights into the development of the Lyric Players Theatre. Among much else, deals with (inter alia): the origins in the Aquinas Hall in QUB, visits to the Dublin Theatre Festival and acquiring the rights to produce *Long Day's Journey into Night*. There is a note from Sam Hanna Bell praising a production of his play *That Woman at Rathard*; a letter from Brian Boyd to Pearse suggesting that he might resign from the Lyric board; items relating to the conflict with Equity; a telegram from Ingmar Bergman sending good wishes to his 'dear friends'; letters from the Ballymoney Free Presbyterian Church protesting about the Lyric production of *Jesus Christ Superstar*; applications for the post of Artistic Director, 1977; Mary's address at the funeral of Louis Rolston.

Lyric projects T4/959–983

Covers the activities of the Belfast Academy of Music and Drama, the New Gallery, the Irish Handcrafts shop and the production of *A Needle's Eye*, a large-format booklet celebrating ten years in Ridgeway Street.

Threshold T4/984–1120

All thirty-eight issues of the magazine. Submissions include: a Ronald Ayling short story; a collection of Serbo-Croatian poems by various authors; 'An Ulsterman', a poem by Lynn Doyle; a Gabriel Fallon article, 'The House on the North Circular Road'; eleven translations of Galician-Portuguese love songs compiled by Pearse Hutchinson; two poems by Norman Iles, 'The Longing for Fitness' and 'Billie Jean Moffat Defeated Maria Bueno at Wimbledon in 1962'; a novelette entitled *The Night the Bed Fell on Hollywood*; 'Bernie', a short story by Maurice Leitch; a speech by Seán Lemass on 'The European Free Trade Area'; three poems by Raymond Roseliep; a short story by Críostóir O'Flynn,

'Travellers'; a poetry collection by James Simmons, *To a Cigarette*. *Threshold* correspondence includes letters to and from: Mary Beckett, Sam Hanna Bell, Patrick Boyle, Padraic Colum, Denis Donoghue, Seamus Heaney, John Hewitt, Philip Hobsbaum, Pearse Hutchinson, Diana Hyde, Denis Ireland, Ben Kiely, Rudolf Klein, Seán Lemass, John Lewis-Crosby, Roy McFadden, John McGahern, Ewart Milne, Brian Moore, Desmond Ryan

O'Malley family material T4/1124–1316

Letters: early ones to her brother Gerard (starting 1926); to and from Queen's University about the award of an Honorary MA (1968); to Equity about her application for full membership (1981); about her membership of the National Theatre Society.

Invitations: to a PEN luncheon (1953); to meet the Queen at Stormont (1953); to be a guest speaker on the BBC's *The Arts in Ulster* (1959).

Autobiography: many drafts of her *Never Shake Hands with the Devil* (1990).

Speeches: headline notes for 'Theatre in Belfast' delivered to the Irish Association in Dublin (1958); and for 'Can the Individual Survive?' delivered to Technical College students in Rathmines, Dublin, in 1953.

Diaries, shopping lists, chequebooks, press cuttings and correspondence relating to her children.

Political career T4/1317–1389

Speeches: to the Irish Labour Party Conference (1953); notes for various speeches on partition and 'The Moral Standpoint of Republicanism' (1950s); a speech welcoming the creation of the Ulster Folk Museum.

Correspondence relating to her years as a councillor on Belfast Corporation (1951–53): letters to the Irish Labour party and to various agencies on behalf of her constituents

Pearse O'Malley T4/ 1390–1442.

Correspondence: with the Newman Society at QUB; with the Irish Taoiseach about the status of the Mater Hospital in Belfast; and with the European Commission of Human Rights about the treatment of prisoners in Northern Ireland. Medical articles and Clan O'Malley material.

Notes and References

THESE NOTES AIM to help readers to find sources for quotes, and also provide extra information which will help readers to understand the text better. But, in the cause of brevity, they are not comprehensive. I have not referenced every quotation, for example, from Mary's autobiography. Press cuttings are sometimes dated in the text, but not always referenced in these notes.

ABBREVIATIONS

Galway = O'Malley / Lyric archive, Hardiman Library, NUI Galway
OMPC = O'Malley private collection
MH = Mary Hickey
GH = Gerard Hickey
MOM = Mary O'Malley
POM = Pearse O'Malley
KOM = Kieran O'Malley
COM = Conor O'Malley
NSH = *Never Shake Hands with the Devil*, Mary O'Malley's autobiography

INTRODUCTION

p. viii   The task was made even harder …' Roy Connolly, *The Evolution of the Lyric Players' Theatre, Belfast*, p. 70

1 YOUGHAL

p. 1   'lopsided …' MOM, *NSH*, p. 1

(**Note:** Other quotations from Mary's autobiography in this chapter are from *NSH*, pp. 1–11.)

p. 3   'I hope you are …' MH, letter to GH, 1926, Galway T4/1174

p. 4   By 1922–23 the euphoria of the Treaty had evaporated, and the division of Ireland led de Valera's followers to challenge the new Irish Free State. A civil war followed, and it may have been a skirmish in this conflict which Mary saw outside her house.

p. 5   Joe Higgins (1885–1925) came from Cork but spent much of his life teaching in Youghal. He did statues of Pearse and Collins and his sculptures of children can be seen in Fitzgerald Park in Cork.

p. 6   O'Brien was a bitter opponent of partition, but earlier he had been a practical reformer who, by his advocacy of the Irish Land Act (1903), had helped many Irish tenant farmers to buy their farms.

2 ST MICHAEL'S

p. 8   'school-girl's black cloth coat …' Undated prospectus for St Michael's, Navan, Galway T4/1270, pp. 12–24

p. 9   'He clipped mine …' *NSH*, p. 12 (this chapter: *NSH*, pp. 12–24)

'just outside the town of Navan …' School prospectus, Galway T4/1270

p. 10   The sources, other than the autobiography, are few: a rather dull diary, the odd letter, her school reports – not much more.

3 DUBLIN, WAR, THEATRE

p. 14   'He was my second father …' *NSH*, p. 25 (this chapter: *NSH*, pp. 24–40)

p. 15   Mary transcribed the terrible ending of the Connolly story: 'They carried him from his bed in a stretcher to an ambulance and drove him to Kilmainham Jail. They carried the stretcher from the ambulance to the jail yard. They put him in a chair. He was very brave and cool … "Will you pray for the men who are about to shoot you? …" … "I will say prayers for all brave men who do their duty." … And then they shot him.'

p. 15   'Irish poets, learn your trade
Sing whatever is well made.'

p. 16   'the wedding was OK …' James Bayley Butler, letter to MH, Galway T/1175

p. 17   'the beginning of a cultural watershed …' Terence Brown, *Ireland: A Social and Cultural History*, p. 168

p. 18   'If neutrality was dangerous …' Clair Wills, *That Neutral Island*, p. 43

p. 20   'a nonentity state …' Frank O'Connor, quoted in Wills, p. 8
'a land outside time …' Kate O'Brien, quoted in ibid., p. 10

p. 21   'a corduroy panzer division …' Terence de Vere White, *A Fretful Midge*, p. 110

p. 22   Kavanagh as a poet encapsulated better than anyone else the miserable frustrations of Irish rural life in the 1930s and '40s.

p. 27   'plays that for various reasons …' New Theatre minutes, Galway T4/1274
Harry Craig (1921–1975), son of a Limerick vicar, excelled in New Theatre productions, helped O'Faoláin to edit *The Bell*, wrote plays for the BBC Third Programme and became a well-known radio voice in England in the 1950s, and then swerved away to Rome where he became a highly paid film scriptwriter (*Lion of the Desert*).

p. 28   'because the cast is so large …' New Theatre minutes, Galway T4/1274

4 SUITORS

p. 30   'I was taken with his ideas …' *NSH*, p. 36 (this chapter: *NSH*, pp. 36–46)

p. 31   A dance where, traditionally, women may ask men to dance.
'Let the philosophers explain …' Note preserved in OMPC

p. 32   'Agreement, August 11, 1944 ...' Preserved in OMPC

p. 33   This address suggests she was no longer living with her mother.

'Dear Pearse ...' MH, letter to POM, OMPC

'Dear P ...' MH, letter to POM, OMPC

p. 34   Perhaps as a result, Pearse was a lifelong teetotaller.

p. 36   'My chief regret ...' POM, letter to MOM, 1957, OMPC

5 BELFAST

p. 37   'I had grown to love Dublin ...' *NSH*, p. 46 (this chapter: *NSH*, pp. 46–64)

'I'm looking forward very much ...' Val Iremonger, letter to MOM, 29/10/47, Galway T4/833

p. 38   'It is nice to read in your letter ...' ibid.

'Well, how are you ...' ibid., T4/833

p. 39   'he had not a Roman Catholic ...' Lord Brookeborough, quoted in Jonathan Bardon, *A History of Ulster*, p. 538

p. 41   'for the 10% of the Ulster audience ...' Hubert Wilmot, quoted in Sam Hanna Bell, *The Theatre in Ulster*, p. 112

p. 44   Cathal Daly – Later a bishop, then Primate of all Ireland and ultimately a cardinal.

p. 45   'Belfast will be what ...' Val Iremonger, letter to MOM, 29/10/47, Galway T4/833

p. 46   'Ladies and gentlemen ...' linking script for *The Nativity*, Galway T4/1

p. 47   'If I wasn't ready to play ...' Sheelagh Flanagan, author interview

'It was a stage ...' Frances McShane, quoted in Bell, op. cit., p. 115

p. 48   'lived in a kind of vacuum ...' Sheelagh Flanagan, author interview

6 POLITICS

p. 50   'stir things up ...' *NSH*, p. 60 (this chapter: *NSH*, 64–84)

'Political and administrative discrimination ...' MOM, letter to George Thomas, 29/5/51, Galway T4/1176

p. 53   'I wish to beg your assistance ...' Patrick Flynn, letter to MOM, 12/1/53, Galway T4/1319

p. 54   'Dear Cllr. O'Malley...' Patrick Flynn, letter to MOM, 8/4/53, Galway T4/1319

p. 55   'The suggestion that the support ...' MOM, speech in council, Galway GT4/1378

p. 56   'It may interest delegates ...' Quote from PEN statement, Galway T4/1378

p. 59   'insufficient interest in the care ...' MOM report on Belfast Zoo, Galway T4/1378

'rats in the monkey cages ...' MOM, quoted in *Belfast Telegraph*

p. 61   'to remedy obvious wrongs ...' Bardon, op. cit., p. 608

'draw Catholics into ...' ibid., p. 608

'that Catholics could become ...' ibid., p. 610

'his tremendous charm ...' Terence O'Neill, quoted in ibid., p. 621

p. 62   Sheehy-Skeffington had been banned by the Vocational Education Committee (which had jurisdiction over the college) because of an incident a month before, when, at a meeting about the persecution of Catholics under the Tito regime in Yugoslavia, Sheehy-Skeffington had called for a general debate, which had become so heated that a visiting papal nuncio walked out. The committee had remembered this outrage, blamed Sheehy-Skeffington and banned him. Afterwards the committee did not apologize for the exclusion, saying, 'One thing the citizens of Dublin will never tolerate is any disrespect, or semblance of disrespect, to the Pope's representative.' A long controversy in the press ensued.

p. 63   'On stage-left ...' COM, *A Poets' Theatre*, p. 23

p. 64   Mary was careful to put membership forms in the programme for the Christmas extravaganza. She soon got members, but it was to be a while before she and Pearse got any return on their expenditure.

p. 65   'Mary couldn't sit still ...' Sheelagh Flanagan, author interview

p. 67   'She was a very striking individual ...' Sir Kenneth Bloomfield, author interview

p. 68   'At first I could not believe ...' Arthur Brooke, letter to MOM, Galway T4/1203

7 FLOWERING

p. 69   'learning … how to cope with …' *NSH*, p. 85 (this chapter: *NSH*, pp. 85–90)

'luxuriating in despondency …' Norman Stevenson, letter to MOM, 1/7/55, Galway T4/1179

p. 70   'an actors' forum …' John Boyle, Lyric brochure, *The First Five Years*, Galway T4/476

p. 73   'very suggestive and crude …' Moya, letter to MOM, n.d., Galway T4/1199

p. 74   'there was a body …' Sam McCready, *Baptism by Fire*, p. 45

Helen's remarkable memoir, *A Time to Speak*, was published in 1992.

'to understand that strange place …' Helen Lewis, *A Time to Speak*, p. 131

p. 75   'To the Lyric she brought many gifts …' McCready, op. cit., p. 123

'My dear Mary …' Helen Lewis, letter to MOM, n.d., Galway T4/1179

'It was like walking …' McCready, op. cit., p. 47

p. 76   'On no account was I to move …' ibid., p. 71

Cantillating – Mary's actors sometimes used a singsong, chanting delivery in Yeats plays.

p. 77   'The theatre's success …' Connolly, op. cit., p. 58

p. 78   *Threshold* – See Appendix A, which contains an account of *Threshold* giving through extracts, some of the flavour of its often-remarkable contributions and outlining its development over three decades.

p. 79   'a certain temerity …' *Threshold* 1, Galway T4/984

8 PRESSURE

p. 81   'I was detailed to go in …' Mary Pengelly, author interview

'We have had ten good years …' POM, letter to MOM, 4/7/57, OMPC

p. 82   'the spill over into the house …' *NSH*, p. 103 (this chapter: *NSH*, pp. 96–128)

p. 83   'Because I am from Ireland …' John Hewitt, letter to MOM, 10/4/57, Galway T4/1130

p. 85 'a wild Highland accent ...' Norman Stevenson, letter to MOM, 10/7/56, Galway T4/1179

p. 86 'he brought brilliance and intelligence ...' McCready, op. cit., p. 65
'I had been part of the reason ...' ibid., p. 65

p. 87 'I really behaved very badly ...' Nuala O'Faolain, letter to MOM, 7/1/59, Galway T4/1180
'it is wonderful to be able, once in a while ...' Alice Berger Hammerschlag, letter to MOM, 7/5/59, Galway T4/809

p. 88 'reduce sets to their simplest form ...' GH to MOM, n.d., Galway T4/1174
'You know this is a very blasphemous play ...' Denis Johnston, quoted in *NSH*, p. 103

p. 90 'Do you remember that day ...' Raymond Warren, letter to MOM, n.d., Galway T4/1204

p. 91 'Last night gave me the impression ...' Rutherford Mayne, letter to MOM, 9/12/58, Galway T4/849

9 EXPANSION

p. 96 'his chair pushed well back ...' *NSH*, p. 132 (this chapter: *NSH*, pp. 132–68)

p. 98 'was like a homecoming ...' McCready, op. cit., p. 74
'More often than not one had to be content ...' COM, op. cit., p. 40

p. 99 'an intense, highly emotional actor ...' MOM, article in *Threshold* 19 (Autumn 1965), Galway T4/987
'as proficient in movement as in speech ...' ibid.
'Each Yeats play ...' COM, op. cit., p. 44

p. 100 'monody, a single melodic line ...' ibid., p. 45

p. 101 'I had a very strong Northern accent ...' KOM, author interview

p. 102 'I have never been so cold in my life ...' Elsebeth Orntoft

p. 110 'We made hundreds of papier-mâché eggs ...' McCready, op. cit., p. 110

10 LOYALTY

(**Note:** The background to this chapter and chapter II comes from *NSH*, pp. 169–203.)

p. 113 'irascible and paranoid, identifying ...' McCready, op. cit., p. 119

p. 114 'She gave you the moon ...' ibid., p. 124

'First two exhibitions ...' Alice Berger Hammerschlag, report on New Gallery, June 1963, Galway T4/809

p. 115 'You have always been stressing ...' Alice Berger Hammerschlag, letter to MOM, 29/11/65, Galway T4/809

'What a pity ...' ibid., 18/12/65

It is quite possible that Mary did pay tribute to her team in the interview with Mary Holland, but this praise did not appear, for whatever reason, in the final article.

p. 116 'with a psychiatrist's consulting room ...' KOM, author interview

'Two people arrived ...' COM, author interview

'One day I came back from Clongowes...' Donal O'Malley, author interview

'running around the house with the dog Grainne ...' COM, author interview

p. 117 'One of my favourite things as a child ...' COM, author interview

p. 121 'I dedicate to speech, to pomp and show ...' Extract from a celebratory Seamus Heaney poem, quoted in *NSH*, p. 213

11 STRUGGLE

p. 123 'This Romish man of sin ...' Quoted in Bardon, op. cit., p. 631

'Our idea was, since we lived in ...' Conn McCluskey, quoted in ibid., p. 643

'To write a good satire, one must ...' Brian Friel, letter to MOM, 18/11/64, Galway T4/825

p. 126 'Isn't this theatre divine? ...' Micheál MacLiammóir, quoted in McCready, op. cit., p. 131

p. 127 'CAST RULES: "Cast to be ..."' Handmade Lyric in-house notice, Galway T4/103

'with satisfaction ...' Trustee report, Galway T4/502

'We are quite unanimous ...' Peter Montgomery, letter to MOM, 12/2/68, Galway T4/860

p. 128 'privately to you both ...' Daphne Bell, letter to MOM, n.d., Galway T4/959

p. 129 'The Trustees took the unprecedented step ...' COM, op. cit., p. 28

'on the basis of the resources available ...' ibid., p. 28

p. 130 'The architect has been over-enthusiastic ...' Press cutting, Galway T4/645

'unhappy to be associated ...' Neil Downes, letter to MOM, 10/3/68, Galway T4/817

'little more than that required ...' COM, op. cit., p. 30

p. 132 'For half its history ...' George Mooney, on a sound recording, OMPC

p. 133 'so intensely was she ...' McCready, op. cit., p. 136

'He is a quiet, fastidious ...' Micheál MacLiammóir, letter to MOM, 12/7/68, Galway T4/846

'in the event of opposing viewpoints ...' Trustee letter to Christopher Fitz-Simon, n.d., Galway T4/823

p. 134 'Mam was hopeless at interviewing people ...' COM, author interview

'The generous contract terms ...' COM, op. cit., p. 30

p. 135 'The rise in the cost of the theatre ...' Arthur Brooke, report in trustee minutes, 1968, Galway T4/813

p. 136 Interestingly, *Threshold* does not seem to have been threatened; by now it was plugging into a sudden surge in creativity in Ulster writing, particularly in poetry.

12 LAUNCH

p. 137 'somewhat self-indulgent ...' Christopher Fitz-Simon, letter to trustees, 1/8/68, Galway T4/823

p. 138 'The question of the Anthem ...' Trustee minutes, 8/10/68, Galway T4/502

p. 139 'affect artistic independence ...' *NSH*, p. 215 (this chapter: *NSH*, pp. 213–27)

p. 140   Evidence that, despite falling out, Helen and Mary were still able to work together.

p. 142   'Yeats's drama aimed for this effect ...' Seamus Heaney, transcript of BBC Northern Ireland broadcast, 31/10/68, Galway T4/646

p. 143   'sincere regret that we find ourselves...' MOM and POM, letter to trustees, 29/10/68, Galway T4/502

           'people had made contributions ...' MOM, quoted in McCready, op. cit., p. 141

           'She would either run her theatre ...' ibid., p. 142

p. 144   Playing the anthem had been an issue in the North for some time. When Catholic/nationalist organizations received Arts Council money, they were required to play 'GSTQ'. There had been complaints about this, and the anthem was probably on its way out as a regular feature of live performance, although some Unionists remained acutely sensitive to any suggestions that it should disappear.

13 CRISIS (1)

(Note: The background for this chapter and the next comes from *NSH*, pp. 228–44.)

p. 146   'To begin with, I struck ...' John Montague, letter to MOM, 2/3/70, Galway T4/850

           For more on the Sweeney piece, see p. 268.

p. 147   'The Downing Street declaration ...' Bardon, op. cit., p. 672

p. 148   'no indication was given after ...' Kenneth Darwin, letter to POM, 8/11/68, Galway T4/815

           'When you questioned the Minutes ...' POM, letter to Arthur Brooke, 4/11/68, Galway T4/1188

p. 149   'If the Lyric was not going to be an independent theatre ...' COM, author interview

p. 151   'I simply have no time for the Lyric as well ...' Arthur Brooke, letter to POM, 8/1/69, Galway T4/813

p. 152   'one of the worst moments of my life ...' Arthur Brooke, letter to MOM, 1990, Galway T4/1203

p. 153 'She wasn't witty …' Christopher Fitz-Simon, author interview

p. 154 'the confusion between capital and revenue accounts …' Roger McHugh, letter to POM and MOM, Galway T4/843

p. 157 'I sincerely hope all the theatre's problems…' Equity letter to MOM, Galway T4/819

'An aspiring actor …' COM, op. cit., p. 33

p. 158 'a happy amateur…' Bernadette Keenan, author interview

p. 160 'The trustees now stand possessed …' Letter from Purvis Bruce of Atkinson Boyd, Lyric accountants, 5/6/69, Galway T4/913

'The Tate Gallery has asked …' Alice Berger Hammerschlag, letter to Frank Benner, 14/3/69, quoted in COM, op. cit., p. 79

p. 163 'compelling speech …' Bardon, op. cit., p. 673

14 CRISIS (2)

p. 164 'The Lyric is still politically suspect …' Patrick Shea, letter to trustees, 2/9/69, Galway T4/914

p. 165 'What has gone wrong …' John Hewitt, letter to POM, 14/11/69, Galway T4/1130

p. 166 'What is the position …' John Hewitt, letter to POM, 30/11/69, Galway T4/1130

'it was decided …' POM statement, quoted in COM, op. cit., p. 144

'There is also the danger that …' ibid.

15 TROUBLES

p. 172 Sam McCready had appeared in *Phaedre* and had such difficulties with the director that he decided in future to concentrate on directing and teaching. Within the year he had left to take up a drama post at the Bangor University in North Wales. His leaving was a huge loss to the embattled theatre, although he came back later.

'cheerful, happy audiences …' *NSH*, p. 244 (this chapter: *NSH*, pp. 243–53)

'I think we'll have to cover …' Stella McCusker, author interview

'She was always feeding people ...' ibid.

Mary's disguises must have been transparent, but for the rest of her time at the Lyric she continued to use various stage names, including at one point 'Sally Noggin'. She tried to avoid attracting the attention of political opponents – some of whom now had guns which they were using ruthlessly.

p. 175   'I take it you are reasonably happy ...' MOM quotes from the James Callaghan letter in *NSH*, p. 259

p. 178   'Very undisciplined ...' Patrick Brannigan, author interview

p. 179   'efficient operation of all ...' Production director contract, Galway T4/503

16 SURVIVAL

p. 184   'Bloody Sunday made its mark on the calendar ...' *NSH*, p. 255 (this chapter: *NSH*, pp. 255–71)

      'He had worked in Bristol ...' COM, author interview

p. 185   'One of his patients was ...' KOM, author interview

      'would be disposed ...' COM, author interview

p. 188   'in a way no other plays did ...' COM, op. cit., p. 98

17 BOMB

p. 194   'a frontal assault ...' COM, op. cit., p. 62

p. 195   'The Security man dashed in ...' *NSH*, p. 275 (this chapter: *NSH*, pp. 275–84)

p. 198   'I am out to get back to the poetic ...' Seán O'Casey, quoted in *NSH*, p. 279

p. 201   'Would you ever consider ...' Linda Wray, author interview

      'We did it in long, black costumes ...' ibid.

18 TRIUMPH

p. 203   'a play about Belfast ...' *NSH*, p. 285 (this chapter: *NSH*, pp. 285–89)

p. 204   'An amalgam of prose and verse ...' Patrick Galvin in programme for *We Do It for Love*, Galway T4/218

'If you hate the bleeding Troubles …' *We Do It for Love*, in *Threshold* 27, Galway T4/988 (Same source for all subsequent quotations from the play.)

p. 208 This is where the Northern version of *We Do It for Love* ends, but in performance the cast sang 'When the sun begins to shine' to the tune of 'The Saints'. Conor O'Malley gives a first-hand account of the production in *Navigating the Archives* (see sources).

p. 209 The event was referred to by Linda Wray in her interview.

19 FINALE

p. 211 'insinuating himself …' Marilynn Richtarik, *Stewart Parker: A Life*, p. 140

'*Deirdre* needs acting …' Stewart Parker, quoted in ibid., p. 140

p. 212 'Although she was not on the Lyric's payroll…' ibid., p. 142

'The occasional production …' Parker, quoted in ibid., p. 143

Galvin was from Cork, but the two plays mentioned drilled deeply into Ulster life and attitudes.

p. 213 'Nothing has ever really come out of the Lyric …' Parker, quoted in Richtarik, op. cit., p. 163

'He did send two plays…' *NSH*, p. 291 (this chapter: *NSH*, pp. 291–99)

p. 217 'lacks cohesion and purpose …' Patrick Galvin, letter to MOM, 11/4/76, Galway T4/827

20 DEPARTURE

p. 218 'got the feeling that …' *NSH*, p. 300 (this chapter: *NSH*, pp. 300–19)

p. 222 In *Navigating Ireland's Theatre Archives* (Barry Houlihan, ed.), Conor O'Malley gives an entertaining account of working on the production.

Such rigid attitudes were not always encountered by English theatres in their dealings with the union.

p. 224 'the agreement …' Paraphrase of André Morell, letter to MOM, n.d., Galway T4/819

21 DISENGAGEMENT?

p. 229　'Can Belfast live with a poet's theatre? …' Article in a Lyric booklet, *A Needle's Eye*, 1979

I eventually found McKeown through a kindly intermediary. But the time for dialogue was to be short; sadly McKeown died in September 2019.

p. 230　'They were highly conscious of the fact …' Ciaran McKeown, 'draft memoir' sent to me in response to questions.

p. 231　'Basically, theatres should be run …' Robert Hutchison, author interview

p. 232　'The difficulty … finally came to a head …' Sam McCready, mail to author in response to questions, 2017

p. 234　'Well before it opened …' The main source for this paragraph is McKeown's 'draft memorandum'.

'It had a large cast …' Patrick Brannigan, author interview

My Silver Bird was not a disaster; the evening was memorable for Stella McCusker's singing of the song 'My Silver Bird'.

p. 235　'it is necessary to express uneasiness …' POM memorandum to the board, June 1981

'The date indicates that …' Sam McCready, mail to the author, 2017

p. 236　'Despite his regard …' Richtarik, op. cit., p. 252

p. 237　'As I was leaving the house …' COM, author interview

A quarter of a century later Sam referred to this incident regretfully, when he was launching his book on Mary and the Lyric, *Baptism by Fire*.

p. 239　'I think we should reconsider …' Leon Rubin, letter to the trustees, late 1982

22 RETIREMENT

p. 242　'The concept was to create …' COM, author interview

p. 243　'Mum struggled …' KOM, author interview

p. 244　This account of their social life after 1976 is not strictly chronological.

p. 245 'Brendan Behan has taken ...' Val Iremonger, letter to MOM, 23/7/56 Galway T4/833

p. 247 'I would like to see a bronze head ...' Deborah Browne, letter to MOM, Galway T4/814

23 ENDINGS

p. 250 'When I arrived, a nurse ...' McCready, op. cit., p. 18

p. 251 'She sat on a chair ...' ibid., p. 23

'He probably wouldn't have married...' Mary Pengelly, author interview

p. 252 'He was always a modest, courteous man ...' McCready, op. cit., p. 150

'a simple box ...' ibid., p. 151

'Mary O'Malley was ...' ibid., p. 152

24 CODA

p. 255 'Mary, supported by Pearse ...' Summary of MOM and POM's achievement – provided by Lionel Pilkington.

APPENDIX A

The sources of this chapter are in *Threshold* issues 1–39, Galway T4/988–991

p. 257 *Over the Bridge* – a play about sectarianism in the shipyards unfortunately brought about the demise of the Group Theatre.

p. 261 'Could I withdraw ...' Seamus Heaney letter to MOM, 11/8/63 Galway T/4 1129

'Irish politics, Irish art, Irish music ...' Seamus Heaney, *Hibernia*, April 1963, Galway T4/646

APPENDIX B

The source of this appendix is Conor O'Malley's *A Poets' Theatre*.

INDEX